Unfinished Leninism

Unfinished Leninism
The Rise and Return of a Revolutionary Doctrine

Paul Le Blanc

Haymarket Books
Chicago, IL

First published by Haymarket Books in 2014
© 2014 Paul Le Blanc

Haymarket Books
PO Box 180165
Chicago, IL 60618
773-583-7884
info@haymarketbooks.org
www.haymarketbooks.org

ISBN: 978-1-60846-366-4

Trade distribution:
In the US through Consortium Book Sales and Distribution, www.cbsd.com
In the UK, Turnaround Publisher Services, www.turnaround-psl.com
All other countries, Publishers Group Worldwide, www.pgw.com

Special discounts are available for bulk purchases by organizations and
institutions. Please contact Haymarket Books for more information at
773-583-7884 or info@haymarketbooks.org.

This book was published with the generous support of Lannan Foundation and
the Wallace Action Fund.

Cover design by Rachel Cohen. Text design by Eric Kerl.

Printed in Canada by union labor.

Library of Congress CIP data is available.

10 9 8 7 6 5 4 3 2 1

RECYCLED
Paper made from
recycled material
FSC® C103567

Contents

To those, now gone, who taught me about Leninism,
to those, very much here, who might make
good use of it, and to those yet to come . . .

ACKNOWLEDGMENTS

Among those whom I must thank, for various kinds of supportiveness around my engagement with the ideas (and the sharing of their own ideas) reflected in these essays, over the past several years, are: Anthony Arnove, Sebastian Budgen, Tom Bias, Sandra Bloodworth, Roland Boer, Peter Boyle, David Castle, Kunal Chattopadhyay, Luke Cooper, Ted Crawford, Paul D'Amato, Neil Davidson, Alexy Gusev, Shaun Harkin, Jonathan Harris, He Ping, Brian Jones, Geoffroy de Laforcade, Li Dianlai, Lars Lih, Michael Löwy, Soma Marik, Kevin Murphy, Manny Ness, Benjamin Opratko, John Rees, John Riddell, Pierre Rousset, Helen Scott, Ahmed Shawki, George Shriver, Ashley Smith, Debbie Smith, Michael Smith, Sharon Smith, Hillel Ticktin, Terry Townsend, Tom Twiss, Nat Weinstein, Suzanne Weiss, Susan Weissman, Wu Xinwei, Xiong Min, Michael Yates, and Dave Zirin. Special thanks for the thoughtful and helpful editorial work by Dao Tran. (Apologies for the incompleteness of this list.)

I have been sustained in many important ways, as I have labored over these writings, by my friend Nancy Ferrari, my sisters Patty and Nora Le Blanc, my sons Gabriel Le Blanc and Jonah McAllister-Erickson, and activist comrades of six continents who are too numerous to name.

These essays have accumulated, mostly over a six-year period, in ways indicated below.

"Lenin's Return" appeared in *Working USA: The Journal of Labor and Society* 10, no. 3, September 2007.

"One for the Encyclopedias" was first published in the now defunct *Colliers Encyclopedia* in 1995, and a refurbished version appeared in the remarkable eight-volume *International Encyclopedia of Revolution and Protest* (Wiley-Blackwell, 2009). A variant is also included in my introduction to the selection of Lenin's writings *Revolution, Democracy, Socialism*, published by Pluto Press in 2008.

"Travesties, Statues, and Laughter" came out of a panel discussion at Princeton University in 2012, after a performance of Tom Stoppard's play *Travesties*, which includes Lenin as a character. The essay first appeared in *International Socialist Review*, May–June 2012.

"Still Kicking: Lenin and His Biographers" first appeared in *International Socialist Review*, November–December 2012. The title's word play refers to Lenin's influence as "alive and kicking" and to the fact that he is recurrently kicked by unfriendly biographers.

"Revolutionary Democracy" was first published under the title "Lenin and Revolutionary Democracy," in *Critique: Journal of Socialist Theory* 38, no. 4, November 2010. It originated as a paper presented at the Boston Convention of the American Association for the Advancement of Slavic Studies, November 12–15, 2009.

"The Great Lenin Debate of 2012" appeared in the online journal *Links, International Journal of Socialist Renewal*, September 1, 2012; it originated as a presentation given at an educational conference in London of the Communist Party of Great Britain, August 20–26, 2012.

"Enduring Legacy" first appeared online with the title "The Enduring Value of Lenin's Political Thought" at the Europe Solidaire Sans Frontières site on February 8, 2012, in response to a review by Charles Post of Lars Lih's biography *Lenin*; a few additional comments are added in light of Post's more recent essay "What Is Left of Leninism? New European Left Parties in Historical Perspective," completed and circulated late in 2012 prior to its publication in *Socialist Register 2013*.

"Luxemburg and Lenin Through Each Other's Eyes" appears here for the first time, although an abbreviated version was published online in *Links, International Journal of Socialist Renewal*, January 3, 2012. It was prepared (and presented in the abbreviated form) for an international conference, "Lenin's Thought in the 21st Century: Interpretation and Its Value," sponsored by the Rosa Luxemburg Foundation, as well as the Department of Philosophy, the

Institute of Marxist Philosophy, and the Institute of Western Marxist Philosophy at Wuhan University in the People's Republic of China, October 20–22, 2012.

"Caution: Activists Using Lenin" is published here for the first time. It was presented at an educational conference of the Communist Party of Great Britain in London, August 20–26, 2012. It first appeared online as a video on October 16, 2013, under the title "Building a Revolutionary Party in the USA," on the website of the Communist Party of Great Britain.

"Leninism Is Unfinished" first appeared in the online version of the US publication *Socialist Worker* on February 1, 2013.

"Leninism for Dangerous Times" was presented at the "Dangerous Ideas for Dangerous Times" conference in London and appeared online at *Counterfire*, June 2, 2013, http://www.counterfire.org/index.php/theory/37-theory/16477-leninism-for-dangerous-times. The additional piece appended to this first appeared June 23, 2013, on the website of the International Socialist Network at http://internationalsocialistnetwork.org/index.php/ideas-and-arguments/organisation/152-paul-le-blanc-moving-forward-to-build-a-mass-socialist-movement.

"Organizing for Twenty-First Century Socialism" was initially composed for a seminar of the same name, which took place during June 8–9, 2013, organized in Sydney, Australia, by Socialist Alliance. It appeared online in *Links, International Journal of Socialist Renewal*, June 12, 2013, http://links.org.au/node/3394.

I have taken the liberty, in this volume, of introducing minor changes in some of these essays.

INTRODUCTION

As of this writing in 2013, there have been increasingly intense stirrings of discontent in the face of the deepening problems of global capitalism, an extended upsurge of protest and insurgency, and yet a sense of disappointment and frustration as the problems of global capitalism persist. One can find as synonyms for the word *doctrine* either *dogma* or *guidelines*—and the rising tide of young activists today, having little appetite for dogma, are increasingly seeking guidelines for their efforts.

Conservative and neoliberal policies, social-liberal and social-democratic reformism, Islamic and Christian fundamentalism, the individualist dissidence of libertarians and anarchists, and ideologies less defined have all failed to eliminate the problems—so the discontent persists, spreads, and deepens. This is the case in the United States and elsewhere in the Americas. It is the case throughout Europe. It is the case from South Africa to Egypt and throughout the Middle East. It is the case in India and in China. There is a need— a "market"—for ideas that address this reality. This has caused, as I have been arguing for the past few years, a significant uptick, a renewal among scholars and intellectuals and activists, of interest in and studies of the ideas and the long-ago activities of Vladimir Ilyich Ulyanov—known to the world as Lenin—and of his early twentieth-century comrades.

Back in 1989, as what passed for "Communism" seemed to be disintegrating throughout the world, an old friend accused me, with considerable exasperation, of being "the last Leninist." Not really true then, it is even less so today. This fact finds reflection in the growth of what might be called "Lenin studies." Among the examples of this phenomenon (in addition to my own modest efforts) are the essays gathered in the 2007 volume edited by Sebastian Budgen, Stathis Kouvalakis, and Slavoj Žižek entitled *Lenin Reloaded*, putting forward the work of an impressive and diverse collection of scholars and intellectuals. One can also find more of the same in the impressive British journal *Historical Materialism* and the flood of books it has been providing over the past several years.

There are also the Herculean efforts of John Riddell and his collaborators in making available, and helping to popularize, in multiple volumes, the remarkable proceedings of the early Communist International, which Lenin helped to found and lead. One of the earliest innovators was Kevin Anderson, whose *Lenin, Hegel, and Western Marxism* helped pave the way for taking Lenin's thought more seriously than was common in the era of the so-called collapse of Communism. From India we have the revolutionary feminist Soma Marik, whose impressive study *Reinterrogating the Classical Marxists Discourses of Revolutionary Democracy* focuses its attention on Lenin and his Bolshevik Revolution.

A retrieval of the profoundly democratic qualities of Lenin and Bolshevism and an exploration of how these were shattered under the impact of historical calamities were offered in Arno J. Mayer's magisterial work *The Furies: Violence and Terror in the French and Russian Revolutions*.

One of the most powerful and penetrating contributions has been Lars Lih's massive work *Lenin Rediscovered: "What Is to Be Done?" in Context*. We should also note some of the new studies of the Hegelian Leninists of Western Marxism, Antonio Gramsci and Georg Lukács also fit into this category, as does the renewed scholarly interest in Leon Trotsky. The growing work on and interest in Rosa Luxemburg is also part of this phenomenon. As I will argue later in this volume, it is a mistake to portray Lenin and Luxemburg as opponents—despite real and important differences, they can more accurately be seen as close comrades and cothinkers in the project of the workers' revolution for socialist democracy.

It is not the case that Lenin is simply of scholarly interest to me. *Lenin was tough, and he was for the workers*. That's what my father told me when I was in my early teens, as we drove in a car one summer, while I accompanied him on one of his many trips as a union organizer. I was asking about, and he was explaining, his understanding of how the world was, and the ideas he believed in. When I asked him about Lenin, that is what he said. Not long after, I read a few of Lenin's writings in a book by C. Wright Mills, *The Marxists*, and then *The State and Revolution*. A few years after that, as a New Left activist who felt a need to find more ideas, better ideas, on how to struggle for positive social change, I began reading more Lenin—*What Is to Be Done?* to start with, and then more and more of his writings, and also about Lenin's life and times.

When I was a young militant in the Socialist Workers Party, which at the time was the leading Trotskyist organization in the United States my reading continued, and was linked with practical experience. When I was thirty-five years old, and very bad things were happening in that organization, one of my mentors—George Breitman—asked me to write something about Lenin. He wanted it to be shown that Lenin's ideas and the quality of his thought were much better than what was passing for "Leninism" in this deteriorating, increasingly undemocratic organization. He wanted people—especially young activists of the future—to understand what was what, and to not be turned off by Lenin's ideas because bad things were done in Lenin's name. In consultation with George, I wrote *Lenin and the Revolutionary Party*. He liked it very, very much, and that made me feel incredibly proud. (He was a working-class intellectual of high caliber, with a meticulous approach to scholarship.) When younger activists now tell me that they have read and liked this book, I tell them that it was written especially for them, which is true. That is also the case with the essays in this volume.

I have shared much of my life with this person whose life force has made him like family. I was born thirty years after the 1917 revolution he led. The tremors and vitality of his example and ideas, of his accomplishments and mistakes, have continued to animate much of my life almost a hundred years after so many workers and peasants and students and others reached out with all that they had to make that revolution. They wanted peace, bread, and land. They wanted to create a republic in which the political and economic and cultural realities of society would be ruled by the democratic councils of the laboring majority. They wanted what Marx had promised—that the free development of each will be condition for the free development of all. This is what Lenin wanted, and fought for, and helped others to fight for. And it didn't happen—in fact, almost the opposite happened. There has been much to wrestle with as I have tried to make sense of that, and to sort through, as best I can, what Lenin did, experienced, and said that might be useful in struggles for a better future.

While the reader can meander through the essays in this volume however she or he wishes, I have put them in a certain order that makes sense to me. The first essay introduces Lenin as someone whose relevance for our own time is becoming increasingly evident. The second offers a succinct account of his life. The third focuses more on his personality. How various biographers of our century have dealt with him (many seeing him as the ruthless architect of totalitarianism, and others not) is the subject of the fourth essay, and the fifth offers a sustained look at what I believe is the revolutionary-democratic thrust of his thinking and of what he attempted—contrasted to the horrific dictatorship that congealed after his death under Joseph Stalin. The sixth essay focuses on recent controversies (in which I was a participant, with Lars Lih and Pham Binh) about how Lenin did and did not go about trying to build a revolutionary party—and it also has something to say about the art and craft of writing history. The seventh, in a somewhat similar vein, takes up some differences with a prominent US Marxist analyst, Charles Post, on how (and how not) to understand "Leninism." I have known Charlie as a comrade in the socialist movement for many years, and as is the case with many comrades down through many years, we are able to take issue with each other on important questions while continuing to join together in struggles against oppression and exploitation. I see Rosa Luxemburg as one of the greatest revolutionary socialists ever (Lenin would have agreed with that, by the way), yet she and Lenin, Marxist comrades that they were, sometimes sharply differed, and the eighth essay explores that. I do not believe Lenin and his ideas are merely of historical interest, but his times were very different than ours—so the ninth essay suggests how his approach might be useful to activists in the United States in the early twenty-first century. An unanticipated development in the British Left, generating a storm of controversy and animated discussion, inspired essays ten and eleven, regarding the open and necessarily unfinished nature of Leninism, which reflects the nature of social reality itself, in our dangerous times. More positive developments in Australia—where potential mergers rather than new splits seemed in the offing—contributed to the final consideration of what is to be done.

There is more than one way in which Leninism can be understood as being unfinished. At the very least, there is the continuing stream of scholarship, adding more information and insights on Lenin, his historical context, and various aspects of his thought. This precludes the possibility of this volume, or any volume at this moment, having "the last word" on Lenin and his ideas.

I have already made reference to the still unfinished efforts of John Riddell and his coworkers in regard to the early Communist International, and there will be more to expect from Lars Lih and others who are able to make even more Russian-language sources available to us. Lars and Ben Lewis have recently made available an important work and partial reassessment of Lenin's comrade Gregory Zinoviev (much criticized—in some cases justifiably so—by many) that may force some rethinking among some inclined to accept him as simply a whipping-boy for Leninism gone wrong. The writings and initial scholarly exploration of an important follower of Rosa Luxemburg and pioneer leader of German Communism Paul Levi (in the volume edited by David Fernbach, *In the Steps of Rosa Luxemburg: Selected Writings of Paul Levi*), who embraced and then rejected Lenin, have just begun to be engaged with by serious activist-scholars.

There are no signs that this will close off any time soon. I have had an opportunity to read through manuscripts of others—the translation from Hungarian of an interesting new work by Tamás Krausz, which makes available Eastern European perspectives and debates on Lenin, a significant interpretation by Alan Shandro on the notion of hegemony as a distinctive element in Lenin's thought, and Roland Boer's remarkable work *Lenin, Religion, and Theology*, published in 2013 (just before the present volume was being prepared), which will take time to be adequately absorbed into Lenin studies. In addition, August Nimtz, who has made important contributions on the political thought of Marx and Engels, has written a major study on Lenin, providing the first scholarly exploration of Lenin's quite serious approach to electoral politics in a two-volume work *The "Ballot" or "the Streets"—or Both*. There is also a collection, to be published by the Rosa Luxemburg Foundation in conjunction with Wuhan University, offering presentations given at an International Conference on Lenin and His Thought that took place in the People's Republic of China in 2012.

We can expect much more scholarly work to help us better comprehend Lenin and Leninism. No less significant, however, will be new applications, misapplications, and practical political experiences related to Leninism that can be expected to emerge since there are many around the world who will seek not simply to interpret reality in various ways—but to change it.

Chapter One
LENIN'S RETURN

This is a review of the following books: *Lenin Rediscovered: "What Is to Be Done?" in Context*, by Lars T. Lih (Leiden/Boston: Brill, 2006); *James P. Cannon and the Origins of the American Revolutionary Left, 1890–1928*, by Bryan D. Palmer (Chicago: University of Illinois Press, 2007); *Lenin Reloaded: Toward a Politics of Truth*, edited by Sebastian Budgen, Stathis Kouvelakis, and Slavoj Žižek (Durham, NC: Duke University Press, 2007).

About forty years ago, my great-uncle George Brodsky (now long dead) gave me an old handbill printed in red ink, issued by District 2 of the Workers Party, which proclaimed LENIN LIVES! It urged us to "Come En Masse" to Madison Square Garden to a Sunday afternoon event chaired by Ben Gitlow (a central leader of US Communism who later devolved into a professional anticommunist on the far right. The event that included the four-hundred-voice Freiheit Chorus, a one-hundred-piece symphony orchestra, and speeches from William Z. Foster, C. E. Ruthenberg, Moissaye Olgin, and Jack Stachel—for an admission fee of fifty cents (not a negligible sum in 1925) and with an exhortation at the handbill's bottom: LONG LIVE LENINISM!

"Lenin Lives!" He had died, in fact, but was alive in the hearts and minds of those rallying in Madison Square Garden, alive in the very nature of that culturally vibrant assemblage, and the relevance of the handbill is reflected in the three remarkable books above, while also posing sharp questions about the terrible times in which we live. Consider three films that capture aspects of our reality as we feel our way toward the close of the new century's first decade. The poignant German comedy *Goodbye Lenin!* (2003)—reflecting on the beautiful, tarnished, murderously corrupted, deadeningly bureaucratized dreams of the Communism that proved so utterly unsustainable throughout Eastern Europe—shows a monstrous statue of Lenin being carried away, through the air, by a helicopter, as a stunned female Communist-idealist (herself close to premature death) watches with uncomprehending wonder.

The edgy thriller *Syriana* (2005) shows us ruthless machinations of Communism's triumphant and relentlessly profiteering adversary, as the corporate-capitalist driven empire "takes out" a thoughtful, progressive, radical-nationalist of an oil-rich country, perpetuating the global exploitation and misery of millions, which—in turn, thanks to the absence of revolutionary alternatives—generates suicidal fundamentalist violence.

Fast forward to the year 2027 portrayed in the uncompromising *Children of Men* (2007): in the absence of a socialist alternative (protest movements for global justice were not enough), the world has begun its downward slide into barbarism, a vast cemetery, with the final enclave of "civilization" standing as an increasingly authoritarian and exclusionary (anti-immigrant, anti-refugee) husk whose inhumanity infects many who struggle against it—but images of Lenin appear, in the midst of religious icons, in an obscure, nurturing haven of those who hope and reach for humanity's future.

But surely the images of Lenin as nurturing hope are misplaced—even radicals agree with liberals who quote conservatives who assure us that Lenin was a monster. In his little essay on Lenin in *Time/CBS News People of the Century: One Hundred Men and Women Who Shaped the Last One Hundred Years*, David Remnick explains to us that the great revolutionary held a "view of man as modeling clay and sought to create a new model of human nature and behavior through social engineering of the most radical kind," and he goes on to quote Richard Pipes that "Bolshevism was the most audacious attempt in history to subject the entire life of a country to a master plan. It sought to sweep aside as useless rubbish the wisdom that mankind had accumulated over millennia." Such an inhuman approach to humanity inevitably breeds nothing but inhumanity—unless the liberal/conservative allegation is a lie.

As my book *Marx, Lenin, and the Revolutionary Experience* was about to be published in 2006, I was unable to shake the feeling that what I was doing in that book hardly reflected my own thoughts alone. Against what had become so standard an interpretation of Lenin, as I was writing in the post-9/11 world, it felt that dominant ideologies were being undermined by political and social crises that would be generating insurgent forces ready to connect with the ideas of the "universally" dismissed revolutionary. Perhaps, I thought, we are about to see a Lenin revival. The appearance, at approximately the same time, of these three volumes (two of which I was able to quickly take note of on my book's page proofs) reinforce that sense.

Lenin Reloaded

Taking the most recent first, *Lenin Reloaded* presents a remarkable set of essays by an impressive set of twenty-first-century intellectuals—with contents causing the working-class child in me to recoil in panic, fearing that I will be too dull-witted to understand what all these learned people, using strange words and esoteric allusions, are saying with such apparent fluency. As I labor over what they have written, I bump into the militant young activist within me who scoffs at such "over-intellectualizing," yet the aging scholar in me feels unable to follow the young comrade's impatient advice to close this book—in part because what many of these people are saying is so interesting, so strikingly put, and (yes) so mind-expanding.

Frederic Jameson, beginning with an account from Trotsky's 1932 diary of a dream-conversation with Lenin, describes Lenin's formidable writings as coming from a man who is unaware that he is dead—

> He doesn't know that the immense social experiment he single-handedly brought into being (and which we call Soviet Communism) has come to an end. He remains full of energy, although dead, and the vituperation expended on him by the living—that he was the originator of Stalinist terror, that he

was an aggressive personality full of hatred, an authoritarian in love with power and totalitarianism, even (worst of all) the rediscoverer of the market in his NEP—none of those insults manage to confer a death, or even a second death, on him. How is it, how can it be, that he still thinks he is alive?

This imagery is an eloquent way of stating the simple premise that "Lenin still means something," but it gains one's attention, nonetheless. So does Slavoj Žižek's description of a Slovenian Communist who led a heroic uprising in a fascist prison, an uprising that became part of the mythology of a triumphant Communist state, a state that then arrested and imprisoned the same man and assigned him to a forced-labor work brigade that was creating a monument glorifying the antifascist uprising that he had led—"a perfect metaphor for the twists of Stalinism." There is Terry Eagleton's challenging and clever essay—with wonderful turns of phrase (he describes Lenin's *Materialism and Empirio-Criticism*, while defending it, as "a work in which one can hear the occasional gurgling of a man well out of his depth"). Eagleton reflects on Lenin's much-maligned notion of a "revolutionary vanguard" (commonly dismissed as the arrogant elitism of a middle-class intellectual) with this fine point:

> Those members of the Citizen Army and Irish Volunteers who fought with James Connolly against the British imperial state in the Dublin Post Office in 1916 constituted a vanguard. But this was not because they were middle-class intellectuals—on the contrary, they were mostly Dublin working men and women—or because they had some innate faculty of superior insight into human affairs, or because they were in serene possession of the scientific laws of history. They were a vanguard because of their relational situation—because, like the revolutionary cultural avant-gardes in contrast with modernist coteries, they saw themselves not as a timeless elite but as the shock troops or front line of a mass movement. There can be no vanguard in and for itself, as coteries are by definition in and for themselves. And a vanguard would not be in business unless it trusted profoundly in the capacities of ordinary people, as elites by definition disdain them.

It is hardly the case that all of these writers are in agreement with each other. Antonio Negri argues "not only must Lenin's thought be re-examined with energetic fidelity, but it must also be reframed—as it were—'beyond Lenin.'" Of course, in going beyond Lenin, Negri and cothinker Michael Hardt presented a notion of the world, in their stimulating best-seller *Empire*, that argued for the obsolescence of Lenin's classic *Imperialism: The Highest Stage of Capitalism*. This is in stark contrast to what Georges Labica argues in *Lenin Reloaded*— "contemporary globalization is nothing other than Lenin's 'new imperialism,' now reaching a still higher stage of development." It is worth pondering how this yet "higher stage" is described:

> If we finally take into account elements unknown to the old "new imperialism," since they simply did not exist, or at least in some cases not on such a scale, such as the weight of debt controlled by international monetary institutions, which has led to the ruin of an entire continent (Africa), we have such things as the threat of nuclear weapons, the dangers to the environment, the foreseeable shortage of drinking water, and the general commodification that extends to the sale of organs and the massive prostitution of children, so that we should not be afraid to speak of a regular "criminalization of the world economy." The drug trade, another element previously unknown, stands at the head of world commerce, narcotics being the commodity with the highest rate of profit.

Also in these pages are prominent leaders of would-be Leninist parties, such as Alex Callinicos of the British Socialist Workers Party (SWP), and Daniel Bensaïd of the French Ligue Communiste Révolutionnaire (LCR)—capable intellectuals from substantial organizations. Callinicos articulately challenges, among other things, what one might call traces of Stalinist residue among others in this volume, yet with a comradely tone and with a respect for the common ground they share in relation to what has been the sterile anti-Leninist consensus. He usefully concludes his contribution with a serious-minded discussion of Lenin's relevance to today's Left—having to do with what he sees as 1) Lenin's strategic analysis of capitalism, 2) his perspective of the specificity and centrality of politics, and 3) his view on the necessity of political organization. This seems remarkably consistent with points made in Bensaïd's own distinctive essay, which concludes with the thought that "a politics without parties (whatever name—movement, organization, league, party—they are given) ends up in most cases as a politics without politics: either an aimless tailism toward the spontaneity of social movements, or the worst form of elitist individualist vanguardism, or finally a repression of the political in favor of the aesthetic or the ethical."

As suggested in Negri's earlier-noted comments, there are those who emphasize how one can use Lenin to go beyond Lenin. In exploring Lenin's radical engagement with Hegel of 1914–16, Kevin Anderson comments that "by widening the orthodox Marxian notion of the revolutionary subject, he helped pave the way for later attempts to widen this still further, to embrace not only, as Lenin had begun to do, national and ethnic liberation movements, but also those of women, ecologists, gays and lesbians, and youth." At the same time, Anderson goes out of his way to stress that one can "still appreciate the many attractive features of this great revolutionary leader without in any way self-identifying as a Leninist, which in the dominant discourse usually means an adherence to his elitist concept of the vanguard party." We have noted that some of Anderson's fellow contributors differ with him here—but none so completely as another scholar who also avoids "self-identifying as a Leninist," Lars T. Lih, who buoyantly argues (against critics like Anderson and against more than one defender in this volume) that the Lenin of the 1902 classic *What Is to Be Done?*—no elitist at all—got his perspectives on organization from none other than Karl Marx himself, "but more concretely and effectively from *Marx as incarnated by European Social Democracy and the German SPD in particular*."

All of this is interesting, and yet we happen to live in a time when, as the editors of this collection observe, "global capitalism appears to be the only game in town and the liberal-democratic system as the optimal political organization of society, [and] it has indeed become easier to imagine the end of the world than a far more modest change in the mode of production." Their response: "For us, 'Lenin' is not the nostalgic name for old dogmatic certainty; quite the contrary, the Lenin that we want to retrieve is the Lenin-in-becoming, the Lenin whose fundamental experience was that of being thrown into a catastrophic new constellation in which old reference points proved useless, and who was thus compelled to *reinvent* Marxism."

The rich, diverse contributions offered in this book—in some cases jostling aggressively against each other, while unified around the common perspective voiced by the editors—is a challenge for all serious intellectuals and activists of our time.

Lenin Rediscovered

A limitation of *Lenin Reloaded* is that the essayists do not have an opportunity, between its covers, to demonstrate amply the virtues embodied in Lenin that are implied in their provocative, sharp-edged assertions. This cannot be said, however, about the volume that one of them has recently produced. Lars T. Lih's *Lenin Rediscovered: "What Is to Be Done?" in Context* reminds me of a saying a Swedish comrade once shared with me—"enough to choke a horse." It is massive, almost overwhelming—and yet, it is a magnificent contribution to our understanding of Lenin, Bolshevism, Marxism, and the history of the Russian revolutionary movement and of Communism.

Clearly written, well reasoned, and effectively documented, it is a work that no scholar seriously examining the life and thought of Lenin will be able to ignore. More than this, it is a gift to serious political activists seeking to draw on traditions and lessons of the past in order to get present-day and future possibilities into sharper focus. It is unfortunate that this book's price is prohibitive for most activists, and that the sheer bulk of the volume (more than 860 pages) will be daunting for many. But those who seek to bridge the gap between serious scholarship and serious activism by helping deepen their comrades' understanding through the development of more widely accessible educational materials will certainly want to draw on this outstanding resource.

Lih's primary target for criticism is "a strong consensus of informed experts" who "at least from the mid-1950s" have put forward a reading of *What Is to Be Done?* that "has found its way into textbooks of political science and of Russian history, and, from there, into almost any secondary account that has reason to touch on Lenin. The two or three famous passages that form the textual basis of this reading are endlessly recycled from textbook to popular history to specialized monograph and back again." He sums up: "Putting all the assertions of the textbook interpretation together, we realize that WITBD is a profound theoretical and organizational innovation, the charter document of Bolshevism, and the ultimate source of Stalinism"—a set of contentions unable to withstand this scholarly onslaught.

Lih presents a Lenin who is absolutely committed to the establishment of political democracy as essential to the struggle for and the realization of socialism, a Lenin who has immense confidence that the working class has a natural capacity for absorbing revolutionary socialist ideas and committing itself to the struggle for a radically better world, a Lenin who is determined to help build a broad working-class party with a principled socialist program flowing from a Marxist understanding of the world. He demolishes the notions that Lenin diverged qualitatively from Marx, that he distrusted the workers and their "spontaneity," that he was an elitist and an authoritarian.

There is, however, a problematical feature of *Lenin Rediscovered*. While his primary anticommunist target is effectively dealt with, he also has a bone to pick with how Lenin has been understood by "activists in the Trotskyist tradition" (specifically "writers such as Tony Cliff, John Molyneux, and more recently Paul Le Blanc"—here referring to my 1990 book *Lenin and the Revolutionary Party*). The activists, he claims, have been inclined to give too much ground to the academics' positing an elitist and authoritarian content in Lenin's 1902 classic. While he does have some nice things to say about us, he suggests that the activists are swayed by the unfair and inaccurate anti-Lenin polemics of 1904 advanced by Rosa Luxemburg and Leon Trotsky (which are also employed by many of the academics). As I argue in a review that appeared in the journal *Historical Materialism*, aspects of this argument strike me as too broadly put and somewhat off-base. Yet this strikes me as a minor problem within what remains a splendid achievement.

Lih is able to demonstrate, with scholarly thoroughness, that this vision is at the core of Lenin's *What Is to Be Done?* and other writings from the mid-1890s up to the revolutionary upsurge of 1905. Thanks to his knowledge of Russian, he is able to comb through existing English translations to identify problematical formulations that do not exist in the Russian original. In fact, about one-third of the text consists of a retranslation of *What Is to Be Done?*, with two sections of detailed annotations—an incredible contribution by itself. He also combs through an immense quantity of other Russian-language materials that he utilizes to help bring the context of Lenin's writings into clearer focus than ever before. For those of us laboring without Russian language skills, this in itself is a precious offering.

More than this, noting that Lenin unambiguously projected a Russian version of the German Social Democratic Party as the kind of organization to bring about socialism in Russia, Lih focuses sustained attention on the German party and its powerful influence on the Russian Marxists. In doing this, he gives well-merited respectful attention to the early contributions of Karl Kautsky and to his importance for the revolutionary Left, Lenin most of all.

One might argue that he "bends the stick" too far—being rather dismissive of the powerful critique of "so-called fatalistic Marxism" of the Second International advanced in the 1920s by the likes of Lukács, Korsch, and Gramsci, and not being alert to the critical insights that Rosa Luxemburg and other revolutionary Marxists (Pannekoek, Riazanov, Parvus, Trotsky, Radek, Rakovsky, and others) were developing at the time. These critical insights found confirmation in the debacle of 1914, causing Lenin himself to revise his earlier positive judgments and to recast and sharpen his own Marxism. But a serious understanding of Lenin and the other Russian Marxists of the early 1900s can be advanced by setting these matters aside in order to fully comprehend *the understanding they had at the time* of the Marxism of the Second International and of German Social Democracy. And as he does this, Lih helps us to see the strengths and grandeur of these truly impressive entities.

What, according to Lih, was the Leninist vision of the revolutionary party as put forward in Lenin's 1902 classic? His view of Lenin's orientation could be summarized this way: The creation of a revolutionary workers' party, guided by a serious-minded utilization of socialist theory and scientific analysis, drawing increasing numbers of working people into a highly conscious struggle against all forms of oppression—this could not be expected to arise easily or spontaneously. It had to be created through the most persistent, serious, consistent efforts of revolutionary socialists. The working class would not automatically become a force for socialist revolution, but it could develop into such a force with the assistance of a serious revolutionary workers' party. Such a party—making past lessons, the most advanced social theory, and a broad social vision accessible to increasing numbers of workers—would be a vital component in the self-education and self-organization of the working class, helping to develop spontaneous working-class impulses toward democracy and socialism into a cohesive, well-organized, and powerful social force.

The greatest limitation in this huge study, perhaps, is that it is not three or four times as huge—that is, it stops in 1904. It needs to be extended two more decades to help us see how Lenin's party, and his ideas, continued to evolve in ways that brought about the workers' revolution of 1917, and what happened in the revolution's aftermath to help transform Lenin's party into something other than what he intended. It might be good to add the consideration of an additional ten years, to examine the further transformation of what had been the revolutionary party of Lenin into the bureaucratic tyranny of Stalin. Those are realities that must also be understood if we are to comprehend the "Leninism of Lenin" in a manner that will be useful for those who wish to change the world for the better.

American Revolutionary

Those arguing in *Lenin Reloaded* that we need to consider how to translate Lenin into our own distinctive realities can do little—again because of space limitations—to illustrate what such efforts might look like. To get a sense of how some have tried to do this very thing (with complex and often mixed results, to be sure), it is worth looking at the history of the early Communist movement that arose in the wake of Lenin's revolution in Russia.

Bryan Palmer's *James P. Cannon and the Origins of the American Revolutionary Left* is one of the finest books yet produced on the

early Communist movement in the United States. This is not surprising given the nature of Palmer's work to date. He was a young
colleague of the incomparable British labor historian E. P. Thomp-
son, of whom Palmer has written a rich and insightful biography
worthy of its subject. In his writing a fluid and clear literary style
seems always to be matched with a searching and disciplined analytical mind. His mastery of the secondary literature on US Communism is matched by his own cutting-edge research, pushing the
edge of scholarship significantly outward.

Cannon is a figure often dismissed by academics, intellectuals,
and political opponents as unworthy of serious consideration. But
Palmer cuts through the dismissive tangle to reveal a remarkable
figure. The young Cannon was intensely active in the Socialist Party
led by Eugene V. Debs and the colorful and rambunctious Wobblies—the Industrial Workers of the World (IWW)—before becoming a key founder and a central leader of the early Communist
Party in the United States. (Cannon's role in the later Trotskyist
movement will be the focus of a projected second volume, but what
we are offered here stands quite well on its own.)

The wonderful blend of literary and scholarly skills greatly enhances Palmer's achievement. The first two chapters on Cannon's
boyhood—which unearth new material—are written with considerable charm, giving a sense of a boyhood reminiscent of Tom Sawyer
or Huckleberry Finn. Other early chapters convey a sense of what
the early Socialist Party was like on the local level as Cannon was
coming of age in a socialist household in Rosedale, Kansas. The
young activist soon struck out on his own, attracted with many others
of his generation to the rough-and-tumble revolutionary unionism
of the Wobblies, and Palmer gives a marvelous on-the-ground picture of the IWW during the Progressive era in such places as New
Castle, Pennsylvania, where Cannon edited a Wobbly paper and
helped provide leadership in organizing and strike struggles. Also
very well done is the account of the merging of local radical streams
(under the impact of World War I, government repression, and the
Russian Revolution) into the early US Communist movement.

The historiography of US Communism has been a minefield.
The contributions of Theodore Draper—in two volumes focused on

the first ten years of American Communism—long dominated the field, and this terrain was extended into the 1930s by Draper protégé Harvey Klehr. Draper and those identifying with him strongly emphasize the decisive influence of the Soviet Union in shaping and dominating American Communism, telling a grim story of authoritarian corruption and wasted idealism. This "traditional" orientation (compatible with traditional Cold War liberalism and more recent neoconservatism) has been sharply challenged over the years by a very substantial and incredibly rich body of "revisionist" scholarship (compatible with "New Left" and socialist perspectives). The "revisionists" have insisted on the indigenous roots of US Communism and—while not denying negative influences emanating from the Soviet Union—highlight inspiring struggles and positive contributions on American soil.

Palmer stakes out a new position in this highly contentious field. He does not allow the story of triumphant Stalinism to obliterate the fact that capitalism is an oppressive system, and that the early Communists were often insightful, creative, and heroic in confronting it—both drawing from and contributing to the rich traditions of the US labor and radical movements. In contrast to many of the "revisionists," however, the story of American Communism's subordination to the vicious Stalin dictatorship that came to dominate the Soviet Union and the world Communist movement is no less central to Palmer's account than it was to Draper's.

Most historians of American Communism have focused on other periods: the first moments, when John Reed and others respond with joy and boundless optimism to the Russian Revolution of 1917; the mass struggles and growing influence of the 1930s; the shift from significant influence during World War II to the disasters of the anticommunist Cold War era; the crisis and collapse in the wake of the revelations of Stalin's crimes. Here we are offered a coherent and detailed story about the converging streams of vibrant labor radicalism that resulted in US Communism's beginnings, its initial growth in the glow of the Russian Revolution, and its painful disorientation and corruption as the revolutionary promise of Lenin and the Bolsheviks was replaced by the bureaucratic tyranny of Stalin's regime.

One of the great strengths of Palmer's book is that it so effectively challenges a common misconception perpetrated by many latter-day students of US Communism, to some extent beguiled by rationalizations of many who embraced the Stalinist dilution of Communism prevalent from the mid-1930s onward. According to such accounts, the US Communist Party of the 1920s was little more than a hotbed of sterile sectarianism that was only overcome by the broad-based reformism of the later "people's front" era. Palmer shows us, however, that this movement represented, "for all its internal divisions, a leading edge of the labor Left, as well as an important force in defending civil rights for oppressed minorities and class-war prisoners"—all in all "a momentous advance for the revolutionary Left, albeit one that would soon stumble and eventually fall backward."

The formation of the US Communist Party had been the culmination of half a century of experience since the Civil War, involving the cumulative development of a vibrant labor-radical subculture, and the corresponding evolution of three generations of labor-radical activists. Uneven, full of contradictions and sometimes absurdities, the Communist Party of the 1920s, with a membership fluctuating between seven thousand and twelve thousand, exercised significant influence in labor, radical, and even liberal circles. Under William Z. Foster's leadership, and with the assistance of Cannon and others, an influential network was created in the American Federation of Labor through the Trade Union Educational League (TUEL), to which many progressive union leaders and activists rallied. (Palmer's critical assessment of Foster's missteps and limitations provides worthwhile insights into TUEL failures.)

The party was also involved in defending human rights and civil liberties in the United States, particularly those of workers, through the International Labor Defense (ILD), which was conceived of during 1925 discussions between Cannon, his companion Rose Karsner, and the legendary IWW leader "Big Bill" Haywood. Indeed, Palmer's book offers the first sustained examination of the ILD (which has generally been subjected to scholarly scrutiny primarily only around the Herndon and Scottsboro cases later in the 1930s). There were many other components of the Communist movement—focusing on the rights of oppressed racial and national groups, women's rights, immigrant rights, the interests of young people and aspirations of students, the opposition to war and imperialism and militarism. Significant attention was given to educating around and building support for the Soviet Union, where many felt a bright socialist future was being built. There were a variety of publications, educational efforts, cultural activities, and more.

He described Cannon as "a figure stamped with the unmistakable marks of the native-born proletarian agitator, [who] nevertheless cultivated relations with some of the more cosmopolitan and theoretical elements in the communist movement, such as Alexander Bittleman, just as he rubbed shoulders with the cultural wing of the revolutionary Left, reviewing books by Mike Gold, drinking and breaking bread with the likes of Tom Tippett and Joseph Freeman, and impressing a youthfully radical Claude McKay with his acumen at a Comintern gathering in Moscow."

Although rich in material on the internal workings of the Communist Party, as well as on the interesting details of Cannon's life, this big book goes much further. Connections with larger economic, social, and cultural developments in the United States are frequently made, with contextual explications, as well, of both national and international political realities. A discussion of the interplay between shifting dynamics within the Communist International and factional fluctuations among the early US Communists is central to the latter part of the narrative (and is a key to Palmer's own interpretation) without, however, obliterating the larger narrative. One gets a vibrant sense of problems and struggles among workers, with the importance of the Passaic strike and the Sacco and Vanzetti case, for example, shining through—and helping to illuminate—the internal conflicts that wracked the Communist Party in the same period.

Palmer does not hold back from tackling larger issues of US labor radicalism, including such questions as Why is there no socialism in the United States? and—at least by implication—how obstacles to an effective socialist movement might be transcended. He explores the relationship of the Soviet Union, as opposed to indigenous traditions, to US Communism, while tracing contributions of the Communist movement to social struggles and social changes in the larger society. He also gives attention to the "organization question" and how different ways of dealing with it have had a significant impact on the fortunes and effectiveness of a political organization and movement. In this last matter, he is part of the rising current of sharp-thinking left-wing scholars who are moving well beyond the fashionable bashing of "the Leninist vanguard party" as the root of all evil. The example and influence of Lenin and the Bolsheviks are far more positive than negative in this narrative. Cannon's stubborn adherence to the early revolutionary ideals is what gets him into trouble with the bureaucratic-authoritarian degeneration of international Communism with the advance and consolidation of the Stalin regime.

The book concludes with the decision of Cannon and a few handfuls of comrades to adhere to the Left Opposition headed by Trotsky. Their expulsion from the Communist mainstream (with even former adherents such as William Dunne and Gil Green turning against them) was engineered by leaders of a rival faction, Jay Lovestone, Bertram D. Wolfe, and Ben Gitlow, who soon were expelled themselves for being insufficiently Stalinist, and who a couple of decades later were prominent Cold War anticommunists. The distinguishing characteristic of Cannon and many others who rallied around Trotsky's banner was that they would remain true to the revolutionary and working-class socialist ideals that had animated the early Communists, in the face of incredibly more powerful and ugly yet "relevant" forces—the totalitarian lure of Stalinism and the exploitative materialism of capitalism.

Lenin Lives

If the words "LENIN LIVES!" are to be more than rhetorical posturing, they will have to go beyond the intellectual constructions contained in essays of the eighteen intellectuals represented in *Lenin Reloaded*. Some of that volume's essayists insist on this themselves. "Without revolutionary theory there is no revolutionary movement, to be sure, which at one level means no more than that you can't have a women's movement without the idea of feminism," Eagleton tells us. "But at the same time, according to Lenin, there is no adequate theory without revolutionary practice. Correct revolutionary theory, he insisted, assumes final shape only in close connection with the practical activity of a mass revolutionary movement."

Living "Leninism" is not encompassed in one and a half dozen intellectuals (the number associated with this book)—they are not "the revolutionary vanguard" of which Lenin spoke, nor is an organization of eighteen hundred activists that has simply declared itself to be so. The words "mass movement" suggests that the vanguard Lenin has in mind constitutes a more substantial, measurable percentage of the working class. My uncle's old handbill, an artifact from the time of which Palmer writes, reflects the fact that serious efforts to implement Lenin's perspective were rooted in a political, social, cultural phenomenon adding up to a section (or vanguard) of the working class. This seems so alien to our own reality!

Yet long before radical academics were intoning the mantra of "race, class, and gender" and to exploring even more diverse and dynamically intersecting identities, such sensibilities could be seen (despite inadequate vocabularies and the inevitable clumsiness of beginners) within the Leninist tradition. The Workers Party of America sought to represent women as well as men, young and old and everyone in between, workers of all colors and cultures and ethnicities, each and every person who suffered oppression under capitalism. It sought to draw more and more of the working class into an independent economic, social, and political force capable of effectively challenging the multifaceted power of capitalism. Its goal was to transfer that power into the hands of the working-class majority— to allow the free development of each to become the basis for the free development of all.

"For Lenin, the knowledge that the working class can have of itself is indissolubly linked to a precise knowledge of the reciprocal relations of all classes in contemporary society, a knowledge which is not only theoretical, we should say is less theoretical than founded on the experience of politics." This according to Bensaïd, who adds: "It is through the test of practical politics that this knowledge of the reciprocal relations between classes is acquired. To paraphrase Lenin, this makes 'our revolution' into a 'revolution of the whole people.'" Callinicos—challenging the notion prevalent among many activists that "the dispersal of campaigning energies serves to confuse the corporate establishment and keep it on the defensive," which he warns could lead to "confusion and exhaustion among activists"— adds that "any effective radical movement requires some means of fitting together specific grievances into some more comprehensive picture of what is wrong and how to remedy it and some systematic means of translating this vision into reality."

As smart as these leftist intellectuals are, they are not the only ones to whom such ideas are occurring. Our world is in trouble. "Mainstream" politics and the logic of the market seem unable to keep things from getting worse. Varieties of reformism, anarchism, and fundamentalism (secular as well as religious) have been tried, continue to be tried, and yet the times in which we live seem to grow more terrible. There is a growing unease, questioning, searching for new pathways of thought and action. These books, which ten or fifteen years ago might not have been taken seriously, will today still not be read by masses of people. But what masses of people are experiencing and feeling and thinking today gives these books a greater resonance than before, and so they may find a greater "market"—a broader and more intense readership—than before. It is even possible that these intellectual stirrings will contribute to thinking and activity among an emergent layer of activists that, in turn, could facilitate larger political shifts.

Lenin has returned, possibly to be followed by a reemergence/revitalization of some variant (or variants) of Leninist politics. Whether this will advance struggles for human liberation, with activists learning from (not repeating) sectarian and tragic derailments of the past—this is a question that may yet become relevant.

Chapter Two
ONE FOR THE ENCYCLOPEDIAS

Vladimir Ilyich Ulyanov was born on April 22, 1870 (April 10, according to the Old Style calendar then used in Russia), in Simbursk (later renamed Ulyanovsk), a provincial town on the Volga River. He was the third of six children in what was at first a relatively happy family. His father, Ilya Nikolaevich Ulyanov, was a respected director of public schools. His mother, Maria Alexandrovna Blank, was the daughter of a physician and taught her children a love of reading and music. His father died in 1886, and in 1887 his beloved older brother, Alexander, was arrested and hanged for involvement in an unsuccessful plot by revolutionary university students to assassinate Tsar Alexander III.

At the end of 1887, Lenin himself was briefly arrested for involvement in a peaceful demonstration against the oppressive tsarist regime and for membership in a radical political group. A brilliant student, he had just entered the University of Kazan, but his involvement in protest activities resulted in his immediate expulsion and banishment to a small village near Kazan, where he lived under police surveillance. In 1888 he was permitted to return to Kazan, but he was denied entry to any university and therefore embarked on his own rigorous course of study. In 1891 he passed law examinations at the University of St. Petersburg. Lenin worked as a lawyer for only a few months before becoming a full-time revolutionary.

The Making of a Revolutionary

At the time when Lenin became a revolutionary, impoverished peasants made up about 90 percent of Russia's population. An expanding class of wage workers and their families, created through the country's substantial industrial growth in the late nineteenth century, made up another 7 percent. There was also a small "middle-class" layer of professionals and well-to-do businessmen (the bourgeoisie), and at the very top, a powerful landed aristocracy capped by an absolute monarchy. The country was characterized by a complete absence of democracy, limits on freedom of expression, the persecution of all religious minorities outside the official Russian Orthodox Church, severe limitations on the rights of women, and oppression of more than one hundred national minorities that inhabited the Russian Empire—a notorious "prison-house of nations" (in which a variety of national groups were oppressed by their Russian conquerors). Such conditions generated many revolutionary currents.

Lenin was deeply influenced by earlier nineteenth-century Russian revolutionaries, especially the writer Nikolai G. Chernyshevsky, as well as by the underground revolutionary populist movement known as the People's Will (Narodnaya Volya). This current was made up of idealistic activists who specialized in clandestine methods and sought to organize a peasant-based revolution and to establish a socialist society that would be based largely on the traditional commune, sometimes known as the "*mir*," that had existed in peasant villages throughout Russia. Lenin drew upon this tradition, especially in his underground organizational concepts, but he was most profoundly attracted to the Western European working-class orientation developed by Karl Marx and Frederick Engels in such works as *The Communist Manifesto*, *Capital*, and *Socialism: Utopian and Scientific*. This orientation had been most forcefully injected into the Russian revolutionary movement by Georgi Plekhanov. Lenin became an influential voice among Russian Marxists through his study *The Development of Capitalism in Russia* (1897) and many other works.

The Marxists argued that Russia was undergoing a capitalist transformation, that industrialization was creating a factory-based proletariat, and that this working class would become the most effective force in the struggle to overthrow tsarism. Instead of engaging in terrorist activities (assassinations, and so forth) against the tsar and his officials, as the People's Will had done, the Marxists argued that the working class should build trade unions to fight for better working conditions and living standards, should organize mass demonstrations to pressure for broader democratic and social reforms, and should organize their own political party to lead the struggle for a democratic revolution. Such a revolution would clear the way for the economic and political development of Russia (presumably through a capitalist economy and democratic republic). Then, when the working class became the majority, the process would culminate in a second revolution with a socialist character. The workers would take control of the economy and run it for the benefit of all. The Marxists believed that workers in other countries should and would be moving in a similar direction.

The Rise of Bolshevism

In 1898, the Marxists organized the Russian Social Democratic Labor Party (RSDLP) to advance their orientation. Later, in 1901–02, the Populists organized the competing Socialist Revolutionary (SR) Party. Both parties joined the international federation known as the Socialist (or Second) International. Lenin aimed many polemics against the SR, but soon he also developed serious disagreements with others in the RSDLP. In the pages of the newspaper *Iskra* ("The Spark"), Lenin, Plekhanov, Julius Martov, and others criticized the so-called Economists, who urged that workers should concentrate only on economic issues at the workplace and that leadership of the democratic struggle should be left in the hands of pro-capitalist liberals. Lenin and the other "Iskraists" argued in favor of building a strong centralized party that would draw the various layers of the working class into a broad economic and political struggle to oppose all forms of oppression, overthrow tsarism, and advance the workers' interests.

Lenin popularized these ideas in *What Is to Be Done?*, published in 1902. The "Iskraists" won the day at the second congress of the RSDLP, held in Brussels and London in 1903. But before the congress was over they themselves had split into two organized factions—the Bolsheviks (from the Russian *bolshe*, meaning "more," since they had gained a plurality of votes) and the Mensheviks (from the Russian word *menshe*, meaning "less"). This split was analyzed in Lenin's *One Step Forward, Two Steps Back* (1904). The Bolsheviks, led by Lenin, insisted on a more disciplined party than favored by the Mensheviks, who became associated with Martov and Plekhanov. In addition, the Mensheviks favored a coalition between workers and capitalists to overthrow tsarism, whereas Lenin (for example, in his 1905 polemic *Two Tactics of the Social Democracy in the Democratic Revolution*) insisted that a worker-peasant alliance, and the subsequent creation of a "democratic dictatorship of the proletariat and the peasantry," would be necessary to achieve a genuinely democratic revolution in Russia.

In this period Lenin maintained a precarious existence in the revolutionary underground (where he met and married one of his closest comrades, Nadezhda Krupskaya, in 1898), in prison and Siberian exile, and in frugal circumstances as an exile outside Russia. He lived in Munich from 1900 to 1902, in London from 1902 to 1903, and in Geneva from 1903 to 1905. Lenin and Krupskaya played an essential role in coordinating the work of the underground Bolshevik organization of the RSDLP, also facilitating the production and distribution of such revolutionary newspapers as *Vperyod* ("Forward") and *Proletarii* ("The Proletarian").

From the 1905 Revolution to 1914

In 1905 a revolutionary upsurge sparked by a spontaneous uprising among the workers, after the tsar's troops fired on a peaceful demonstration in St. Petersburg, and fueled by hundreds of strikes and peasant insurgencies, forced the tsarist regime to grant a number of important reforms, including greater political liberties and the creation of a weak parliamentary body called the Duma.

Although Lenin at first rejected participation in the Duma (he changed his position in 1906), he supported participation in the soviets (councils) of workers' deputies, spontaneously formed democratic bodies arising in workplaces and workers' communities that directed revolutionary activities. He also strongly favored opening up the RSDLP, especially its Bolshevik wing, to a dramatic influx of radicalizing workers. The political gap between Bolsheviks and Mensheviks narrowed, and the membership of the RSDLP soared. One left-wing Menshevik, Leon Trotsky, head of the St. Petersburg soviet, even advanced (in articles written from 1904 through 1906) the idea of *permanent revolution*—that is, the concept that the democratic revolution would lead to workers taking political power with support from the peasants, initiating a transitional period to socialism, with the Russian Revolution helping to generate workers' revolutions in more advanced industrial countries. While Lenin did not fully accept this notion at the time, it was later reflected in his perspectives for the 1917 revolution.

In late 1905 and throughout 1906, however, the forces of tsarist conservatism were able to stem the revolutionary tide and rescind many of the reforms granted earlier. Revolutionaries were once again forced underground or into exile, and many left-wing intellectuals became demoralized.

Differences between the Bolsheviks and the Mensheviks once again sharpened, yet Lenin also found himself in conflict with a group of Bolsheviks led by Alexander A. Bogdanov. These "ultraleft" Bolsheviks denigrated trade union work and other reform activities (to which they counterposed "armed struggle"), and also questioned the wisdom of the Bolsheviks' running in elections and participating in the Duma. Lenin insisted that involvement in the Duma gave revolutionary socialists a powerful tool for legal agitation and education and that reform struggles enabled the working-class movement to grow in experience and political effectiveness. He wrote a philosophical work, *Materialism and Empirio-Criticism* (1909), arguing against what he saw as serious philosophical revisions of Marxism being advanced by Bogdanov and others. At the same time, he was conducting a fierce struggle against the "Liquidators," an influential current among the Mensheviks that wanted to replace all revolutionary underground organizational forms with strictly legal and reform-minded structures. Lenin was also sharply critical of "conciliators," such as Trotsky and even of some in the Bolsheviks' ranks, who attempted to maintain RSDLP unity. He had concluded that a cohesive and disciplined organization, based on a revolutionary Marxist program combining both legal and underground activity, could not be created by seeking compromises with socialists having a variety of orientations.

In 1912 Lenin and those who agreed with him sought to reorganize the RSDLP on a clear, cohesive basis—which resulted in a split with all other currents in the RSDLP. The new Bolshevik RSDLP published the newspaper *Pravda* ("Truth"). They had not only a coherent strategic orientation but, above all, a clear program, highlighted by three demands: an eight-hour work day, beneficial to the workers; land reform, beneficial to the peasants; and a democratic constituent assembly. These three demands were used to dramatize the need for a worker-peasant alliance in the democratic revolution. The Bolsheviks also had a serious and disciplined organizational structure that integrated legal reform efforts with revolutionary work. Between 1912 and 1914 Lenin's Bolsheviks outstripped all other currents in the Russian revolutionary movement, enjoying predominance among the organized workers.

Bolshevik successes coincided with a new wave of radicalization among the dramatically growing Russian working class. Government violence against striking workers in the Lena gold fields in 1912, combined with population growth in the country's industrial centers marked by intensive exploitation of workers, generated considerable ferment and growing protests. By 1914 some observers concluded that Russia was on the verge of another revolutionary outbreak.

Imperialist World War

This militant upswing was checked, however, by the eruption of World War I, which was used by the tsarist authorities to suppress all dissent. The socialist movement split into "patriotic" and antiwar fragments, not only in Russia but in all countries involved in the conflict. In Russia only the more moderate "patriotic" socialists were able to operate openly, thus managing to eclipse the now repressed Bolsheviks in the labor movement.

Lenin had moved to Krakow, in Austrian Poland, in 1912. After the outbreak of war in 1914 he was deported to Switzerland. Lenin, like many Marxists, had expected the outbreak of war. However, he was deeply shocked by the capitulation of the Second International's mass parties before the "patriotic" demands of their respective ruling classes—in particular that of the German Socialist Party (SPD), which he had previously considered the very model of an orthodox Marxist party in a more or less democratic parliamentary system. With the exception of Rosa Luxemburg, Karl Liebknecht, and a few others, the bulk of the SPD leaders either endorsed German war aims or refrained from opposing the war effort. Lenin, along with Luxemburg and others on the revolutionary left, saw imperialism—the aggressive economic expansionism of the various "great powers"—as the underlying cause of the ensuing slaughter. He was outraged that workers of the rival countries were being encouraged to kill each other in this conflict, and he never forgave Karl Kautsky, the German symbol of "orthodox Marxism," for rationalizing the betrayal of working-class internationalism.

In the period from 1914 to 1917 Lenin concentrated on efforts to build a revolutionary socialist opposition to the war. He joined with various antiwar socialist currents at the Zimmerwald and Kienthal conferences in criticizing the failure of the Second International to remain true to its uncompromisingly antiwar statements, and he called for a new, revolutionary Third International. He also produced a study that explored the economic roots of World War I, *Imperialism, the Highest Stage of Capitalism* (1916). In addition, he developed a critical analysis of nationalism, distinguishing between the nationalism of advanced and oppressive capitalist "great powers" (which revolutionaries should not support) and the nationalism of peoples oppressed and exploited by the "great powers" (which revolutionaries should support).

Lenin at this time also took issue with those non-Bolshevik revolutionaries, notably Luxemburg and Trotsky, whose policies were, in fact, closest to his own. Rejecting the emphasis of Luxemburg (in *The Junius Pamphlet*) and Trotsky (in *War and the International*) on calling for immediate peace and advocating a "Socialist United States of Europe," he advanced the most intransigent possible slogan: "Turn the Imperialist War into a Civil War." Though only his closest associates, such as Gregory Zinoviev, accepted this slogan, it was very important to Lenin because it would make impossible any compromise with "centrist" Social Democrats such as Kautsky and (in France) Jean Longuet, who by 1916 inclined toward a moderately antiwar posture yet were quite unwilling to make a clear break with the pro-war majorities of their parties. Only by splitting revolutionary socialists away from such compromisers would it be possible, he believed, to provide leadership to war-weary masses for a genuine socialist transformation.

The Fall of Tsarism and the Rise of "Dual Power"

Within Russia, a growing disillusionment with the war generated a new upsurge of radicalism among the workers and peasants. A spontaneous uprising initiated by women workers on International Women's Day in Petrograd (as St. Petersburg had been renamed in 1914) in March 1917 turned into a successful revolution when the Russian Army—largely "peasants in uniform"—joined with the insurgent workers and turned against the tsarist government. A situation of "dual power" arose as the powers of the state were assumed by democratically elected councils (soviets) of workers' and soldiers' deputies and also by a pro-capitalist Provisional Government set up by politicians in the Duma. Many SRs and Mensheviks, and even some Bolsheviks, supported the Provisional Government. Lenin returned from exile in April 1917 to challenge this widespread orientation.

Immediately after the overthrow of the tsarist regime, Lenin had desperately sought to find ways to return to Russia. He was refused permission to travel by way of Great Britain and France, since the governments of those countries saw him as a threat to Russia's continued participation in the war. However, the German government—for similar reasons—allowed Lenin and all other Russian exiles to travel through Germany. Later, those hostile to Lenin were to use this (and also funds from Germany allegedly secured by the Bolsheviks) in order to slander him as a "German agent."

Upon his arrival in Petrograd, Lenin pointed out that the Provisional Government was unable to end Russian involvement in the war, could not guarantee that the workers in the cities would have enough to eat, and was unprepared to break up the nobility's large estates to give land to the peasants. Therefore, he argued, workers and revolutionaries should give no support to the Provisional Government. Instead they should demand "all power to the soviets" and insist on "peace, bread, and land." The democratic revolution had to grow into a working-class revolution supported by the peasantry. This development would stimulate the war-weary and radicalizing workers of such countries as Germany, Austria-Hungary, and France to join their Russian comrades in socialist revolution.

These "April Theses" shocked most of Russia's socialists, including many leading Bolsheviks, but quickly won over the rank and file of Lenin's party, as well as such former opponents as Trotsky. By July 1917 the Bolsheviks were in the lead of a militant mass demonstration against the Provisional Government, which was now headed by Alexander Kerensky, a moderate socialist. The demonstration erupted in violence, leading to repression by the Provisional Government. Many Bolsheviks (including the prestigious new recruit Trotsky) were arrested, and Lenin fled across the border to Finland. There he began writing his classic Marxist study *The State and Revolution*, which presented a libertarian and democratic vision of working-class revolution and the socialist future. Before he could complete this study, events had evolved to the point where Lenin found it possible to issue a practical appeal to the Bolshevik Central Committee for a revolutionary seizure of power.

Counterrevolutionary opponents played a key role in bringing about this turn in events. In September 1917 General Lavr Kornilov mounted a right-wing military coup designed to oust both the Provisional Government and the soviets. The Provisional Government freed all revolutionary militants from prison and gave them arms. Bolsheviks joined with Mensheviks, SRs, anarchists, and others to defend the revolution. Kornilov was defeated, his troops melting away under the influence of revolutionary agitators.

Bolshevik Revolution and Russian Civil War

From hiding, Lenin urgently insisted to his comrades that the Bolsheviks launch an uprising to establish soviet power. Two of his own close followers, Gregory Zinoviev and Lev Kamenev, argued against so audacious a move, but they found themselves overwhelmed by revolutionary enthusiasm not only within the party but among growing sectors of the working class and peasantry. A split among the SRs resulted in a substantial left-wing faction that supported the Bolshevik demands. The soviets themselves now adopted the position of "all power to the soviets" and organized a Military Revolutionary Committee under Trotsky's direction, which prepared an insurrection to overthrow the Provisional Government.

The stirring but relatively bloodless October Revolution in Russia, which was actually carried out on November 7, 1917 (according to the modern calendar), was seen as a beacon of hope by the discontented throughout the world. One of the central developments of the twentieth century, it led to the formation of the Union of Soviet Socialist Republics and to the rise of modern Communism.

Lenin was the leader of the first Soviet government, the Council of People's Commissars (Sovnarkom), which consisted of a coalition of Bolsheviks (who soon renamed their organization the Communist Party) and Left Socialist Revolutionaries (commonly referred to as Left SRs). The new regime entered into peace negotiations with Germany to secure Russia's withdrawal from World War I. The German government made harsh demands for territorial and financial concessions as a precondition for a peace settlement. Many revolutionaries, including the Left SRs and even a Left Communist faction in Lenin's own party, opposed the concessions and called for a revolutionary war against German imperialism.

Trotsky, who as leader of the Russian negotiating team at Brest-Litovsk had used the peace talks to expose German imperialist war aims and to appeal to the German masses "over the heads" of their government, took an intermediary position, hoping that German military action against the infant Soviet republic would be blocked by mutinies and strikes by the German working class. Trotsky advocated refusal either to sign the Germans' Brest-Litovsk diktat or to resume the war with a virtually nonexistent Russian Army. This compromise position was initially adopted by the Soviet government, but the hoped-for mass strikes and mutinies failed to materialize, and, when the German military launched a devastating offensive, Trotsky withdrew his "neither war nor peace" proposal and sided with Lenin.

Against angry opposition among many Bolsheviks and most Left SRs, Lenin insisted on Russia's need for peace and narrowly won acceptance of what were now even stiffer German demands, resulting in the Treaty of Brest-Litovsk (March 3, 1918). The Left SRs withdrew from the government and assumed a stance of violent opposition. The Right SRs and even some Mensheviks were openly hostile as well. Pro-capitalist and pro-tsarist forces committed themselves to the overthrow of the new regime, as did a number of foreign governments, notably those of Great Britain, France, the United States, and Japan. In all, fourteen foreign countries intervened with military forces and aided counterrevolutionary Russian forces in an escalating, brutal civil war. Masses of workers and peasants joined the new Red Army to defend the gains of the revolution. Their efforts were hampered by economic collapse—hastened by premature nationalizations—and also by the inexperience and inevitable mistakes of the new government.

In 1918 some SRs carried out assassination attempts in which Lenin was badly wounded and other prominent Bolsheviks were killed. In response, a Red Terror of arrests and executions was launched against all perceived "enemies of the revolution" by the Cheka (special security forces), set up on Lenin's initiative and directed by Felix Dzherzhinsky. Early in 1918 the Sovnarkom had dissolved what it felt to be an unrepresentative constituent assembly on the grounds that this institution had been superseded by a more thoroughgoing soviet democracy. By 1919, however, this democracy had largely evaporated. As a result of Communist repression of opposing left-wing parties and the relative disintegration of the working class as a political force (because the economy itself had largely disintegrated), the soviets were transformed into hollow shells that would rubber-stamp the decisions of the Sovnarkom and the Communist Party.

Brutal Communist policies were deepened in response to the murderous campaigns of anticommunist counterrevolutionaries (often known as "the Whites" as opposed to the left-wing "Reds"). Increasingly under the leadership of reactionary and pro-tsarist army officers, the Whites often combined anticommunism with antidemocratic, anti–working class, anti-peasant, and anti-Semitic violence. Nonetheless, the Whites were given substantial material support from foreign governments hoping to put an end to what was a "bad example" to their own working classes.

Lenin and the Russian Communists were convinced that the spread of socialist revolution to other countries was essential for the final victory of their own revolution. In 1919 they organized the first congress of the Communist International (the Third International), initiating the formation of Communist parties in countries throughout the world. Concerned that these new parties might fall prey to "ultraleft" errors (such as attempting to seize power without majority working-class support or refusing to fight for "mere" reforms), Lenin wrote *"Left-Wing" Communism: An Infantile Disorder* in 1920. At the second and third congresses of the Communist International he argued in favor of the "united front" tactic, whereby Communists would join forces with more moderate Socialists to protect and advance workers' rights against capitalist and reactionary attacks. (This would also win support among growing numbers of workers for the Communists who would prove to be the most effective fighters for the workers' interests.) Lenin never gave up on the belief that the future of the new Soviet republic could be secured only through the spread of working-class revolution to other countries, but he never lived to see his hopes realized.

From "War Communism" to New Economic Policy

During the Russian Civil War, in Lenin's opinion, he and his comrades had made terrible mistakes. In pushing back the foreign invaders, for example, the Red Army—with Lenin's support but over the objections of Red Army commander Trotsky—invaded Poland in hopes of generating a revolutionary uprising among the Polish workers and peasants. Instead, a fierce counterattack drove the Russian forces from Polish soil.

Some of the greatest mistakes involved the implementation of what was called "War Communism." Sweeping nationalizations of industry formally placed the economy in the hands of the inexperienced state, and attempts at strict centralized planning introduced authoritarian and bureaucratic elements into the economy. Efforts were also made to pit "poor peasants" against allegedly "rich peasants" in order to establish state controls over agriculture. Such policies resulted in red tape, bottlenecks, and shortages, growing discontent among the workers and bitterness among the peasants.

These policies were even theorized by some as providing a positive "shortcut" to the ideal Communist society of the future (which Marx had insisted could be achieved only after an extended period of high economic productivity, abundance, and genuinely democratic social control of the means of production). In fact, the policies of War Communism could reasonably be justified only as desperate emergency measures in the face of civil war and invasion. By 1921 the experience of War Communism had generated peasant revolts and an uprising of workers and sailors at the previously pro-Bolshevik Kronstadt naval base outside of Petrograd.

Lenin now led the way in adopting more realistic policies that had been urged by some Communists, including Trotsky. In 1921 the New Economic Policy (NEP) was established to allow small-scale capitalist production in the countryside and the reintroduction of market mechanisms into the economy as a whole. One Bolshevik theorist, Nikolai Bukharin, became closely identified in later years with the preservation of the NEP reforms. Such changes, together with the end of the civil war and foreign intervention, led to improvements in the economy and to the possibility of implementing important health, education, and social welfare policies beneficial to millions of people in the battered Soviet republic.

Yet at the same time, the Communist Party under Lenin also took measures to strengthen its monopoly of political power and even, as an emergency measure, to curtail democracy within the party itself, for the first time banning factions. In particular, a Workers Opposition headed by union leader Alexander Shlyapnikov and feminist intellectual Alexandra Kollontai—calling for greater working-class control over the state apparatus and economy—was prevented from expressing its views, but smaller oppositional currents were repressed as well. These measures established precedents and the framework for the development of a permanently narrow and repressive dictatorship.

Lenin's Final Defeat and Legacy

Lenin grew increasingly alarmed that the Soviet republic was becoming "bureaucratically degenerated," as he put it. Suffering from a stroke in May 1922, he recovered sufficiently in autumn to return to work, only to be felled by a second stroke in December. Throughout this period and into the early months of 1923 he focused attention on ways of overcoming the bureaucratic tyranny that was gripping the Communist Party and the Soviet government and of strengthening controls by workers and peasants over the state apparatus.

Lenin opposed the inclination of some party leaders to adopt repressive policies toward non-Russian nationalities. Chief among these particular leaders was Joseph Stalin, who became the party's general secretary in 1922. Also, while Lenin had seen the concept of "democratic centralism" as involving "freedom of discussion, unity in action," Stalin and others who were now in charge of the party apparatus distorted the concept—so that a bureaucratic "centralism" crowded out inner-party democracy—to inhibit questioning of and suppress opposition to their own policies.

Lenin sought an alliance with Trotsky to fight for his positions in the party, and he broke decisively with Stalin, whom he identified as being in the forefront of the trends he was opposing. In his last testament he urged that Stalin be removed from his positions of party leadership. But a third stroke in March 1923 completely incapacitated him. At his country home in the village of Gorki, outside Moscow, he suffered a last, fatal stroke on January 21, 1924. After an elaborate state funeral, Lenin's embalmed body was placed in a mausoleum in Moscow's Red Square.

He was mourned by millions in the Soviet Union and by Communists and other revolutionaries throughout the world, but much of Lenin's work was undone by (yet bombastically identified with) the later policies of the Stalin regime. Even in his lifetime, what he viewed as the "dictatorship of the proletariat"—political rule by the working class—had, under difficult conditions, degenerated into a one-party dictatorship. But after his death it evolved into a ruthless bureaucratic tyranny that defended above all else the material and other privileges of the bureaucratic rulers.

Those who had been closest to Lenin found their authority eliminated by Stalin's political machine, and most of them were eventually killed in the purges during the 1930s, when many hundreds of thousands of real and imagined dissidents among the Communists and others were destroyed. Alternatives to this Stalinist version of "Leninism" were put forward, particularly by Trotsky and by Bukharin; but throughout the Communist International and the world Communist movement Stalin's orientation dominated. Even when later Communist leaders denounced Stalin in 1956, the bureaucratic system and undemocratic methods with which he was associated remained in place.

With the collapse of the Soviet Union in 1991, questions arose about how much influence Lenin would continue to have as a symbol and as a theorist. Lenin concerned himself with many dimensions of political theory, but his distinctive contribution involved the conceptualization and organization of a party that proved capable of carrying out a socialist revolution in Russia in 1917. Even for many of his most severe critics, Lenin's political integrity and personal selflessness are beyond dispute, as is his place in history as one of the greatest revolutionary leaders of the twentieth century. What is hotly contested across the political spectrum, however, is his relevance for the future—which is, of course, related to how we are to interpret his life and thought and actions.

Chapter Three
TRAVESTIES, STATUES, AND LAUGHTER

Politics (revolutionary politics included) is the art of the possible, and since politics involves the actions and relationships of human beings, political possibilities are often reflected in the interplay of personality and politics. To the extent this is true, it is meaningful to consider personalities of leading political figures in order to gain insights into their political perspectives and practice. This is certainly the case with Vladimir Ilyich Lenin, the Russian revolutionary intellectual who led the Russian Revolution of 1917 that has been seen by many as the starting point of modern Communism.

These comments are stimulated by a marvelous intellectual romp by Tom Stoppard entitled *Travesties.* In that play Lenin is one of three major revolutionaries—the only political one (and political to his very core), the other two, novelist James Joyce and Dadaist pioneer Tristan Tzara, being artistic radicals. As one would expect, the play is permeated with crackling dialogue and delicious humor, as when the rather silly conservative hero, charmed by Lenin's aversion to modern art, tells us "there was nothing wrong with Lenin except his politics."[1]

An exuberant and brilliantly executed revival of the play at Princeton's McCarter Theatre in 2012 (more than three decades after it was first produced) has particular resonance in our own time, a point made by more than one participant in a stimulating panel discussion after one of its final performances. Stoppard is one of the most interesting contemporary playwrights, particularly since, with absolutely no pretense of being a revolutionary, he is drawn—over and over and over again—to both literate and entertaining engagements with questions of politics and revolution: not only *Travesties* but also the remarkable trilogy The Coast of Utopia, which focuses on Russia's nineteenth-century revolutionary intellectuals, and *Rock 'n' Roll* (dealing with Communism, dissidence, and "the velvet revolution" in his native Czechoslovakia).[2]

Stoppard clearly has no desire to rally theatergoers around the banner of "Leninism." Yet it is one of the functions of his plays, just as clearly, to generate thought and discussion of the ideas that collide and confront each other in what he presents to theatergoers. Through him many more people than would otherwise have been the case consider some of Lenin's ideas.

It is quite striking, however, that of the three revolutionaries in *Travesties* (and of all the other characters in what is such a vibrantly funny piece of theater), only Lenin is given exclusively humorless lines. Of course, just as Shakespeare's historical plays present historical figures not as they were but as a means for telling his own story, so Stoppard's Lenin is presented not as he actually was, but as a symbol first of social-political insurgency, and then—more imposingly—as a symbol of the bureaucratic authoritarianism that Communism became. Just as Shakespeare's plays are not diminished as works of art by his artistic license, so *Travesties* retains its great charm despite limitations in its portrayal of the historical Lenin. The fact remains that the actual personality of Lenin is flattened in this play. That is, arguably, no fault of Stoppard's. It is the way Lenin has commonly been seen not only by hostile journalists and historians but also, for many decades before 1990, by loyal citizens in Communist countries where immense statues of Lenin were erected to justify and glorify bureaucratic tyrannies.

Yet the inadequacy of this, for those wishing to understand the actual Lenin, is suggested when we compare the ponderous talking statue in *Travesties* with other portrayals closer to the historical Lenin. Consider Edmund Wilson's description (in his 1940 classic *To the Finland Station*) of how Lenin appears "in an old historical film patched together from old newsreels, *From Tsar to Lenin*, a short sturdy man with a big bald boxlike brow, leaning forward as if on the edge of his chair, arguing, insisting, smiling, screwing up his eyes in the shrewd Russian way, gesturing to drive his points home: a rapid fire of lips, eyes and hands in which the whole man is concentrated."[3] Such animation seems absent from the Lenin of *Travesties*.

With the play's debut in1974, Stoppard's "Leninism" symbolized a powerful challenge to artistic freedom. Since Communism's collapse in the 1990s, the power of this "Leninism" has seemingly passed away. Yet in a sense, Lenin lives on—certainly in his writings.

The great Russian novelist Maxim Gorky, an intimate friend but sometimes also a fierce critic of Lenin, once commented: "Outwardly he is all wrapped in words, as a fish is covered with scales." Gorky protested: "There was another Lenin," certainly different from Stoppard's—as Gorky put it, "the splendid comrade, the cheerful person with a live unflagging interest in everything in the world, with an astonishingly kind approach to people."[4]

But the words—revolutionary writings, political analyses, polemics—are inseparable from this person, nonetheless. Another one-time intimate turned fierce critic, Angelica Balabanoff, put it this way: "From his youth on, Lenin was convinced that most of human suffering and of moral, legal, and social deficiencies which torment and degrade humanity were caused by class distinctions. He was also convinced that class struggle alone . . . could put an end to exploiters and exploited and create a society of the free and equal. He gave himself entirely to the attainment of this end and he used every means in his power to achieve it."[5]

The 1917 revolution that Lenin led was influenced by the radical-democratic and socialist ideas of Karl Marx. It was carried out by Russia's small but highly organized working class, supported by enough of the peasant majority to make it stick. It was opposed, attacked, and undermined in innumerable ways by the world's most powerful countries, but it cleared its way past the carnage of World War I and the Russian Civil War, and a global superpower called the Union of Soviet Socialist Republics (or Soviet Union) emerged. The word "Communism" had originally meant an economy of abundant resources, controlled by all of the people, in which the free development of each would be the condition for the free development of all. Far from being a beacon of freedom and socialist democracy, however, the Soviet Union became known as one of the most repressive dictatorships in human history, particularly under Lenin's successor, Joseph Stalin, who took power in the late 1920s.[6]

"People tend to think of Stalinism as being . . . a perversion of Leninism," Stoppard commented in 1974. "That is an absurd and foolish untruth, and it is one on which the Left bases itself. Lenin perverted Marxism, and Stalin carried on from there." This is as common a view as the notion of the humorless Lenin. The engaging cultural-anarchist poet, Andrei Codrescu—a truly splendid, independent-minded social commentator—in like manner challenges the image (passed on by a British journalist in 1919) of Lenin as having "a joyous temperament" prone to laughter.

Instead, Codrescu suggests, Lenin was somewhat "boring," living up to Alexander Solzhenitsyn's portrait as (in Codrescu's summary) "a dour, overwrought, frowning, anxious micromanager who becomes apoplectic and enraged over small details, and has no time for shared pleasure, unless it is sharing a mean joke with co-conspirators, a joke that moreover advances the cause of the Revolution." This seems to match Stoppard's own portrayal of Lenin in Zurich (except there is not even malicious joking). It will be worth taking up the question of Lenin and laughter later, but any inclination to smile freezes when Codrescu, like Stoppard, essentially puts Lenin on the same plane as Stalin, characterizing him as "a mass murdering ideologue."[7]

This equation of Lenin and Stalin has been challenged by insightful observations of more than one knowledgeable anticommunist. In his classic *The Great Terror*, Robert Conquest tells us: "Lenin's Terror was the product of the years of war and violence, of the collapse of society and administration, of the desperate acts of rulers precariously riding the flood, and fighting for control and survival." The situation was quite different under Stalin, "who attained complete control at a time when general conditions were calm. . . . It was in cold blood, quite deliberately and unprovokedly, that Stalin started a new cycle of suffering." The qualitative break involved Stalin's so-called revolution from above beginning in 1929. This rapid industrialization and forced collectivization of land rode roughshod over the workers and peasants. It generated millions of deaths, the regimentation of culture, intensified repression, mass arrests, and bloody purges. To declare that "Stalinism was the outcome of Leninism," Hannah Arendt has argued, obscures "the sheer criminality of the whole regime" that made bloody purges and the gulag its centerpieces. Whittaker Chambers made a similar point in 1956: "To become the embodiment of the revolutionary idea in history Stalin had to corrupt Communism absolutely. . . . He sustained this corruption with a blend of cunning and brute force. History knows nothing similar on such a scale."[8]

The authoritarian personality that both Stoppard and Codrescu perceive, however, finds corroboration in Stefan Possony's biography *Lenin: The Compulsive Revolutionary*, which offers—if anything—an even more severe judgment: "Self-righteous, rude, demanding, ruthless, despotic, formalistic, bureaucratic, disciplined, cunning, intolerant, stubborn, one-sided, suspicious, distant, asocial, cold-blooded, ambitious, purposive, vindictive, spiteful, a grudgeholder, a coward who was able to face danger only when he deemed it unavoidable—Lenin was a complete law unto himself and he was entirely serene about it."[9]

Often a biographer's judgments of his subject's personality, however, are related to political considerations. A dyed-in-the-wool conservative such as Possony is confident in the knowledge that some people, some classes, and some races are superior to others, as he argued in another study, *The Geography of Intellect*. Revolutions designed to overthrow those of superior intellectual and cultural qualities, in the name of utopian notions of equality and "rule by the people," he informed his readers, destroy the very fabric of civilization, paving the way for chaos and tyranny. Obviously, from this standpoint, Lenin—committed to overturning the present social order to create a new and radically democratic society of the free and the equal—is a monster.[10]

This naturally stands in contrast to the view of someone such as Leon Trotsky, a revolutionary comrade, who disagreed with the assertion that Lenin had made great sacrifices for the revolutionary cause. "Lenin did not sacrifice himself," Trotsky insisted. "On the contrary, he lived a full life, a wonderfully abundant life, developing, expanding his whole personality, serving a cause which he himself freely chose." One need not be a revolutionary, however, to perceive such positive characteristics in Lenin. A shrewd and knowledgeable anticommunist, US diplomat George F. Kennan, has insightfully suggested the difference between the leadership qualities of Lenin and Stalin, commenting that Lenin "was spared that whole great burden of personal insecurity which rested so heavily on Stalin. He never had to doubt his hold on the respect and admiration of his colleagues. He could rule them through the love they bore him, whereas Stalin was obliged to rule them through their fears."[11]

The personal qualities to which both Trotsky and Kennan allude were noted by many others in a position to know. The highly respected Lenin scholar Carter Elwood (if anything anti-Leninist in his own orientation) has emphasized in his new collection of penetrating essays, *The Non-Geometric Lenin*, that political idolaters and many critics who focus exclusively on his revolutionary politics miss "a man with non-revolutionary interests and human foibles," but that "neither the hagiographic nor the linear Lenin was a very interesting individual." Elwood notes "he was at times considerate and friendly, or on other occasions condescending and demeaning, in the same fashion as many other people are when confronted with complex personal problems." He adds that "a balanced and comprehensive view of Lenin" requires going beyond politics "to study his relations with those around him" and as "a person with normal interests in food, drink, holidays and tramping through the mountains."[12]

Essential details on this "non-geometric Lenin" have, in fact, long been available. According to so sharp a political opponent as the prominent Menshevik Raphael Abramovitch, who knew him personally and spent time visiting with him and his companion Nadezhda Krupskaya in their 1916 Swiss exile, "it is difficult to conceive of a simpler, kinder and more unpretentious person than Lenin at home." Another Menshevik leader, Julius Martov, concurred that there were not "any signs of personal pride in Lenin's character," that he sought, "when in the company of others, an opportunity to acquire knowledge rather than show off his own."

Isaac Don Levine cited these comments in a 1924 study of Lenin. A Russian-born US journalist who was uncompromisingly critical of

Lenin but quite familiar with the details of his life, Levine commented that the Communist leader "derived genuine pleasure from associating with children and entertaining them," and that he had an "effeminate weakness for cats, which he liked to cuddle and play with." The knowledgeable Levine reported that other enthusiasms included bicycling, amateur photography, chess, skating, swimming, hunting—though Lenin was sometimes not inclined to actually shoot the animals he hunted ("well, he was so beautiful, you know," he said of a fox whose life he refused to take). According to one acquaintance, British diplomat Bruce Lockhart, he was "the father of modern 'hiking'. . . a passionate lover of outdoor life." And, of course, Lenin loved music. "During his life in Switzerland Lenin immensely enjoyed the home concerts that the political emigrants improvised among themselves," the journalist reported. "When a player or singer was really gifted, Lenin would throw his head back on the sofa, lock his knees into his arms, and listen with an interest so absorbing that it seemed as if he were experiencing something very deep and mysterious."[13]

Other, more explicitly, political qualities were naturally also emphasized by the shrewd anticommunist Levine—those of a personality "concise in speech, energetic in action, and matter-of-fact," with an unshakeable faith in Marxism, although "extraordinarily agile and pliant as to methods," with an "erudition" that could be termed "vast." His "capacity to back up his contentions [was] brilliant." While he had an ability "to readily acknowledge tactical mistakes and defeats," he was never willing to consider "the possible invalidity of his great idea" (revolutionary Marxism). Years later, the US State Department's most capable "old Russia hand" George F. Kennan—in no way a Marxist or socialist—would offer the opinion that Lenin represented "a critical intelligence second to none in the socialist movement." Levine's conclusion summarizes: "The extraordinary phenomenon about Lenin is that he combined this unshakeable, almost fanatic, faith with a total absence of personal ambition, arrogance or pride. Unselfish and irreproachable in his character, of a retiring disposition, almost ascetic in his habits, extremely modest and gentle in his direct contact with people, although peremptory and derisive in his treatment of political enemies, Lenin could be daring and provocative in his policies."[14]

Among the more provocative of Lenin's political writings, at least in retrospect, was his 1905 article "Party Organization and Party Literature," from which Stoppard draws for some key Lenin dialogue in the play *Travesties*—as Stoppard puts it, "there's a sense in which Lenin keeps convicting himself out of his own mouth." In his study of Stoppard's plays, John Fleming emphasizes that the playwright was becoming "personally and artistically involved in condemning Eastern Bloc repression," especially political restraints imposed on free artistic expression, policies that seem to be advocated in Lenin's 1905 essay. Stoppard's understanding of this essay mirrors that of the triumphant Stalinist bureaucracy of the 1930s and 1940s. In his 1934 classic *Artists in Uniform*, however, Max Eastman—denouncing the Stalinist regimentation of the arts (in contradiction to the relative cultural freedom and creativity of the 1920s)—emphasized that Lenin's 1905 essay "was written under capitalism and tzarism, and was, even so, devoted solely to the question of whether '*party literature*,' having been in the previous illegal period free from control of the party, should in the new legal period come under that control." As Robert C. Tucker commented years later, although "it seems clear from the article that Lenin was speaking primarily of political writings," Stalin's bureaucratic regime appropriated the article for its own purposes—claiming "Leninist authority for the established practice of party control and censorship of all cultural expression in Soviet Russia."[15]

Anatoly Lunacharsky, people's commissar of education in the Soviet Republic, pointed out "Vladimir Ilyich never made guiding principles out of his aesthetical likes and dislikes." His cultural tastes tended to be relatively conservative. As he explained to the seasoned German Communist leader Clara Zetkin (who tended to agree with him): "It is beyond me to consider the products of expressionism, futurism, cubism and other 'isms' the highest manifestation of artistic genius. I do not understand them. I experience no joy from them." But far from seeking to repress them, he said in the next breath: "Yes dear Clara, it can't be helped. We're both old fogies. For us it is enough that we remain young and are among the foremost at least in matters concerning the revolution. But we won't be able to keep pace with the new art; we'll just have to come trailing behind." Adding that "our opinion on art is not the important thing," he emphasized: "Art belongs to the people. . . . For art to get closer to the people and the people to art we must start by raising general educational and cultural standards."[16]

It may be worthwhile returning to the question of laughter—which was observed by more than one stray British journalist. "I have never met anyone who could laugh so infectiously as Vladimir Ilyich," commented Maxim Gorky. "It was even strange that this grim realist who so poignantly saw and felt the inevitability of great social tragedies, the man who was unbending and implacable in his hatred of the capitalist world, could laugh so naively, could laugh to tears, barely able to catch his breath." Trotsky agreed: "At some gatherings at which there were not many people, Lenin would sometimes have a fit of laughter, and that happened not only when things went well, but even during hard and difficult moments. He tried to control himself as long as he could, but finally he would burst out with a peal of laughter which infected all the others." Lunacharsky agreed: "Life bubbles and sparkles within him." The cousin of Winston Churchill, the sculptor Clare Sheridan, saw the same thing as she labored to mold a likeness of the revolutionary leader. Lenin's condition for allowing her to do this was that he not be interrupted in his work—for example, when a worker came in to discuss important matters with him. She offered this description: "The Comrade remained a long time, and conversation [with Lenin] was very animated. Never did I see any one make so many faces. Lenin laughed and frowned, and looked thoughtful, sad, and humorous all in turn. His eyebrows twitched, sometimes they went right up, and then they puckered together maliciously."[17]

The personal qualities we have been reviewing here had political impact. It is interesting to return to the insightful reflection offered by George Kennan:

> Endowed with this temperament, Lenin was able to communicate to his associates an atmosphere of militant optimism, of good cheer and steadfastness and comradely loyalty, which made him the object of their deepest admiration and affection and permitted them to apply their entire energy to the work

at hand, confident that if this work was well done they would not lack for support and appreciation at the top of the Party. In these circumstances, while Lenin's ultimate authority remained unquestioned, it was possible to spread initiative and responsibility much further than was ever the case in the heyday of Stalin's power.[18]

Lenin's leadership style was organically connected not only with his personality, of course, but also with his political orientation. His starting point was the elemental Marxist belief in the necessary interconnection of socialist theory and practice with the working class and labor movement. The working-class majority cannot adequately defend its actual interests and overcome its oppression, in his view, without embracing the goal of socialism—an economic system in which the economy is socially owned and democratically controlled in order to meet the needs of all people. Inseparable from this is a *basic understanding of the working class as it is*, which involves a grasp of the diversity and unevenness of working-class experience and consciousness. This calls for the development of a practical revolutionary approach seeking to connect in serious ways with the various sectors and layers of the working class.

This fundamental orientation is the basis of other key perspectives that one can find in his writings. One involves socialist and working-class support for struggles of all who suffer oppression, and a conception of forging social alliances and united fronts to advance these and other struggles. There is also an approach of integrating reform struggles with revolutionary strategy, a remarkable understanding of the manner in which democratic struggles flow into socialist revolution, as well as the need for working-class supremacy (or hegemony) if such struggles are to triumph. Lenin's vibrant, revolutionary internationalist approach involves the interconnection of working-class struggles in all countries, also encompassing a profound analysis of both nationalism and imperialism. All this is drawn together in a coherent conception of organization that is practical, democratic, and revolutionary.[19]

Ours is a time of social, economic, cultural, and political crises that, in multiple countries, have been generating a variety of insur-

gencies, occupations, and militant struggles to challenge the globalization policies of the powerful business corporations dominating our
planet and to mobilize increasing layers of the 99 percent to challenge
the oppressive and exploitative power of the wealthy 1 percent.[20]

Recalling Frederic Jameson's notion of a Lenin who is unaware
that he is dead, it is possible to conceive of a renewal of the ideas
and politics that Lenin actually represented. It is intriguing that precisely at this time there has been the revival of a play having Lenin
as a major character. Lenin may symbolize something different now
than was the case either twenty or forty years ago. Just as Shakespeare plays experience new interpretations and new meanings at
different points in history, so might future incarnations of this Tom
Stoppard play take on a new meaning—with Lenin as a revolutionary symbol, associated with liberating ideas (and perhaps a bit more
humor), taking on new life in our time of troubles.[21]

Chapter Four
STILL KICKING:
LENIN AND HIS BIOGRAPHERS

Vladimir Ilyich Lenin remains an object of interest to people around the world even today. The fire of revolutionary Marxism, after the amazing flare-up that Lenin helped orchestrate, has been reduced to glowing embers nurtured by unpredictable breezes. Many people have no clear conception, or no conception at all, of who this man was, but there are significant numbers who do. For some he remains an object of fear and hate, for others of passionate hope, for some of disappointment—with others defined by yet other categories. "Tell me what you think of Lenin," writes historian Christopher Read, "and I will tell you who you are." One of the most challenging and idiosyncratic political theorists of the twentieth century, Hannah Arendt, commented in her 1963 reflection *On Revolution*, that "it is perhaps noteworthy that Lenin, unlike Hitler and Stalin, has not yet found his definitive biographer, although he was not merely a 'better' but an incomparably simpler man; it may be because his role in twentieth-century history is so much more equivocal and difficult to understand."[1]

The full-scale biographies emerging in the last half of the twentieth century were all problematical. Those produced in the Soviet Union presented a granite statue of greatness, used to justify the existing order: the icon had been wonderful in every way and correct about everything, and universally loved by all people except for those who were enemies of humanity. After the collapse of the Soviet

Union, academic careerists switched to "catch up" with the worst of US works from an earlier era—Stefan Possony's *Lenin: The Compulsive Revolutionary* and Robert Payne's *The Life and Death of Lenin*, bent on portraying Lenin as an evil genius, consistent with so much of Cold War anticommunism. David Shub's *Lenin* was the Cold War product of a former Menshevik opponent of Lenin's—better than those just mentioned, but with obvious biases and in different ways also serving the anticommunist purposes of the time. Louis Fischer, an ex-leftist journalist, produced a critical but not hostile *Life of Lenin* that focused on his later years, after the 1917 revolution, in the period when Fischer was a Russia correspondent for the US press. Adam Ulam's work of popular scholarship, *The Bolsheviks*, in which an account of Lenin's life was embedded, described an authoritarian Lenin who had never really been a Marxist.

Better than fussing with any or all of these would be to read three works, in the following order, by people with a surer grasp of who and what Lenin was: Leon Trotsky's *The Young Lenin*, Nadezhda Krupskaya's *Reminiscences of Lenin*, and Moshe Lewin's *Lenin's Last Struggle*. There are also non-biographical works that focus on Lenin's political thought: Alfred Meyer's *Leninism*, a Cold War anticommunist study, and two works that were not—Marcel Liebman's *Leninism Under Lenin* and Neil Harding's *Lenin's Political Thought*. Blending an intensive focus on Lenin's political thought with a lightly drawn biography is the three-volume *Lenin*, by Tony Cliff. Utilizing Lenin's *Collected Works* plus various scholarly articles and books, Cliff hoped to guide like-minded activists in their efforts to build the British Socialist Workers Party and its sister organizations around the world. There are varying opinions of the results, with debate still swirling.[2]

The post–Cold War collapse of Communism has not meant the collapse of Lenin studies. With the dawn of the twenty-first century there have been at least six English-language works on Lenin's life, and a proliferating number of examinations of various aspects of his ideas. The two most valuable syntheses are by Christopher Read and Lars Lih, and we can see why, first of all, by briefly surveying the others.

Bad Man

Robert Service was the first out of the gate in 2000 with his five-hundred-page *Lenin: A Biography*. There were a number of us who were hopeful that this would be a very substantial and even path-breaking contribution, and this for several reasons. Here was an experienced historian who knew Russian and had been able to gain entrance into newly opened archives—but there was more. In 1979 he had produced an important study entitled *The Bolshevik Party in Revolution 1917–1923: A Study in Organizational Change*, which dealt with the vitally important issue of how a genuinely revolutionary party of 1917 was transformed by the early 1920s into an increasingly less democratic and bureaucratized structure. It seemed a work by someone whose sympathies were on the left, especially leaning toward the Workers' Opposition in the Bolshevik party, perhaps too quick to make negative judgments of Lenin and sometimes even flippant in tone—but providing important information and ideas. In 1991 the initial edition of his succinct survey *The Russian Revolution, 1900-1927* appeared, and despite a quibble one might have with details, it seemed a good and reliable summary.

More complex, and more impressive, was his three-volume biography of Lenin that appeared between 1985 and 1995. The author became increasingly critical of his subject as the years went by, although by no means dismissive, and for anyone who had combed through Lenin's writings, it was clear from these volumes that Service had also been there. Not inclined to quote, he provided extensive summaries, offering slants one might question but certainly corresponding to what Lenin had written, and connecting texts with historical contexts and critical-minded commentary that one felt merited attention. Also, when Ronald W. Clark—the experienced and very capable biographer—died before finishing his own useful five-hundred-page work entitled *Lenin: A Biography*, Service was the person called in to help prepare this informative and sympathetic account for final publication in 1988.

Lenin's "vision of a future for mankind when all exploitation and oppression would disappear was sincere," Service wrote in the conclusion of his third Lenin volume. "This surely is the central point of his life." He added that Lenin and his comrades were also responsible for the authoritarian reality that took hold in Soviet Russia, but that masses of people around the world had responded to the hopeful vision Lenin represented in response "to the conditions of distress, social and political, in their own countries," adding: "In most of these societies these conditions have not been improved in the years after Lenin's death. Only a minority of the globe's national economies have provided prosperity for most of their people." Given this, he concluded, "it would be foolhardy" to predict that Lenin's influence might not yet be felt in the future—although he clearly did not see this as cause for elation. In his 2000 biography he makes a similar point—but not quite: "It is not even impossible that his memory might again be invoked, not necessarily by card-carrying communists, in those many parts of the world where capitalism causes grievous social distress. Lenin is not quite dead, at least not yet."[3]

Service's new biography seemed focused on finishing him off. The propensity for flippant editorializing and personal denigration (buttressed by superficial references to evidence) was much more pronounced than in his three-volume work. The popularized condensation of the earlier volumes formed the backbone of the new book. Although much was made of new archival material, there was little revelatory material actually presented, and nothing that explained the tone of unrelenting hostility by Service toward his subject. This disappointing book certainly failed to achieve the "balanced" scholarship promised in the introduction, but it said what many wanted to hear, and received accolades as "the most authoritative and well-rounded biography of Lenin yet written—and the one that is, in its quiet way, the most horrifying" (according to one blurb on the back cover of the paperback edition). But for those who were familiar with the other biographies of Lenin, with the scholarship on the Russian Revolution, with the specifics of Marxist theory, and who—like the younger Service—felt that an oppressive and exploitative capitalism should be replaced by the democratic humanism at the heart of socialism, the praise seemed hollow.

A newer contribution that appeared in 2010—*Conspirator: Lenin in Exile*—is premised, in part, on the intelligent insight that since most of Lenin's life, from 1902 to 1917, was lived in exile, that period (more than the brief years of revolution and power—1917–23) is the obvious focal point for a biographer who wants to understand the person Lenin was. The problem is that author Helen Rappaport felt she already "understood" the person Lenin was, and she despised him. Among her strengths is that she is fluent in Russian and has a feel for Russian culture (and consequently served as a consultant to playwright Tom Stoppard for his remarkable Coasts of Utopia trilogy on nineteenth-century Russian intellectuals), all of which was obviously helpful for someone who confesses that she is not a professional historian. And she does seem to have read a considerable amount in preparation for this book—which may be the meaning of the Shakespeare quote she offers at the beginning of *Conspirator*:

POLONIUS: What do you read, my lord?

HAMLET: Words, words, words.

Indeed, Rappaport is not particularly interested in the "words, words, words" of Marxist theory and revolutionary polemic that were at the center of Lenin's life, nor is she particularly interested in the labor movement, the class struggle, the lives of workers, or the plight of the oppressed that were the focal point of all that he did. She is much more interested in the places where he lived in exile, many of which she has made a point of visiting. She also is interested in speculations that he spent a lot of time with prostitutes (with minimal evidence, she concludes that he did) and contracted venereal disease (she spends significant time on this "probability"—as does Service, incidentally—based on inconclusive accounts and latter-day medical conjectures). But beyond that, Rappaport helps us see Lenin as a "narrow authoritarian," who frothed at the mouth when speaking, who gloried in political manipulations, surrounding himself with yes-men and hatchet-men helping him rise to power, and was a man whose "mobile, malicious little eyes" revealed "something ruthless and predatory."[4] For those who want to loathe Lenin, this book is invaluable. For those wanting to get a firmer grasp on what happened in history, it isn't.

Scholarly Gems

Perhaps this is the place to discuss the work of Carter Elwood's important and influential series of essays gathered in *The Non-Geometric Lenin: Essays on the Development of the Bolshevik Party 1910-1914*.[5] This collection is a gem for any serious-minded scholar. Like Service and Rappaport, Elwood is hostile to what he understands as key aspects of Lenin's politics—but unlike them, he is a meticulous researcher, not inclined to jump to conclusions, inclined to take very seriously the specifics of the workers' and socialist movements in pre-revolutionary Russia, time and again demonstrating a scholarly integrity that demands respect from anyone who cares about the history that Elwood is studying. In addition to this collection of essays, he has written three extremely valuable books—one on the underground activity of the Russian Social Democratic Labor Party, focusing on the Ukraine from 1907 to 1914, another on an agent-provocateur in the top leadership of the Bolsheviks, Roman Malinovsky, and finally a biography of an outstanding leading activist and feminist in the Bolshevik ranks, Inessa Armand. (Armand is rumored to have had a fleeting affair with Lenin—in the biography Elwood says it's not true, but in a new essay contained here he concludes that it is.[6])

Elwood is inclined to accept aspects of what Lars Lih has denounced as "the textbook version" of Lenin developed in the days of Cold War anticommunism—that Lenin was inclined toward an undemocratic, elitist, manipulative mode of functioning and organization-building. This influences much of the way that he interprets the evidence he presents—but he also presents a considerable amount of evidence that doesn't fit neatly into this schema (with Bolshevik comrades over and over disagreeing with him, not taking his advice, outvoting him, not agreeing to print his articles, and so on). More than that, Elwood displays a genuine interest in the actual people he is writing about, including Lenin. The book of essays is divided into two sections, one primarily political (focused on Lenin's efforts to build the Bolshevik Party), the other focused more on Lenin's personality and daily life. The meaning of the book's title—*The Non-Geometric Lenin*—highlights what Elwood sees as a "non-linear" and more lifelike complexity in Lenin, with discontinuities between his political practice and his more complex human qualities (for which Elwood displays more sympathy).

Recent contributions by two other serious scholars also add to the human dimensions of this revolutionary figure. It is illuminating, as we try to understand the humanity of a historical figure such as Lenin—to rescue him from being a statue—to be able to see him in relation to his parents and siblings, in the dynamic family context within which he grew up. There were three sisters and two brothers in Lenin's life, and we are fortunate to have studies of the sisters and of the elder brother.

In her fascinating book *Forgotten Lives: The Role of Lenin's Sisters in the Russian Revolution*, Katy Turton complains of what she calls "the solar system myth." Many accounts by Lenin worshippers and haters alike picture Lenin as "the sun in the planetary system in the Ulyanovs," around which the others orbited in awe and adoration. In focusing on Anna, Olga (to whom Lenin was closest, and who died in 1890) and Maria Ulyanov, she portrays distinct personalities and independent lives. Highly educated and cultured, on their own terms they became—like so many of their generation—part of "the revolutionary community, in which women and men worked together, formed friendships and families, and campaigned to bring about the transformation of Russian society." Anna was the older sister and became deeply involved in revolutionary activity in the mid-1880s (well in advance of the teenaged Volodya, the future Lenin). Olga Ulyanova, a few years later—when she and Volodya were in close contact and still getting their political bearings—wrote that "the aspiration towards truth and to the ideal is in people's souls," adding: "One must always believe in people, in the possibility of something better on earth, despite personal disappointment. . . . If one doesn't believe in people, doesn't love them, then what is one living for?" When she died, a classmate wrote to her own brother: "Oh Arsenii, if only you knew what sort of person Ulyanova was. How much hope was placed in her! It is safe to say that in Ulyanova Russia has lost an honest, tireless activist. . . . She was a person of brilliant mind, intellectual maturity, education, talent. . . . She read the best works on political economy and sociology."[7]

Philip Pomper, in *Lenin's Brother*, tells the story of Alexander Ulyanov, born two years after his sister Anna, like her drawn into revolutionary activity, and swept up in arrest and execution in the late 1880s due to a revolutionary conspiracy to assassinate the tsar. Alexander's own story is the focus of this study, and he had powerful impact on the future of Lenin and his sisters, but particularly interesting for our purposes is information offered on Lenin's childhood. Pomper, not sympathetic to what he tells us about Lenin's mature political orientation, summarizes his own research on the little boy: "Volodya was the most outgoing and playful of the three older children—perhaps the most winning one to outsiders. In fact, one might speculate that he was psychologically the healthiest of the three, though this would be difficult to infer from Anna's memoirs." Anna described the psychological severity of her schoolmaster father on herself, Alexander, and the younger children, explaining:

> Father was against "showering people with praise," as he put it, considering it extremely harmful for people to have high opinions of themselves. Now, as I look back on our childhood, I think that it would have been better for us if this generally applied pedagogical line had been administered less strictly. It was fully correct only for Vladimir, whose vast self-confidence and constantly distinguished achievement in school called for a corrective. In no way affecting his accurate self-assessment, it undoubtedly reduced the arrogance, which children with outstanding abilities are prone to ... and taught him, in spite of all the praise, to work diligently.

Pomper adds that Lenin was "physically the spitting image of his father," and that "just beneath the surface of Ilya Nikolaevich's severity, there was a streak of mischievous humor, a quality completely alien to his older son and characteristic of Volodya."[8]

Hazards of Scholarly Balance

Of course, such gems may contribute to, but cannot substitute for, a more rounded and unified understanding of Lenin. This is attempted by two serious scholars reaching for a greater balance than that achieved by Service's work (not to mention Rappaport's)—Beryl Williams's *Lenin* (2000), and James D. White's *Lenin: The Practice and Theory of Revolution* (2001). In addition, each is packed with a considerable amount of information—both authors have obviously immersed themselves in older sources and especially the more recent scholarship. In a sense, this is one of the reasons that both books fail as durable biographical studies.

What they tend to be "balancing" are the various works of scholarship on Lenin, and one can learn much from that. But sometimes trying to balance the various scholarly studies—particularly at a certain moment in history—cannot provide the much-desired "objectivity" that is the goal of many serious scholars. As the 1990s were fading into the early twenty-first century, it seemed clear to most scholars (including in the former Soviet Union) that Communism had been "the road to nowhere" and that the entire effort had been an insupportable waste of time and life and resources, a fault that could be traced to the very moment of revolutionary conception. The prevailing moods and trends in academe in the 1990s were inclined to embrace the old Cold War anticommunist interpretation of Lenin—in some cases with even darker colors, in others with greater nuance, but most were also more inclined than ever to underscore continuity with the brutality of Stalinism. The effort to "balance" such scholarship, however, gives us more second-hand judgments but less actual Lenin. This may be better than what Rappaport and even Service have produced, but it falls short of "the real stuff" that someone like Elwood seems more adept at working toward.

Their conclusions to some extent reflect the problem. Shortly before the collapse of the Soviet Union, Williams notes, a public opinion poll under Gorbachev asked Soviet citizens who were the most important world figures of all ages. First was the modernizing tsar of the eighteenth century, Peter the Great. Second was Jesus. Third was Lenin. Here is what Williams does with this:

> Like Christ he became for his people a martyr and a saint, whose teachings could not be challenged; like Peter his revolution was one of Westernization and modernization, often

through barbaric methods. His experiment with human nature lasted 74 years. At the end of it, however, Russians and Russia, let alone the world, proved remarkably resistant to his vision of socialism. The brave new world failed to materialize. In the long run, as Russians admitted under Gorbachev, the end did not justify the means.[9]

This is more consistent with the mood of Williams and those around her in the year 2000 than with what Lenin said (he never claimed to have established socialism, nor was he seeking to change human nature) or with the complexities of Soviet experience. But then consider White's conclusion. He starts with the interesting comment by E. H. Carr that (in White's paraphrase) "the Bolsheviks not only made a revolution, but analyzed and prepared the conditions in which it could be made." He goes on to suggest that this is an illusion, that "first Lenin and then Stalin had made great efforts to create that impression," and he concludes: "Before we can know whether a 'self-conscious' revolution of the kind Carr had in mind is at all possible, it is necessary to clear away the confusion that Lenin and his successors have created."[10] Aside from the linkage of Lenin and Stalin, at least as manipulators of the truth who created illusions about Bolsheviks strengths, White's book ends with the "balanced" injunction that we must clear away Lenin's thought before we can know whether a self-conscious revolution is actually possible.

Taking Lenin Seriously

The great strength of Christopher Read's *Lenin: A Revolutionary Life* (2005) and Lars Lih's *Lenin* (2011) is that they take Lenin seriously in ways that most others do not (with the partial exception of Elwood). They give attention to the proliferating array of interpretations and secondary sources, but they are determined to form their own judgments through a serious-minded engagement with primary sources. First of all, they engage with what Lenin himself had to say, both in published sources and correspondence, and they read these in a critical-minded way—not hostile, but not assuming that Lenin's words are the fount of Truth, and also not assuming that Lenin was simply lying and manipulating in order to advance his own dark (dictatorial, proto-Stalinist) designs.

It is interesting to take some time to unpack what it means to take Lenin seriously. Here are two statements that, taken together, often cause confusion. Statement number 1: Lenin wanted to achieve a society of the free and the equal, and he wanted to establish rule by the working class over society's political and economic life. Statement number 2: What ended up being established in the Soviet Union, particularly under Stalin, was one of the worst dictatorships in human history.

Read and Lih understand the truth of both statements. Unlike so many, they do not assume that Lenin was talking about freedom and democracy and workers' control simply in order to establish a brutal dictatorship. Nor do they appear to believe that democracy and socialism are foolish illusions. In this sense, for example, they take Lenin seriously. It then remains to be seen how Lenin's words actually played out in practice, and also how one might explain why things turned out so differently from what Lenin said he was reaching for.

In other ways, too, they show a respect for Lenin's ideas by 1) taking the time to see what they are, 2) placing them in context, 3) seeing what others of the time were saying, and 4) trying to understand how things played out. More than this, they are inclined to see Lenin neither as a demon nor a saint but as the interesting and remarkable person that he was. They look at his life, relationships, and everyday activities in a manner consistent with the rich material gathered in Elwood's *Non-Geometric Lenin*.

In the scholarly apparatus of each book it seems clear that Lih and Read think highly of each other's contributions. At the same time, the two biographies, while sharing much common ground and similarities of approach, are different in significant ways.

There is an oblique quality to Lih's book—focusing on key moments in the history of the Russian revolutionary movement in which Lenin was centrally involved, and often focusing on the impressions and ideas of others in order to contextualize and then zero in on what Lenin was thinking and doing. At the same time, the overall result tends to be a rounded and insightful presentation of Lenin's life and politics. Read, on the other hand, is almost always focused directly on

Lenin's life and ideas—adding context in generous amounts at appropriate points. As he tells us, his key primary source is Lenin's *Collected Works* (including, importantly, his correspondence), supplemented by a generous and critical-minded use of Krupskaya's *Reminiscences* (plus reference to other, less friendly memoirs by former Bolsheviks Nikolai Valentinov and Angelica Balabanoff, as well as the outstanding book-length chronology by Gerda and Hermann Weber, *Lenin: Life and Works*), and only then the scholarship of others.

Read views Lenin as seeking to create a democratic upsurge for socialist revolution, led by the working class in alliance with the peasantry. The problem begins when the Bolshevik Revolution, as a radical-democratic insurgency, is successful in 1917. Then all hell breaks loose, and amid the violence and chaos of counterrevolutionary assault and economic collapse the radical-democratic scenario that had been central to Lenin's Bolshevism falls apart. We then see Lenin and his comrades scramble as best they can to hold things together. In the process, something very different takes shape than what had been projected in the revolutionary upsurge of 1917. A brutality and authoritarianism crystallize as part of the new order, and this creates preconditions for what will become known as Stalinism.

Problems of a Revolutionary Life

Of course, no book is perfect, and in Read's book there are simple factual errors worth noting.

- One of the errors may simply be a bit of unclear writing. On page 67, Read talks about the German revisionist Eduard Bernstein putting forward the notion that instead of resorting to a revolutionary overturn, socialists could just gradually reform the problems of capitalism out of existence. Then he eases into a discussion of Lenin's Menshevik opponents on page 68—but it is simply not the case that a majority of the Mensheviks were adherents of Bernstein's reformism. Like Lenin, they were inclined to line up with the "orthodox" Marxism of Karl Kautsky.

- On page 92, again in regard to the Mensheviks, Read has Lenin referring to them as "liquidationists" because they favored a less centralized party than Lenin—but that was absolutely not the meaning of the term for Lenin or anyone else. Liquidators were that current among the Mensheviks after 1906 who wanted to abandon illegal underground work in tsarist Russia.

- On page 114, in an uncharacteristically fuzzy discussion of Lenin's ideas (specifically on national self-determination), Read mistakenly asserts that for Rosa Luxemburg "Polish independence was a goal in itself" when—as a revolutionary anti-nationalist—she in fact opposed the struggle for an independent Poland, while Lenin, an advocate of self-determination for oppressed nationalities, supported it.

- On page 164, it is stated that Trotsky attacked "Lenin's concept of the Party and associated 'democratic centralism.'" While the young Trotsky more than once attacked Lenin's ideas on party organization, he never attacked "democratic centralism" (the notion of freedom of discussion, unity in action), a term first introduced by the Mensheviks, then embraced by the Bolsheviks. Later it was turned into something entirely different in the Stalinized Communist movement, and in the studies of Cold War academics—but that is another matter.

- On page 167, it is suggested that the nineteenth-century French revolutionary Auguste Blanqui was an anarchist—but he wasn't.

- On page 239, we are told that "Lenin had been uncompromising from the first with any attempt to allow [religious] believers to join the Party." This is not true. In his 1905 article "Religion and Socialism," while he calls religion "the opium of the people," he also indicates that "we [do] not forbid Christians and other believers in God to join our party."[11]

These errors, the sort that crop up in almost any book dealing with complex themes ranging over a significant swath of history, are not central to Read's narrative and analysis. Much more important is the way he defines "Leninism." Although plausibly suggesting that Lenin was partly shaped by the Russian traditions of revolutionary populism (and, perhaps less plausibly, by elements of Bakunin's anarchist thought), Read is very much of the opinion that Lenin's thought was thoroughly grounded in the principles of revolutionary Marxism, with its belief in the possibility and need for working-class revolution and its socialist goal envisioning a radical democracy and society of the free and the equal. And yet Read wrestles, as we all must wrestle, with a disturbing truth: "From our perspective of examining Lenin's life, perhaps the most extraordinary and ironic feature is that, while he retained such ultra-democratic ideas in his head, Lenin presided in practice over the emergence of one of the most intrusive bureaucratic state structures the world had ever seen."[12]

Read believes that the answer to the riddle, in part, can be found in a fatal flaw at the very heart of Leninism. In addition to the "ultra-democratic" perspectives of Marxism that he acknowledges were central to Lenin's theoretical orientation, Read believes another element was no less essential to Leninism—something that hardened in him during his early Siberian exile, adding an "extra steel" that was indispensable to "Lenin's own distinctive revolutionary theory and practice." He therefore became the truly "Leninist" Lenin only when "his manipulativeness and dogmatism were in full flow."[13]

Amid the balanced discussion of Lenin's personality, his serious-minded engagement with Lenin's Marxism, his thoughtful discussion of positive and reasonable qualities of what Lenin thought and said and did, there is this darker element that Read sees as essential for understanding who Lenin was and how he impacted history. In taking this analytical turn, he employs a more sophisticated variant of the old "textbook" version of the undemocratic Lenin that Lars Lih has done so much to demolish.

"The problems began to arise," Read tells us, "when the culture of centralization and secrecy inculcated by autocratic conditions became a habit which could not be shaken off even when the conditions no longer prevailed." The Bolshevik/Menshevik split at the Second Congress of the Russian Social Democratic Labor Party revealed "a new side of Lenin, the ruthless, stop-at-nothing side. He had not hesitated to split the movement though he does not appear to have foreseen the development coming." In building Bolshevism he sought "a personally loyal instrument which, he hoped, would never let him down," and so he was determined to build a "party in his own, self-made likeness."[14]

Another contributing factor was Lenin's notion that "no one but Lenin had ever really understood Marxism," so his loyalty to Marxism necessarily meant "his failure to accept opposition." He could not be patient in allowing reality to teach comrades the validity of his own Marxist understanding—"Leninism was Marxism in a hurry." In fact, his great weakness was inseparable from his great strength: "the energy and power of his intellectual creativity . . . was the feature that attracted his supporters and repelled his enemies."[15]

Theoretical rigidities apparently begat organizational rigidities. Read tells us that between 1902 and 1904 Lenin's "notion of the vanguard, elite party was becoming increasingly divisive" and that "as time went by Lenin was carving out a more and more radical and solitary path." Lenin was continually engaged, according to Read (with no clear documentation) in "purging his party of heretics," and he could not be stopped from continuing "his favorite pastime, splitting an ever smaller party." Read gets carried away with such formulations: "To see his beloved Party adopting what he considered suicidal principles of broad membership was too much for him to accept." Such an orientation actually eroded his Marxist convictions regarding the role of the working class—for him there were recurrent "ambiguities about the revolutionary potential of the Russian working class," causing him more than once to fret over "working-class backwardness." Reaching for a link between Lenin's allegedly undemocratic notions in the prerevolutionary period and the post-revolutionary Communist dictatorship, Read even suggests that "arguably . . . the elite began the Revolution in 1917, not the masses" (though this flies in the face of much evidence and even the thrust of Read's own account). Perhaps the Bolsheviks actually meant to establish "a one-party dictatorship" in 1917.[16]

This "textbook" distortion of Lenin and his politics is contradicted—and (it seems to me) refuted—by material in such well-documented studies as Lars Lih's *Lenin Rediscovered* and my own *Lenin and the Revolutionary Party*, and it stands as the most serious defect in Read's work, at certain points tending to bend it out of shape. There is ample evidence that Lenin was far more open, proved able to tolerate and endure disagreement from his comrades, and, if anything, was supremely confident in what Lih calls a "heroic" conception of the workers' inherent revolutionary potential. Rather than governing over his own shrinking organizational kingdom, Lenin coordinated a party-building orientation that ultimately resulted in the impressive growth, vitality, and class-struggle relevance of the Bolsheviks. And as has been widely documented (including in material that Read himself presents to us), the 1917 revolution was essentially "ultra-democratic," not authoritarian.

As indicated, the defect in Read's interpretation is contradicted by evidence that Read himself presents. He is compelled more than once in this biography to puzzle over Lenin's "un-Lenin-like" behavior. In a "stunning" letter to Plekhanov in October 1905, he wrote: "We are in agreement with you over nine-tenths of the questions of theory and tactics, and to quarrel over one-tenth is not worthwhile." Read comments that Lenin's "new sense of urgency over reconciliation" between Mensheviks and Bolsheviks "was clear as was its motivation" amid the revolutionary opportunities of the 1905 upsurge. Nor was this a one-time fluke. "The years were filled with intense squabbles with three opponents—Trotsky, Bogdanov and the Mensheviks," Read tells us. "Time after time Lenin announced a complete break with one or another of the groups, only, bewilderingly, to hold out hopes of unity shortly thereafter." He also notes that the Bolsheviks—absolutely committed to a government based on the democratic councils of workers and other popular forces in 1917—were on record as wanting to share power, in the soviets, with others committed to such a soviet government.[17]

Plausible arguments can be made, given his humanity and the historical record, that Lenin was sometimes supremely overconfident (or arrogant), sometimes intolerant, sometimes inclined to indulge in polemical overkill, sometimes naïvely short-sighted, sometimes afflicted with blindspots that could have dire consequences. Such qualities were not the whole of Lenin, nor are they *essential* to the body of theory that can be associated with the actual "Leninism" of Lenin. Nonetheless, given the complexity of the historical process, and Lenin's centrality to aspects of it, one could argue that Lenin's shortcomings (no less than his strengths) were a factor in problems that emerged in the Russian revolutionary experience. What Read does not successfully demonstrate, however, is that these shortcomings were as consistent and potent as he suggests. There were too many countervailing tendencies (in the Russian revolutionary movement, in Lenin himself, and so on) for that to be so.

Revolutionary Tragedy

Good historian that he is, Read provides sufficient evidence for an alternative explanation as to how the Russian Revolution "went wrong"—one that even factors in Lenin's actual shortcomings. As Read notes, in the four-year period following the 1917 revolution, there was "a series of three strategies pursued by Lenin": first, the establishment of what could be called a "Commune-state" (combined with a mixed economy that would gradually transition from capitalism to socialism); second, the severe policies of "war communism" that combined an authoritarian one-party dictatorship with the rapid (and damaging) nationalization of the economy; and third, a New Economic Policy that maintained one-party rule but shifted back to the utilization of market relations to build up the economy. What is key for us—though Read often seems to forget it—is that up to 1918 Lenin's ideal, his first choice, was the Commune-state.

This means that Lenin's initial intention was far from setting up a dictatorship of the Russian Communist Party (the new name adopted by the Bolsheviks early in 1918). As Read points out, the revolution had been led by the Bolsheviks, but also involved were anarchists, the Left Socialist Revolutionaries, and even some Mensheviks, as well as many nonparty workers—active in the soviets, factory committees, unions, and workers' militias. This corresponded with what Lenin projected in *The State and Revolution* and other writings of 1917. The model of the Paris Commune of 1871 indicated what the post-insurrectionary transition was supposed to look like. Read notes that "Lenin called for 'abolition of the police, army and bureaucracy', that is, the smashing of the existing state machine." It was to be replaced by the democratic soviets and the workers' militias. "The people would be armed and therefore they could not be forced into submission by armed external agencies," is how he explains Lenin's perspective. "Bureaucratic and judicial functions would also be democratized by enforcing a regular rotation of administrative tasks in which the whole population would participate." Read adds that "all 'political' functions could . . . be reduced to accounting and control within the grasp of the average, literate intelligence."[18]

Read makes clear that Lenin did not believe socialism was possible in Russia unless it was aided by world revolution. Even before the Bolshevik Revolution he was emphasizing the point, and as late as 1922 he was still emphasizing it:

> 1917: "Russia is a peasant country, one of the most backward of European countries. Socialism cannot triumph there directly and immediately. But the peasant character of the country . . . may make our revolution the prologue to the world socialist revolution, a step toward it."
>
> 1922: "We have always urged and reiterated the elementary truth—that the joint efforts of the workers of several advanced countries are needed for the victory of socialism."[19]

Read's accusation—at least in this section of his book—is not that Lenin is a manipulative authoritarian, but that his actual revolutionary-democratic vision is incredibly naïve and unrealistic. He also suggests that Lenin and his comrades concealed from the masses the Bolsheviks' ultimate goals. "Mass support came to the Bolsheviks as the only significant agents of what the masses wanted—peace, bread, land and all power to the soviets," he asserts. "It was emphatically not a conversion to Bolshevik values and to the dreams embodied in *The April Theses* and *The State and Revolution*."[20] Yet in all fairness, Lenin and the Bolsheviks, while making "peace, bread, land" and "all power to the soviets" their central slogans, were also very clear about the ultimate goals—world revolution and socialism globally as well as in Russia. Consider Lenin's very public appeal the morning after the seizure of power:

> Comrades, workers, soldiers, peasants and all working people! Take all power into the hands of your soviets. . . . Gradually, with the consent and approval of the majority of the peasants, in keeping with their practical experience and that of the workers, we shall go forward firmly and unswervingly to the victory of

socialism—a victory that will be sealed by the advanced workers of the many civilized countries, bring the peoples lasting peace and liberate them from all oppression and exploitation.[21]

In Lenin's 1917–1918 scenario, then, class-conscious workers and their steadfast allies among the poor peasants establish a revolutionary-democratic commune-state that inspires workers' revolutions throughout the world, setting the stage for the development of a global socialist order of the free and the equal. But "almost from the very first day of the October Revolution," according to Read, "Lenin's hopes and expectations for it began to collapse."[22] There was, of course, the horrific and destructive First World War—still raging when the Bolsheviks took power—combined with a horrific civil war that arose after 1917, nurtured and funded by a number of powerful capitalist governments that also sent in their own troops and orchestrated a debilitating economic blockade. Although there was a wave of revolutionary upsurges in countries around the world, none resulted in the hoped-for working-class socialist triumph, so the new Soviet Republic remained fatally isolated. What's more, the administrative experience and cultural level of the overwhelming majority of ordinary Russian workers and peasants proved woefully insufficient for sustaining the libertarian commune-state envisioned by Lenin and his comrades. The result was chaos, economic and social disintegration, and the dramatic erosion of the vibrant popular upsurge that had given life to the democratic councils, the soviets, which caused the newly named Communist Party, itself ill-prepared for overwhelming tasks of governance and administration under such dire circumstances, to try to step into the breach.

The other two strategies—"war communism" (1918–1921) and the New Economic Policy (1921–1928)—followed. A key feature of both involved replacing the shattered hopes for soviet democracy and the "commune-state" with an emergency one-party dictatorship, buttressed initially by desperate violence and authoritarian justifications (the "red terror"). As Read comments, "one could argue that the cost of survival was the stifling of the revolution," although he also emphasizes that "from 1920 onwards the resort to terror was much reduced and disappeared from Lenin's mainstream discourses and practices."[23] Lenin and his comrades bear considerable responsibility for these developments, as Read shows us, and he goes on to offer challenging insights on the dynamics that made the "temporary" bureaucratic dictatorship increasingly powerful and durable.

Although the Communist dictatorship seemed relatively benign through much of the 1920s, under Stalin's steady hand it turned immense and increasingly stifling, yet also voracious and murderous, as the 1920s gave way to the 1930s. Read by no means equates Lenin with Stalin, and he acknowledges the well-documented facts of "Lenin's last struggle" against the embryonic beginnings of Stalinism—but his partial adherence to the "textbook" interpretation of Lenin encourages him, in the next breath, to suggest a different way of seeing things, stressing (far more strongly than the evidence will allow) that in some ways Stalin could be seen as Lenin's legitimate heir, even though he also denies that "Stalinism was the one and only potential outcome of Leninism." Read insists that the best in Lenin scholarship allows for the revolutionary's humanity—"a more realistic, balance, rounded, human portrayal of Lenin."[24] He himself has done much, regardless of differences one might have with his interpretation, to clear the path for a such scholarship.

Humanity and Revolution

"Oliver Cromwell insisted that his portrait should include 'warts and all,'" comments Lars Lih. "Post-Soviet studies of Lenin often seem to be based on a methodology of 'nothing but warts.'" Like Carter Elwood and Christopher Read, he also has pushed past relentless negativity, and has also—more than most—emphasized the necessity of engaging with the political ideas that animated this twentieth-century revolutionary.[25]

Lih's remarkable, reliable, deliciously readable new biography—*Lenin*—stands as the best of the twenty-first century biographies considered here. We are offered a succinct yet substantial work of scholarship that clearly presents the life of a genuine revolutionary, in stark contrast to the cold-blooded totalitarian monster that recent political fashions have dictated as the appropriate way of seeing Lenin. Lih shattered myths about Lenin in his massive earlier volume, *Lenin Rediscovered: "What Is to Be Done?" in Context*, and he has continued that good work in this informative biography.

We are presented here with someone steeped in Marxist thought, in fact "in love" with Marx's writings (as Lih nicely puts it), maintaining throughout his life the belief in a "heroic working class." To advance this scenario, Lenin labored to develop a revolutionary party around the program of the majority faction (the Bolsheviks) that he led. Fundamentally democratic, evolving through sharp debates and disagreements, sometimes even splits (though sometimes unifications), the Leninist organization Lih reveals is a collectivity of activists in which Lenin was more than once overruled but within which he earned considerable authority. Far from developing a blueprint for an authoritarian order, Lenin's "blueprints" (such as they were) projected a workers' and peasants' republic of democratic councils (soviets) that would, increasingly, replace what he and other Marxists perceived as the economic dictatorship of capitalism with the economic democracy of socialism. Of course, things did not turn out that way.

This richly textured book, graced with a number of splendid and appropriate illustrations, places Lenin securely in context: the context of European and Russian history, the context of the broader socialist movement (a truly mass phenomenon before World War I), the context of truly heroic workers' struggles and of the Russian Social Democratic Labor Party (and later the Communist Party) that contained a number of other experienced and strong-minded individuals. We are given a sense of the qualities that enabled this human being to have the impact that he did in such contexts. An iron will is combined with a brilliant intellect, with a profoundly realistic and practical theoretical and organizational bent, yet also with a desire to learn from others and—by no means inconsequentially— a capacity for charm and humor, and for genuine kindness. At the same time, Lih perceives an overly confident inclination to see a highly complex reality through the distorting lens of Lenin's revolutionary assumptions and his faith that the "heroic working class" could and would overcome all obstacles.

This perspective could not survive the escalation of problems and horrific crises that beset the revolutionary regime after 1917,

Lih insists. True enough, but one wonders if Lih is absolutely on target in concluding that Lenin's revolutionary orientation was "far from realistic." Lenin is likened to the Biblical Noah, confidently building his revolutionary ark as the floodwaters of political, social, and economic catastrophe rose higher and higher. "As it turned out, the ark was leaky because it was built on unsound assumptions, the voyage involved more suffering than anyone had bargained for, and the ark ended up far from where its builder planned."[26]

It is difficult to judge Lenin's purported lack of realism due to Lih's surprising failure (given the contrary emphasis in much of his other work) to give adequate attention to the primary theoretical works produced by this revolutionary who, as Lih himself emphasizes, took theory so seriously. "I am still completely 'in love' with Marx and Engels," Lenin confessed to Inessa Armand in 1917, "and I can't stand to hear them abused. No, really—they are the genuine article."[27] Lenin is presented as being in the mainstream of the pro-democracy, pro-worker Marxism prevalent in the world socialist movement of his time. This was the Socialist International to which socialist parties around the world, including Lenin's own, were affiliated before the First World War tore it apart. Its Marxism embraces the rich contributions of Karl Kautsky up to 1910, as well as those of Rosa Luxemburg, Franz Mehring, David Riazanov, Leon Trotsky, and others. Lenin's distinctive interpretations and analyses were developed very much in the midst of what Lih has termed "the best of Second International Marxism." The thoughtful Russian literary critic D. S. Mirsky once commented in his interesting old biography of Lenin that "Leninism is not identical with the sum of Lenin's outlook. The Marxist precedes in him the creator of Leninism, and the vindication and reestablishment of genuine Marxism was one of his principal tasks in life."[28]

Lih would certainly agree with this. It may be, however, that it is his dogged emphasis on Lenin's affinity to Second International Marxism that contributes to this volume's greatest limitation: how little it offers on distinctive aspects of Lenin's Marxism. This especially comes through in the very light treatment accorded to Lenin's involvement in the deliberations and development of the Communist International. This is especially serious, given that Lenin saw revolutionary internationalism as key as to how to move beyond the excruciating dilemmas coming out of World War I and posed by Soviet Russia's post-revolutionary isolation.

Lih's failure to engage adequately with aspects of Lenin's thought may also help explain why—as is the case with Read—he seems not to take seriously what Moshe Lewin called "Lenin's last struggle" against the beginnings of what would later be called "Stalinism." He is not inclined to acquiesce, however, in Christopher Read's "detection" of embryonic Stalinism in Leninist precedents. Lih stresses exactly the opposite, especially in regard to "the peasant question." (In stark contrast to Lenin's worker-peasant alliance, the full "blossoming" of Stalinism involved the so-called revolution from above, with the murderous and disastrous forced collectivization of land initiated in 1929–30). The fact remains that the question of revolutionary internationalism is a key to what drove some of Lenin's closest comrades into opposition to the Stalinist machine, but it receives rather short shift in this volume. Valuable as Lih's biography is, it seems that Lenin—as Arendt put it years ago—has "not yet found his definitive biographer."

Yet Lih's book deserves, and will probably find, a significant readership. In the midst of proliferating waves of capitalist crisis, growing numbers of people may also be "falling in love" with the ideas of Marx and Engels, and may conclude that Lenin is "the genuine article" as well. A world in which more and more of the population finds itself proletarianized and oppressed will tend to generate people who may be attracted to the kind of Leninist thinking that Lars Lih describes: "The party inspires the workers with a sense of their great mission to lead the *narod* [the oppressed people], and the proletariat then carries out this mission by inspiring the *narod* to join the workers in their crusade to overthrow tsarism, thereby opening up the road that ultimately leads to socialism—this is Lenin's scenario."[29]

Both Lih and Read sense that the study of Lenin is of more than simply historic interest. "The influence of, and interest in, one of the most important figures in the twentieth century is far from exhausted," Read tells us at the end of his own study. "Lenin's future may hold as many surprises as his past."[30]

Chapter Five
LENIN AND REVOLUTIONARY DEMOCRACY

In the introduction to the selection of Lenin's writings that I edited, I argue that Lenin's perspectives were profoundly and radically democratic, and that "the hope for the future may lie with those who are able to utilize the . . . lessons from the Leninist experience in the struggles of the twenty-first century." This goes against influential interpretations of scholars stretching from Bertram D. Wolfe through Leonard Schapiro to Richard Pipes, interpretations also informing the views of many liberal and left-wing scholars and commentators. That view sees Lenin as an authoritarian elitist bearing primary responsibility for the totalitarian order established under his presumed disciple and heir, Joseph Stalin.[1]

In disputing that interpretation, I will give attention to the Bolshevik tradition, the historical reality that has sometimes been referred to as "Leninism." As with many important terms, this one is highly controversial—there are not only multiple and utterly contradictory meanings, but there have also been those who have argued that the term has no "scientific" value whatsoever. My meaning, when I use the term Leninism, involves the combined theoretical, analytical, strategic, tactical, and organizational approach consistent with the life and thought and political practice of Vladimir Ilyich Ulyanov—popularly known as Lenin. In this presentation I will tilt the balance toward a consideration of Lenin's party, which is seen as the microcosm of the totalitarian order that he allegedly wished to impose.

Those who challenge the commonly held view certainly have some explaining to do. If the Marxism of Vladimir Ilyich Lenin arguably represents a powerful force for political freedom and genuine democracy, there is certainly no denying that it gave way to the murderous bureaucratic tyranny associated with Joseph Stalin. Adherents of Stalinism, perhaps wishing to see promising beginnings of socialism in that tyrannical regime, naturally embraced the notion that Lenin led to Stalin. The negative features of "actually existing socialism," and then its collapse, greatly undermined the credibility of "Leninism" for many. Opponents of socialism and revolution (and also weary, disillusioned one-time partisans) have also emphasized a deep bond between Lenin and Stalin—in order to close off the revolutionary socialist path as anything that a thoughtful, humane person would want to consider.

One of the problems with this, as I argue in *Marx, Lenin, and the Revolutionary Experience*, is that if not enough thoughtful, humane people are prepared to forge a revolutionary socialist path to the future, then political freedom, genuine democracy, a decent life for all people, not to mention the survival of human culture and planet Earth, might not be part of the future.[2]

Lenin and His Revolution

There is much more than discussions of "the organization question" in what this revolutionary has to say to us. In the new selection of Lenin's writings contained in the volume *Revolution, Democracy, Socialism*, one sees the breadth and coherence of his thinking in his emphasis on the need for socialist and working-class support to struggles of all who suffer oppression, and in his way of integrating reform struggles with revolutionary strategy.

Lenin's insistence on the necessity of working-class political independence, and on the need for working-class supremacy (or hegemony) if democratic and reform struggles are to triumph is matched by his approach to social alliances (such as the worker-peasant alliance) as a key aspect of the revolutionary struggle. We also find his development of the united front tactic, in which diverse political forces can work together for common goals, without revolutionary organizations undermining their ability to pose effective alternatives to the capitalist status quo. His profound analyses of capitalist development, and of imperialism and of nationalism utilize, expand upon, and to some extent deepen Marx's own analyses.

Lenin's vibrantly revolutionary internationalist orientation embraces the laborers and oppressed peoples of the entire world in these writings. Especially dramatic is his remarkable understanding of the manner in which democratic struggles flow into socialist revolution. Challenging commonplace perspectives in the socialist movement of his time, Lenin analyzes the nature of the state in history, with a conceptualization (rooted in Marx and Engels yet at the same time remarkably innovative) of triumphant working-class struggles generating a deepening and expanding democracy that would ultimately cause the state to wither away.

Of course, Lenin became the model revolutionary leader of the twentieth century because he was the leader of the first revolutionary working-class seizure of power in Russia. It is instructive to see how John Reed summarizes this in his classic eyewitness account *Ten Days That Shook the World*. At one point the focus is on Lenin as heroic mass leader: "So, Lenin and the Petrograd workers had decided on insurrection, the Petrograd Soviet had overthrown the Provisional Government, and thrust the *coup d'etat* upon the Congress of Soviets. Now there was all great Russia to win—and then the world!"[3] Later on, however, we will see that Reed refocuses our attention on the Bolshevik party—a splitoff from the old Russian Social Democratic Labor Party in which Lenin's faction had engaged in seemingly endless struggles with not only the more moderate Mensheviks, but with a myriad of other currents as well.

"The comrades grouped around Lenin were far more seriously committed to principles, which they wanted to see applied at all cost and pervading all practical work," as Lenin's companion Nadezheda Krupskaya put it. She added that "Ilyich could not stand this diffuse, unprincipled conciliationism, conciliationism with anyone and everyone, which was tantamount to surrendering one's positions at the height of the struggle." Instead, "the thing was to have a united Party center, around which the Social-Democratic worker masses could rally." The final break—in which the Bolshevik party was established as an independent entity—came at a 1912 conference "at which we were able in a business-like manner to discuss questions relating to the work in Russia and frame a clear line for this work."[4]

It is here that Reed comes to focus his later comments:

> Not by compromise with the propertied classes, or with the other political leaders; not by conciliating the old Government mechanism, did the Bolsheviki conquer the power. Nor by the organized violence of a small clique. If the masses all over Russia had not been ready for insurrection, it must have failed. The only reason for Bolshevik success lay in their accomplishing the vast and simple desires of the most profound strata of the people, calling them to the work of tearing down and destroying the old, and afterward, in the smoke of the falling ruins, cooperating with them to erect the framework of the new.[5]

The Bolshevik Mystique

The interplay of Lenin, the Bolshevik party, the broader Russian working-class movement, and the insurgent masses of workers and peasants animates most serious studies of the Russian Revolution. Those of us who have focused our attention on such studies have been unable to avoid running into what might almost be called the mystique of the Bolshevik party. N. N. Sukhanov, one of Lenin's Menshevik opponents in the Russian Social Democratic Labor Party (who acknowledged Lenin's role as "a herald of the ideas of revolutionary Marxism" and "the most authoritative leader of the Soviet proletarian Left") commented on what he called "characteristic traits of the Bolshevik 'way of life' and of specific methods of Bolshevik party work"—which he described unsympathetically in these terms:

> It became quite obvious that all Bolshevik work was held within the iron framework of a foreign spiritual center [presumably Lenin's ideas], without which the party workers would have felt themselves to be completely helpless, which at the same time they felt proud of, and of which the best

amongst them felt themselves to be the devoted servitors, as knights were of the Holy Grail.[6]

A less knowledgeable and more sympathetic sense of this reality comes through in the accounts of John Reed's fellow left-wing journalist from the United States, Albert Rhys Williams. Reed and Williams, along with Louise Bryant and Bessie Beatty, found themselves traveling to Russia (before the Bolshevik seizure of power) with a small cluster of returning Russian-American revolutionaries, whom he described as "free, young, sturdy spirits," but who "were neither fools nor imbeciles. Knocking about the world had hammered all of that out of them. Nor were these men hero-worshippers. The Bolshevik movement was elemental and passionate, but it was scientific, realistic, and uncongenial to hero-worship." Nonetheless, as Williams later emphasized, their attitude toward Lenin was that, "on the whole, they trusted him to use his subtle and wide knowledge of Marxist theory, checked against his close knowledge of people, and his genius as a tactician to know the moment when the people were ready to seize power, and to lead the way." In addition to this, Williams emphasized other qualities—"their faith in the historic role of the workers, their hardheaded reasoning, their compassion—[and] probably the most essential ingredient: self-discipline. That, and their relentless optimism, a spirit of courage and daring" Williams concluded. "Only with both could they have survived the coming trials."[7]

By 1919, the name of the Bolshevik party was changed from "Russian Social Democratic Labor Party (Bolsheviks)" to the Russian Communist Party (Bolsheviks). The shift from a party seeking the revolutionary overturn of the state to a party holding state power would eventually give way to a fatal transformation (as we shall explore shortly), but the early Communist movement continued to adhere to the old Bolshevik ethos well into the 1920s. To this party, according to Nikolai Bukharin and Evgeny Preobrazhensky in their *ABC of Communism*, "adhere the best of the workers and poorer peasants," adding that "all the interests which a party representing the interests of its class vigorously pursues, constitute the party program," and that "from our successes and failures, from our mistakes and oversights, experience will be gained, not by ourselves alone, but by the whole international proletariat."[8]

In his *History of the Bolshevik Party*, produced in 1923, Gregory Zinoviev made much of the term "professional revolutionary" (a conceptualization often expressed with the synonym "cadre"). "This term—'professional revolutionary'—played its part in the controversies between the Bolsheviks and the Mensheviks," Zinoviev wrote. Lenin's argument was:

> against us . . . there is Tsarist autocracy's enormous force, its whole apparatus which it has created over its 300 year term of office; against us are all the technical resources of the old Russia, its schools and its press; yet we have a completely juvenile workers' movement. If we want to force the working masses together and to merge the separate little fires flaring up here and there into one single big flame, then we need an exceptional, almost miraculous apparatus which is capable of realizing all this. And for this it is no less necessary in turn that people really dedicated to the working class are brought together by us into one organization of professional revolutionaries.[9]

Lenin himself had made the point in the 1900 essay "The Urgent Tasks of Our Movement," insisting, in the language of the classical Marxism permeating the international socialist movement of that time, that the Russian working class must "fulfill its great historical mission—to emancipate itself and the whole of the Russian people from political and economic slavery." But this would not happen, he insisted, unless it produced "its political leaders, its prominent representatives able to organize a movement and lead it." He added that "the Russian working class has already shown that it can produce such men and women." He concluded:

> We must train people who will devote the whole of their lives, not only their spare evenings, to the revolution; we must build up an organization large enough to permit the introduction of a strict division of labor in the various forms of our work. . . . Social-Democracy does not tie its hands, it does

not restrict its activities to some one preconceived plan or method of political struggle; it recognizes all methods of struggle, provided they correspond to the forces at the disposal of the Party and facilitate the achievement of the best results. . . . Before us, in all its strength, towers the enemy fortress which is raining shot and shell upon us, mowing down our best fighters. We must capture this fortress, and we will capture it, if we unite all the forces of the Russian revolutionaries into one party which will attract all that is vital and honest in Russia.[10]

In his profoundly important study of early Bolshevism, *Lenin Rediscovered*, Lars Lih capably shows us that Lenin's model was the German Social-Democratic Party, which he sought to adapt to Russian realities while remaining absolutely true to the revolutionary perspectives of Marx and Engels and (so he thought) to the example of his German comrades. It can be argued, however, that he unknowingly remained more completely and consistently true to Marxist perspectives than did "the grand old man of German Social Democracy" August Bebel and the "pope of Marxism" Karl Kautsky. The political trajectory of both Bebel and Kautsky involved compromises with powerful nonrevolutionary forces that increasingly weakened the revolutionary fiber of the German Social-Democratic Party (and of the Socialist (or Second) International) in ways that were not fully clear to Lenin until 1914.[11]

In a sense, then, there is truth to the 1926 observations of Max Eastman, a close comrade of John Reed and Albert Rhys Williams, when he described Lenin's party in such terms as these, enhancing what I have called the Bolshevik mystique:

It is an organization of a kind which never existed before. It combines certain essential features of a political party, a professional association, a consecrated order, an army, a scientific society—and yet it is in no sense a sect. Instead of cherishing in its membership a sectarian psychology, it cherishes a certain relation to the predominant class forces of society as Marx defined them. And this relation was determined by Lenin, and progressively readjusted by him, with a subtlety of which Marx never dreamed.[12]

A problem with Eastman's portrayal of Lenin as Heroic Individual is that it loses an essential element of the Bolshevik party aptly captured in this observation by the Indian Marxist scholar and revolutionary feminist Soma Marik, who tells us that "the Bolshevik party that emerged by February 1917 was not a personal creation of Lenin. While he was its foremost theoretician, the party was created by protracted interactions between practical workers and theorists, and repeatedly remodeled." She notes that "many ideas and organizational concepts had to be modified and discarded under the pressure of events and under class pressure."[13]

Bolshevism and Its Opposite

Eastman also employed a somewhat dubious label in describing Lenin—"engineer of revolution." From here it would be a short conceptual step to designating the Bolshevik or Communist Party as a collective "engineer of revolution," with humanity as the raw materials to be utilized in social construction. And this relates to what happened in the 1930s: a murderous collectivization of land and intensely exploitative super-industrialization, capped by intensified authoritarian controls established over various realms of culture, the redefinition of socialism to exclude freedom of expression and democracy, the glorification of bureaucratic dictatorship, the personality cult of Stalin, the increasingly fierce repression, the explosive expansion and brutalization of forced labor camps, the infamous "purges" in which phony accusations and torture and show trails led to innumerable executions.

All was done in the name of Communism, under the leadership of the Communist Party of the Soviet Union, causing J. Arch Getty and Oleg V. Naumov to entitle the important study they produced as *The Road to Terror: Stalin and the Self-Destruction of the Bolsheviks, 1932–1939*. Regarding the Communist leadership that saw itself as representing a continuation of Leninist policy, Getty tells us: "In the worldview they had constructed, the future of humanity depended on socialism. Socialism in turn depended on the survival of the soviet revolutionary experience, which depended on keeping the Bolshevik regime united, tightly disciplined, and in control of a society that frequently exhibited hostility to that regime." And yet, Getty acknowledges, something new had been added to realities in the Soviet Union at the beginning of the 1930s. "This 'new situation,' as the Stalinists called it, was the disastrous position in which the Stalinist leadership found itself after the 1929–32 period of famine, repression, and social upheaval that its collectivization and industrialization policies had caused."[14]

As Albert Rhys Williams noted late in life, these policies were described as revolutionary in the 1939 party textbook *History of the Communist Party of the Soviet Union*, which told readers: "The distinguishing feature of this revolution is that it was accomplished *from above*, on the initiative of the state." Williams responds: "It was a far cry from Lenin's constant call for 'initiative from below,' in the much darker days of 1918." More recently, Robert C. Tucker has commented that "the implication was not, or not fully, understood at that time" within the Communist Party, "so habituated was the collective party mind to the idea that building socialism would be an evolutionary process." Indeed, for Lenin "the idea of the construction of socialism as a revolution from above employing repressive means against large elements of the Revolution's constituency, especially in a terror-enforced collectivization against the peasantry, never entered his mind."[15] This notorious "revolution from above" flowed from another Stalinist commitment—that of building "socialism in one country," in sharp contradiction to the internationalist perspectives of Marx, Lenin, the pre-1924 Bolshevik party, and the first four congresses of the Communist International.

In fact, the dynamics and impact of this "revolution from above" contradicted the party organizational principles that had been embraced in 1921 at the Third Congress of the Communist International. Insisting that "the democratic centralism of the Communist Party organization should be a real synthesis, a fusion of centralism and proletarian democracy," this resolution explicitly warned against a division in the party between "the active functionaries and the passive masses" and against "formal or mechanical centralization [which] would mean the centralization of 'power' in the hands of the Party bureaucracy, allowing it *to dominate* the other members of the Party or the revolutionary proletarian masses which are outside the Party."[16]

Seeds of Stalinism

There were elements in the Bolshevik experience under Lenin, however, that could be said to contain seeds of what came to be known as Stalinism. The wonderful quality of Lenin's Marxism, especially between 1915 and 1917, was the unity of revolutionary strategy and revolutionary goal—each permeated by a vibrant, uncompromising working-class militancy, insurgent spirit, and radical democracy. This is worthy of the great symphonies of narrative and analysis that the finest representatives of the revolutionary Marxist tradition have produced. This was Lenin's triumph, culminating in the Bolshevik Revolution.[17]

Lenin's tragedy is that this broke down in practice in 1918—not simply because of the debilitating and murderous violence, but because the simple solution of "workers' democracy" became problematical when the abstract visions were brought down to the level of concrete realities. Workers' committees and councils in the factories and neighborhoods did not have enough information and knowledge to form practical decisions nor enough skill and practical experience to carry out decisions for the purpose of running a national economy, developing adequate social services throughout the country, formulating a coherent foreign policy, or running a factory. This was especially so in the context of the overwhelming destructiveness of World War I, the various and unrelenting foreign military interventions against the revolution, the economic blockade, and the horrors of the civil war.[18]

And in that context the rights of speech, press, assembly, and association—providing the possibility of spreading confusion, or putting forward super-revolutionary but unworkable alternatives, or fomenting counterrevolution—could not be tolerated. This meant the suppression of Mensheviks, anarchists, Left Socialist Revolutionaries, Right Socialist Revolutionaries, liberals, priests, and others. Only the dictatorship of the Communist Party could be tolerated; so Lenin was insisting by 1919.

In some ways, this reflected a powerful element of truth in the situation—but led to terrible contradictions, inevitably to abuses and crimes and corruption. A one-time ally of the Bolsheviks, the great Left Socialist Revolutionary leader Maria Spiridonova, wrote an open letter from a Bolshevik prison giving some sense of this moral disaster. "Your party had great tasks and began them finely," she recalled. "The October Revolution, in which we marched side by side, was bound to conquer, because its foundations and watchwords were rooted in historical reality and were solidly supported by all the working masses." But by November 1918 this had all changed: "In the name of the proletariat you have wiped out all the moral achievements of our Revolution. Things that cry aloud to Heaven have been done by the provincial Chekas, by the All-Russian Cheka. A bloodthirsty mockery of the souls and bodies of men, torture and treachery, and then—murder, murder without end, done without inquiry, on denunciation only, without waiting for any proof of guilt."[19]

This was acknowledged even by partisans of the Bolshevik cause, even as they defended the Bolsheviks. For example, Albert Rhys Williams wrote this in his 1921 classic *Through the Russian Revolution*:

> "Repressions, tyranny, violence," cry the enemies. "They have abolished free speech, free press, free assembly. They have imposed drastic military conscription and compulsory labor. They have been incompetent in government, inefficient in industry. They have subordinated the Soviets to the Communist Party. They have lowered their Communist ideals, changed and shifted their program and compromised with the capitalists."
>
> Some of these charges are exaggerated. Many can be explained. But they cannot all be explained away. Friends of the Soviet grieve over them. Their enemies have summoned the world to shudder and protest against them. . . .
>
> While abroad hatred against the Bolsheviks as the new "enemies of civilization" mounted from day to day, these self-same Bolsheviks were straining to rescue civilization in Russia from total collapse.[20]

Victor Serge later recalled:

> "Totalitarianism" did not yet exist as a word; as an actuality it
> began to press hard on us, even without our being aware of it.
> ... What with the political monopoly, the Cheka, and the Red
> Army, all that now existed of the "Commune-State" of our
> dreams was a theoretical myth. The war, the internal measures
> against counterrevolution, and the famine (which had created
> a bureaucratic rationing-apparatus) had killed off Soviet
> democracy. How could it revive and when? The Party lived in
> the certain knowledge that the slightest relaxation of its au-
> thority could give the day to reaction.[21]

Leninism versus Stalinism

Lenin had always believed that although "the Party, as the vanguard
of the working class, must not be confused ... with the entire class,"
it was the case that a "varied, rich, fruitful" interrelationship with the
working class as a whole must be facilitated by "the full application
of the democratic principle in the Party organization." This meant
that the organization should function according to "the principles of
democratic centralism." The unity and cohesion of the party must be
permeated with "guarantees for the rights of all minorities and for
all loyal opposition ... the autonomy of every [local] Party organization ... recognizing that all Party functionaries must be elected
and subject to recall," and that "there must be wide and free discussion of Party questions, free comradely criticism and assessments of
events in Party life." This would help the proletarian vanguard to link
up "and—if you wish—merge, in a certain measure, with the broadest
masses of working people," but (as Lenin explained in 1920) only
through prolonged effort and hard-won experience that would be
"facilitated by a correct revolutionary theory which ... is not a dogma
but assumes final shape only in close connection with the practical
activity of a truly mass and truly revolutionary movement."[22]

In 1923, Leon Trotsky put forward the image of "Bolshevik"
that was consistent with Williams's observations, the 1921 Com-

intern resolution, and Lenin's writings. He was employing it, how-ever, as an argument against bureaucratic-conservative trends within the now-ruling organization. "A Bolshevik is not merely a disci-plined person; he is a person who in each case and on each question forges a firm opinion of his own and defends it courageously and independently, not only against his enemies but inside his own party. Today, perhaps, he will be in the minority in his organization. He will submit, because it is his party. But this does not always signify that he is in the wrong." And if he is right, by persistently raising his differences, "he will render his party a service." What the party needs is not "sycophantic functionaries" but people "who are strongly tempered morally, permeated with a feeling of personal responsibil-ity." He emphasized: "What is needed is criticism, checking of fact, independence of thought, independence of character, the feeling of responsibility, truth toward oneself and toward one's work."[23]

The comments of Lenin and Trotsky are also consistent with the illuminating description of the Bolshevik Party of 1917 by Victor Serge, who strikingly asserted that "the party is the nervous system of the working class, its brain." Of course, the nervous system—extending throughout the body—carries messages back and forth and to and from the brain. The members of the revolutionary party, Serge tells us, "have to uncover, by scientific analysis of historic processes, the tendency of events and the possibilities that are open in them." More than this, just as the nervous system carries sensations and in-formation throughout one's body, while interacting with our central intelligence, the party comrades "have to grasp the action that is pos-sible and necessary for the proletariat, according with historical ne-cessity and not with its wish or hope of the moment. In a word, they must see reality, grasp possibility, and conceive the action which will be the link between the real and the possible." The measure for what is to be done is "the proletariat's own higher interests." Serge puts it all together like this:

> The October Revolution offers us an almost perfect model of
> the proletarian party. Relatively few as they may be, its mili-
> tants live with the masses and among them. Long and testing
> years—a revolution [in 1905], then illegality, exile, prison,

endless ideological battles—have given it excellent activists
and real leaders, whose parallel thinking was strengthened in
collective action. Personal initiative and the panache of strong
personalities were balanced by intelligent centralization, vol-
untary discipline and respect for recognized mentors. Despite
the efficiency of its organizational apparatus, the party suffered not the slightest bureaucratic deformation. No fetishism
of organizational norms can be observed in it; it is free of
decadent and even of dubious traditions; its dominant tradition is that of the war against opportunism—it is revolutionary down to the marrow of its bones.[24]

What Serge offers here is consistent with the descriptions offered by Williams and Reed and Krupskaya, and with the writings
of Lenin and Trotsky. It has little in common with the ideological
description by J. Arch Getty of the so-called Bolsheviks who pur-
portedly "self-destructed" in the 1930s. "The Bolshevik Party was a
product of idealistic, egalitarian, and socially progressive strands in
the Russian intelligentsia and working class," Getty acknowledges.
"By the 1930s much of the original idealism had been lost or transformed, as Bolshevik revolutionaries became state officials."[25]

Not all of the Bolsheviks were corrupted in the way that Getty
suggests. Of course, some were. In 1932, Trotsky wrote from exile:
"On the foundation of the dictatorship of the proletariat—in a
backward country, surrounded by capitalists—for the first time a
powerful bureaucratic apparatus has been created from among the
upper layers of the workers, that is, raised above the masses, that
lays down the law to them, that has at its disposal colossal resources, that is bound together by an inner mutual responsibility,
and that intrudes into the policies of a workers' government its
own interests, methods, and regulations." Trotsky was merciless in
describing the ex-working-class functionary: "He eats and guzzles
and procreates and grows himself a respectable potbelly. He lays
down the law with a sonorous voice, handpicks from below people
faithful to him, remains faithful to his superiors, prohibits others
from criticizing himself, and sees in all of this the gist of the general line."[26]

In the same period, a dissident Communist in Soviet Russia, Martemyan N. Riutin, was complaining that "Stalin is killing Leninism, [killing] the proletarian revolution under the flag of the proletarian revolution, [killing] socialist construction under the flag of socialist construction." A one-time leader of the Communist Party in Moscow, expelled in 1930 for opposing the forced collectivization of land, Riutin wrote that "the most evil enemy of the party and the proletarian dictatorship, the most evil counterrevolutionary and provocateur could not have carried out the work of destroying the party and socialist construction better than Stalin has done," adding that "the main cohort of Lenin's comrades has been removed from the leading positions, and some of them are in prisons and exile; others have capitulated, still others, demoralized and humiliated, carry on a miserable existence, and finally, some, those who have degenerated completely, have turned into loyal servants of the dictator."[27]

The dilemma of a regime founded in the spirit of socialist democracy evolving as a bureaucratic dictatorship, as Lenin himself recognized, could only be resolved by revolution bringing more advanced industrial countries into the socialist orbit, creating a material basis for the economic and cultural development of a socialist society. As the spread of socialist revolutions was blocked, however, the growing contradictions overwhelmed revolutionary Russia. Moshe Lewin has commented that "the year 1924 [marks] the end of 'Bolshevism,'" adding:

> For a few more years one group of old Bolsheviks after another was to engage in rearguard actions in an attempt to rectify the course of events in one fashion or another. But their political tradition and organization, rooted in the history of Russian and European Social-Democracy, were rapidly swept aside by the mass of new members and new organizational structures which pressed that formation into an entirely different mold. The process of the party's conversion into an apparatus—careers, discipline, ranks, abolition of all political rights—was an absolute scandal for the oppositions of 1924–28.[28]

But these scandalized dissident Communists were swept aside and savagely repressed by what Michal Reiman has aptly described as "a ruling social stratum, separated from the people and hostilely disposed toward it," even (I would add) as this stratum claimed to speak in the name of the people and with the rhetoric of Marx and Lenin.[29]

The Saving Remnant

Among Communists in the Soviet Union it is certainly the case that there were also those who, while adapting to the Stalinist atmosphere, neither became utterly corrupted nor abandoned completely their earlier ideals and Leninist inclinations. (The fate of some of these people has been recounted in such dissident Soviet/post-Soviet scholars as Roy Medvedev and Vadim Rogovin, and also in the brilliant contribution of US historian Wendy Z. Goldman.[30]) The same was true within the international Communist movement. As Marxist theory and revolutionary organizational perspectives became increasingly compromised and debased, there were some—including in the leaderships of certain Communist parties—who for a time were able to remain true to their original perspectives through the 1920s. For a short while, such figures as M. N. Roy in India, James P. Cannon in the United States, Chen Duxiu in China, Antonio Gramsci in Italy, and Georg Lukács in Hungary continued to do important political work. Gramsci and Lukács provided theorizations of their work that stand as particularly influential intellectual and cultural contributions—and are nothing if not vital expressions of Leninist perspectives.

Among Marxists influenced by Leninism but incapable of embracing Stalin's version of Marxism, some returned to the left-wing of the Social Democracy (the Second International), some handfuls joined with Trotsky to form the Fourth International (seeking to develop what Trotsky called a "Bolshevik-Leninist" alternative to Stalinism), some abandoned any pretense of revolutionary politics, and some continued to engage with Marxist ideas while drifting more or less away from political activism. Among those Europeans in this last category there developed something that took the label of "Western Marxism." This often involved rich studies in philosophical, sociological, and historical matters, with analyses of and in a variety of issues having to do with culture and consciousness. By the late twentieth century, many intellectuals and academics were inclined to counterpose such Western Marxism to the perspectives not only of Stalin but also of Lenin (often arguing that the latter had been responsible for the former). But Western Marxism's foundational figures happen to be two highly sophisticated and unrepentant Leninists—Lukács and Gramsci—who wrote their most influential works as they sought to build and give leadership to the Communist parties in their native lands. These writings involve sustained efforts to utilize Lenin's revolutionary political thought in order to carry out tasks of party-building and revolutionary strategy.[31]

Even now, after the much-celebrated "collapse of Communism," it seems possible—given the way the world is going—that these critical Bolshevik and Leninist traditions will continue to attract, and be developed by, revolutionary activists of today and tomorrow.[32] Especially to the extent that they are able to make such traditions relevant in actual protests and political action, it is likely that scholarly debate will swirl around the issue of Lenin and revolutionary democracy.

Chapter Six
THE GREAT LENIN DEBATE OF 2012

The deepening of global crises, the intensification of popular protest and insurgency, and the spread of revolutionary possibilities have been generating renewed interest in Marxism and, along with that, a renewal of Marxism. A key figure in the Marxist tradition—and in the renewal—is the person who was central in the first revolution to be led by revolutionary Marxists: Vladimir Ilyich Lenin. For those who are serious about Marxism, about challenging capitalism, and about revolutionary change, Lenin is a key figure who must be engaged with. Wrestling with and learning from the actual ideas and experience associated with Lenin has become a priority for a significant and growing minority of scholars and activists.[1]

Not surprisingly, efforts to get all of this right have generated different ways of understanding what happened in history and (for some of us) how this can be usefully applied to our own present-day realities and future efforts. One of the most recent controversies, in which I have become involved—at one point, tongue in cheek, I referred to it as the "Lenin wars"—was initiated by a young activist in the United States named Pham Binh.[2] Pham, a former member of the International Socialist Organization (ISO), who left it a few years before I joined it, attacked the late Tony Cliff (a significant figure in the ISO tradition) for writing, a quarter of a century back, a massive political biography of Lenin whose purpose was, in part, to serve as a guide in the building of the British Socialist Workers Party and its international affiliates. Cliff created a historically inaccurate conceptualization of Lenin, Pham tells us, in order to advance his own particular political agenda. Advancing his own political agenda is something that Pham himself is "guilty" of, the purpose of his polemic being to advance his own particular views about the Occupy movement and the tasks of socialists in the United States. (There is, of course, nothing intrinsically wrong with that.) His modest contribution makes use of a few Lenin quotes and of the excellent work of Lars Lih, a serious historian and Lenin scholar.[3]

Lars and I were both drawn into this debate—initially on opposite sides. In the course of our debate, however, there have been fruitful convergences, although certain distinctions and differences remain in our interpretations of the historical material—yet there is between us, I feel, a mutual respect and an openness, related to the fact that we more or less share a common methodology. What I want to do here is, first of all, to indicate what that methodology is. Then I want to map out the two areas in which Lars and I have disagreed—a 1905 debate among the Bolsheviks and the meaning of the 1912 Prague "All-Russia Conference" of the Russian Social Democratic Labor Party (RSDLP). I will indicate my own understanding of where things stand now in that dispute, offering my own take on the historical actualities. Finally, I will give some attention to the lessons—and also the non-lessons—for our own time of issues related to this controversy, and also related issues that go beyond these particular "Lenin wars."

Methodology for Historians and Marxists

A starting point for our understanding of historical methodology is grasping the fact that the word "history" has two basic meanings. As my good friend Wikipedia puts it: "History is the discovery, collection, organization, and presentation of information about past events. History can also mean the period of time after writing was invented." I would rephrase that to say that history is, first of all, all the stuff that happened in the past (in a sense, up to this very moment, which has itself just passed into history). But history is also a discipline, the study of the past. Sometimes this second meaning of history is called historiography, which Wikipedia tells us refers "either to the study of history and methodology of history as a discipline, or to a body of historical work on a specialized topic"—for example, Lenin and the Bolshevik party. In a moment I want to talk a bit more about the methodology of history as a discipline, but first I want to touch on the connection of history and politics.

A starting point for me is to focus on the contributions of Marxism to historiography. A central aspect of Marxism is what has been called the materialist conception of history, or historical materialism, which has had a powerful impact on the discipline of history, just as it has had on so many other intellectual disciplines. There have naturally been raging controversies over how to understand historical materialism and how to use it. I will restrict myself here to summarizing some of how I understand it and use it. If we want to understand human beings, a key thing we need to grasp is how they sustain themselves—the activities and relationships they enter into, and the resources they use, to get the things that they need (such as food, clothing, shelter) and the things that they want. That is, we must look at economics. Because of its centrality to the human condition and to the lived experience of us all, economics is a key to the shaping of human culture and consciousness and institutions. For at least the past five thousand years, there has been sufficient economic surplus in increasing areas of the world to allow for economic inequality, with powerful minorities enriching themselves through exploiting laboring majorities—and history is shaped in large measure by these social-economic classes, and the tensions and conflicts and struggles that inevitably arise between them. History is a dynamic totality of contradictory and interacting factors, moved forward by conflicting and evolving potentialities inherent within it—which has led to the rise and decline of different forms of economy, and these different economic systems can be utilized to develop a coherent understanding of the actual shape of history over the centuries. All of these notions have become truisms in the discipline of history. But there is a key element of Marxism that is more controversial—the unbreakable link between the study of history and the commitment to revolutionary politics.[4]

Although some historians are not inclined to admit it, even to themselves, there is always an interplay of politics and historiography.

If you are a liberal or a conservative or an anarchist or a fascist or a socialist or a racist or a misogynist or an egalitarian or whatever (and some political notions seep into the thinking of even those who see themselves as apolitical), that will influence the way you interpret and study and write history. It influences the questions you ask, the answers you seek, the way you interpret the data you find as you explore historical questions. Marx and those who have embraced his orientation are clear and upfront—they seek an understanding of history in order to help change the world in the interest of the exploited and the oppressed, seeking a future without exploitation and oppression. This shapes the way they study and interpret history—and there is nothing wrong with that, especially if they are conscious and honest about it.

At this point, however, it may be fruitful to make a distinction between serious politics and what many of us have labeled sectarian politics. Serious politics seeks to engage with the world as it really is, and with the potentialities for change that are really there. If it is revolutionary politics, it seeks to connect with the actual lives and consciousness and struggles of the exploited and the oppressed in a manner that can have real impact, bringing into being consciousness and struggles that can positively change lives and create the possibility of an actual revolution. If it is sectarian politics, while the stated purpose may be the same, the actual purpose is to sustain a particular universe that is separate from the actual, real-world lives and consciousness and struggles of those inhabiting the larger society. The primary purpose is to validate and sustain the centrality and importance of one's particular organization and ideas and specialness. This approach to politics often spills over into one's approach to history—a lack of seriousness, the creation of historical narratives on the basis of fragments grabbed from one or another source, but not fully understood, in order to make a particular sectarian point, to validate your own particular notion or argument about what you believe should be done. References to history are utilitarian—an actual immersion in historical sources and interpretations tends to be dismissed as adventures in esoterica, the primary point being to create a sense of historical authority for what we should do—or say—today or tomorrow. This is not good historiography.

For serious Marxist historians, I think it is helpful to have a sense of the integrity of the discipline of history and also a keen sense of what I would call "the activist disadvantage and the activist advantage." I want to connect this to similar and different qualities that I believe can be found in the approach of Lars Lih and myself. Some of the similarities can be found in our approach to the integrity of the discipline.[5]

A serious historian first of all needs to listen to others. This involves having some familiarity with what other historians have to say (that is, secondary sources) and also with what the actual people you are studying have to say (which refers to what we call primary sources). It is important to be able to give a sympathetic reading to what is being said (that is, trying to understand, really and truly, what the person says and means) but also to give it a critical reading (which means considering possible internal contradictions in what is being said and also contradictions between a secondary source and a primary source, or contradictions between one primary source and another). The right kind of listening also involves the insight that someone, whether an historian or a historical participant, may be wrong about many important things but still get some things right.

Related to all of this, a historian needs to reach for coherence, understanding that history is not simply a jumble of interesting or contradictory or annoying facts, or one damn thing after another. What are the meanings, the causes that bring about certain effects that themselves cause new effects? Where do the ever-present contradictions come from, and how do the contradictions fit together into a coherent whole and explain what happened next? At the same time, it is helpful to hungrily seek things that will challenge the coherence. Sometimes, something that seems to contradict your coherent narrative helps to illuminate something "new" that needs to be grasped in order to get the story right. If you take a shortcut to dismiss it or pigeonhole it, you may create a false coherence that distorts the reality.

The secondary sources (that is, the accounts written by historians) that are best are those that utilize and do justice to the primary sources (materials from the period under study—including documents, journals and journalism, recollections from participants, and so on). This raises the question of how one uses primary sources. I have already touched on that, but there is more to be said. For any serious assertion, it is best to have more than one reference point in the pool of historical material, with at least some contextualization of primary texts. Just because Lenin writes something, for example, does not by itself clinch anything. What was the purpose and what was the context of the document, how does it correspond with other documents by Lenin, how does it correspond to what others were saying at the time, and how does it correspond with retrospective overviews provided by other participants? (Of course, latter-day recollections of participants need to be correlated with documents from the time—the mind can play tricks, and memories are not always reliable.) Understanding how such things fit together helps us understand the actual meaning of the particular Lenin quote. In all of this, it is important, as already suggested, to reach for coherence but also to reach for complexity.

Given the kind of complexity involved here, it is important to understand that history is necessarily a collective enterprise. Various historians who immerse themselves in the historical material may provide useful information and interesting interpretations, but they will inevitably get some of it wrong. Others delving into the material and weighing in on what they found and how they understand it all come up with new insights and mistakes, which may be challenged (providing corrections and newer insights, sometimes with mistakes) by someone else. Some aspects of this collective enterprise may result in academic dead-ends, or the collective building up of ideological dogmas (more often than not buttressing the status quo). But some of it results in the collective accumulation of more information, more insights, more understanding of what happened in history.

The Activist Approach: Advantages and Disadvantages

Before turning to the examination of Bolshevism in 1905 and 1912, I want to take a few moments to consider what I have referred to as "the activist advantage and the activist disadvantage." Lars Lih's marvelous book *Lenin Rediscovered* primarily sets out to demolish what he refers to as "the textbook" account of Lenin initiated by Cold War anticommunists. But he also advances, secondarily, a critique of Tony Cliff, John Molyneux, and me (lumping us together despite our differences). In this, he correctly notes that we are political activists, and sometimes refers to us as the activist historians. It seems to me that there are both advantages and disadvantages in such activism for one who is seeking to write about the history of Bolshevism. An obvious advantage is that we passionately care about the history and know something about it (for example, we are actually inclined to read Lenin seriously), and we also are absolutely unsympathetic to the project of the Cold War anticommunists—all of which puts us in the same camp as Lars himself. The additional advantage we have is an intimate, inside knowledge (which Lars cannot have) of the pull-and-tug and swirl of revolutionary politics and of organizational dynamics. Sometimes this can provide insights and clues, an "insider's" familiarity with the practical meaning that certain theoretical texts may possess.

The activist disadvantage seems to me to have two aspects. I want to take some time on the first before moving on to the second. There is a very natural tendency—which I have already noted—to connect the history with what we perceive as the present-day requirements of our own political activity and projects, and this can all too often result in shortcuts and distortions in the way we interpret the history—reading the present into the past in ways that distort what actually happened in the past. Left-wing activists are not the only historians who do this, but it is certainly a temptation and occupational hazard for us.

I think, on the other hand, that there is a strength in this aspect of the "activist disadvantage" that I am criticizing. There is a desire, on our part, to ground our perspectives and activities in what actually happened in history, and to give people—our own comrades and others—a sense of what happened in history as part of a left-wing political education and the development of a socialist class consciousness. There are popularized accounts of history that are consequently developed and shared, in some cases broad overviews such as A. L. Morton's *A People's History of England*, Howard Zinn's *A People's History of the United States*, Chris Harman's *A People's History of the World*, Leo Huberman's *Man's Worldly Goods*, Sheila Row-botham's *Women, Resistance and Revolution*, Peter Fryer's *Staying Power*, my own *Short History of the U.S. Working Class*, and so on. There are also popularized works on the Bolsheviks and the Russian Revolution, the history of May Day, Marxism, and so on. Whatever their limitations or weaknesses, Tony Cliff's multivolume works on Lenin and Trotsky fit into this category, as do a number of popular pamphlets and short books produced by various left-wing organizations. These serve a positive function of providing an entry point for larger numbers of people—activists, workers, students, and others—to an initial understanding of what happened in history and how this might connect to the struggles of today and tomorrow.

Related to such work, however, is the second activist disadvantage: a tendency on our part to settle into a basic, overarching historical narrative—consistent with the traditions in which our organizations are rooted—which we do not question, and which sometimes closes us off from seeking new insights into what actually happened in history. This is in contrast to a historian like Lars Lih. In one of my polemics, I shared my appreciation for Lars by noting that "he is a scholar of considerable integrity, in my opinion, whose work is greatly enhanced by the fact that he is fluent in Russian and has an incredibly fine mind and delicious wit and iconoclastic bent, facilitating a fruitfully critical-minded approach to the study of Lenin." I would repeat the critical side of this too: "being an iconoclast with integrity does not mean that one is inevitably right when he smashes some presumably 'iconic' interpretation of what happened in history." Sometimes he can overstate his case (which enhances the drama of smashing the particular icon), and sometimes even he can get something wrong. But unencumbered by the "activist disadvantage," Lars has been feeding invaluable and challenging contributions into the collective enterprise of comprehending what actually happened in the history of Bolshevism.

Creating Bolshevism

The recent disagreements between Lars and me have involved two issues: the meaning of a debate that arose among the Bolsheviks at a conference in April 1905, and whether the Bolsheviks became a distinct party as a result of a conference in Prague in January 1912. It seems to me Lars has two primary concerns here. One is to defend his interpretation of Lenin's pamphlet *What Is to Be Done?* as a document that is absolutely consistent with the revolutionary-democratic essence of Marxism and that is profoundly optimistic about the capacity of the working class to make a revolution. (I agree with his interpretation.) His other concern related to this is that Lenin's conception of the revolutionary party has nothing to do with the conspiratorial elitism attributed to him by the "textbook interpretation" but was actually the conception agreed upon by most Marxists throughout the world at that time, including the German Social Democrats grouped around August Bebel and Karl Kautsky. (I basically agree with this too.) Others in the debate have sought the authority of Lars's work with a somewhat broader concern in mind—to establish historical-Leninist authority in support of projects involving some variety of socialist unity. If Bolsheviks and Mensheviks were part of the same organization, and if Lenin thought this was fine (as a good Social Democrat embracing—as did the Mensheviks—the orientation of Karl Kautsky), then obviously we should go and do likewise, rejecting the project of building distinctly "Leninist" organizations. Lars has no position on this—he is focused on what actually happened in history.

It seems to me that the dispute between Lars and me has narrowed dramatically on both questions of 1905 and 1912. I will first try to sum up where things stand on the first controversy in a manner that I think Lars might agree with.

In April 1905 at a Bolshevik conference a dispute opened up with Lenin on one side; and on the other stood some practical Bolshevik activists, who were known as committeemen, operating in underground conditions inside Russia. The debate seems to have involved the question of how open the revolutionary party now could and should be, particularly related to the question of bringing more workers onto the party's revolutionary committees in the midst of the 1905 workers' insurgency.

A Belgian historian named Marcel Liebman, in his book *Leninism under Lenin*, argued that this was part of a larger pattern of

Lenin's history—swinging from authoritarian-elitist inclinations (reflected, for example, in *What Is to Be Done?*) to revolutionary-democratic inclinations (reflected in the dispute with his rigid committeemen comrades). Following this interpretation, Tony Cliff argued that the committeemen wanted to adhere to the undemocratic ideas in *What Is to Be Done?* while Lenin wanted to abandon those ideas. It seems clear, however, that the Liebman-Cliff interpretation of Lenin's 1902 pamphlet is wrong—and that their interpretation of the 1905 debate is therefore seriously flawed.

In my writings I have emphasized the importance of the debate and suggested (following accounts by Nadezhda Krupskaya, and others) that Lenin was right in opposing a sectarian tendency among the Bolshevik committeemen. Lars was inclined to see this as giving support to the Cliff misinterpretation, and even to see my position as a hostile attack on the Bolshevik *praktiki* (and he scoffed at a presumed "Lenin versus the Bolsheviks" scenario). It seemed to me, on the other hand, that Lars was intent on denying the existence of a debate that actually happened. Fortunately, the discussion moved past this unproductive wrangle.

It is clear that there *was* a sharp debate in 1905—with Lenin and some Bolshevik comrades on one side and with a number of Bolshevik committeemen on the other—over the question of creating greater openness and worker involvement in the Bolshevik organization inside Russia, and Lenin lost the vote on this question. There are documents from the April conference themselves that show this to be true, and also two "inside accounts" in English—one by Solomon Schwarz, who was a Bolshevik at that time but later became a Menshevik, and another by Lenin's companion and close comrade Nadezhda Krupskaya. Schwarz's conclusions are designed to demonstrate dogmatic, sectarian qualities in Bolshevism that even Lenin was uneasy about, while Krupskaya's conclusion was that these were growing pains in Bolshevism that eventually were overcome in part through Lenin's efforts—but both tell basically the same story, which is critical of the triumphant committeemen. The question remains, who was right—Lenin or the committeemen (a leading spokesman of that time, according to Lars, being Lev Kamenev). Until proof is offered otherwise, I am inclined to trust

Krupskaya's account, with its assumption that Lenin was right. At one point in our debate, Lars leaned toward Kamenev and the committeemen as having a firmer grip on the Russian realities. It's a tantalizing question—and only someone like Lars, who is fluent in Russian, can help us to come closer to a resolution of that question.[6]

Lars Lih is in the forefront of those rejecting the Stalinist notion—propagated in the 1930s (and later embraced by Cold War anticommunists)—that as early as 1902 Lenin set out to establish a "party of a new type" (one that would be qualitatively different from the old Social-Democratic model). At long last this party of a new type came into being, according to that interpretation, with the formal split from the Mensheviks in 1912. More than simply rejecting this notion, Lars, with an iconoclastic flourish, announced in a 2012 polemic that he was revising his own judgment, as presented in his excellent short biography *Lenin*, published one year earlier, and siding with Pham Binh's rejection of (as Pham put it) "the myth that the Mensheviks and Bolsheviks separated into two parties in 1912." Actually, the formulation that Lars advanced was more restrained. He says: "Lenin and the Bolsheviks *did not set out* to organize their faction as a separate party, they vehemently denied that they had done so after the Conference, and they were justified in making this denial."

After a substantial interchange, which included my lengthy and fully documented article entitled "The Birth of the Bolshevik Party in 1912," Lars offered the following judgment, which seems to me to reflect a convergence in our views:

> Recently Paul Le Blanc has written a long and instructive essay on the Prague conference which concludes that "for all practical purposes, the party that emerged from the Prague All-Russian RSDLP conference of 1912 was a Bolshevik party." The key words here are "for all practical purposes." Paul points to a number of reasons for equating Bolshevism and the party: the new central committee was composed overwhelmingly of Bolsheviks; the Bolshevik effort to forge a coalition with "party Mensheviks" never amounted to much; the other factions did not acknowledge the legitimacy of the

central institutions voted in by the Prague conference and they tried (not very successfully) to set up competing institutions; there is direct organisational continuity between the 1912 central committee and the Communist Party of 1918 that added 'Bolshevik' to its official name. All this is true, but in no way clashes with my earlier statement about the *outlook and aims* of Lenin and the Bolsheviks in 1912.[7]

As Lars goes on to say, there remain a number of unresolved issues. One of them he identifies in this way: "I believe that Paul does not sufficiently allow for the possibility that the Bolshevik *outlook* in 1912 cannot be directly deduced from what turned out to be, 'for all practical purposes,' the actual outcome." I think that is an important question, and I think it is even more complicated than what Lars indicates. What did Lenin say in certain polemics and how do some of his formulations compare to what he actually thought (to the extent that this can be determined from correspondence and other documents) is another question. Yet another involves the possibility—probably the inevitability—that what Lenin believed and what some of his Bolshevik comrades believed and said might not be quite the same.

No definitive answers can be provided here, but there are a few things that can be said about the work remaining to be done. To answer these and other questions, it is necessary to give serious attention to what went before, and this in two different ways.

One factor to consider is that the April 1905 Bolshevik conference referred to earlier was actually the Third Congress of the Russian Social Democratic Labor Party. But only the Bolsheviks attended; the Mensheviks boycotted. Christopher Read, in his 2005 biography of Lenin puts it this way:

> It was thus not entirely Lenin's fault that when the Third Congress convened in London on 25 April 1905 all the delegates were Leninists. Lenin used the congress . . . to establish a Leninist grip on key Party institutions. Existing papers—*Iskra* and *Vpered*—were declared disbanded, and a new paper, *Proletarii*, set up as the official Party newspaper under Lenin's ed-

itorship. An all-Leninist Central Committee was elected. . . . Lenin even wrote to the International Socialist Bureau in Brussels in June demanding it recognize *Proletarii* as the only official newspaper and derecognize *Iskra*.[8]

In this situation, of course, Lenin was not inclined to completely and definitively split from the Mensheviks, and there were soon efforts—partially successful amidst the revolutionary turmoil of 1905—to heal the breach. The point is, however, that in 1912 we see a very similar scenario, but Lenin and others had already had this previous experience under their belts and had seen how "unity" turned out in the years following 1905. There were growing frustrations with the growth of liquidationism (abandonment of the revolutionary underground) among a large sector of the Mensheviks, combined with the toleration of and the adaptation toward liquidationism among another large sector of Mensheviks, the passage and flouting of anti-liquidator resolutions, ongoing Menshevik hostility toward the Bolsheviks, and the relative paralysis of the RSDLP.

By 1911 Kamenev and Lenin collaborated in producing the intransigent polemic *The Two Parties* and the Leninist Bolsheviks were committed to organizing an RSDLP conference in Prague—in a manner similar to what happened in April 1905. With a difference—this time there *was* an intention to exclude the majority of Mensheviks, and also the anticipation that there might well be a boycott by others. It is interesting to note the take on the situation according to Rosa Luxemburg, speaking for the Social Democratic Party of the Kingdom of Poland and Lithuania, in the autumn of 1911. By this time, Luxemburg was much closer to Lenin and the Bolsheviks than had been the case six years earlier—but she was alarmed with the practical possibility that two parties would actually be created out of the RSDLP. "In view of the cynical excesses of the factional entities that side with the Liquidators Martov, Dan and Company," she wrote, "Lenin and his friends began to address the question of convening a Party Conference that would exclude the *Golos* tendency [that is, Martov, Dan and company]," adding that "in the political estimation of the Mensheviks, there are no significant differences between our tendency and Lenin's."

This agreement is evident in how Luxemburg described the internal situation in the non-Bolshevik sectors of the RSDLP: "The orgies of opportunism of the 'Mensheviks' and their open support of the Liquidators led . . . to the split in the heart of their own faction and to the secession of the 'party Mensheviks,' led by Georgi Plekhanov." While respectful of the party-Mensheviks, Luxemburg was as scornful as Lenin was toward the ultraleft Bolsheviks—the Forwardists—associated with Bogdanov, and also toward Trotsky's "anti-faction" faction. But she was concerned that the Bolsheviks, in "wanting to form a bloc only with the 'party-Mensheviks,'" were adopting what she considered a destructive effort to shut out the Mensheviks grouped around Martov and Dan and also the smaller groups. "This stubborn Bolshevik war against all other groups even had the result," she noted, "that Plekhanov's group also, made fearful by the isolation of the Leninist faction, definitively backed out from an alliance that Lenin saw as the only possibility."[9]

The Prague conference of 1912 did not declare the existence of a new Bolshevik Party. It declared the reorganization and renewal of the RSDLP—but one as much under Bolshevik control as had been the case in 1905. Except now there were no efforts to backtrack in the interests of unity. As Lars Lih indicates, the formal position of Lenin and his comrades was that this version of the RSDLP would not simply and exclusively be the Bolsheviks. And I think Lars is correct when he says Lenin and his Bolshevik comrades were, "not propagating a 'new type of party,' as later Stalinist historians had it. They were propagating the party principle *as it had always been understood in the Second International*."[10] Their goal was an organization conforming to an idealized notion of the German Social Democratic Party, one that did not compromise away its revolutionary birthright but remained true to revolutionary Marxism. What emerged in 1912 was, nonetheless, a Bolshevik party, with a Bolshevik leadership, following a Bolshevik line. To deny that Lenin could even imagine that such a thing might emerge from the 1912 Prague conference is interesting and worth considering but not entirely persuasive to me. But there is work to be done to clarify what the most plausible answers might be to this and other questions.

Lessons for Our Time (and Non-Lessons)

At this point I would like to turn to the question of finding lessons—and non-lessons—in all of this for our own time. Obviously, if we are being serious about studying and understanding history, we can't be satisfied with an approach through which we construct morality tales to validate ourselves, our organizations, and specific political projects. Nor can we expect to find readymade recipes with which to cook up revolutionary dishes for the here and now. We *can* find lessons and insights that might help us figure out what to do—but we have to be serious as we do that, avoiding uncritical idealizations, and trying to identify similarities and differences between, for example, Lenin's context and our own.

Nothing that we face is just as it was for Lenin and his comrades. Our 1903 and 1905 and 1912 and 1917 may not look at all like theirs, and the sequence of events may differ dramatically. We should avoid acting and talking as if we were in the equivalent of their 1912 or 1917 when, in fact, we may be closer to the equivalent of their 1898 or 1901. More than this, in our present-day contexts, to the extent that the socialist movement and the working class are not intertwined and interacting in significant ways, we have not gotten beyond Square One of revolutionary politics. In some ways, our reality has little to do with the reality in which there was a Second International or Third International—it is in some ways closer to the reality existing before the creation of the First International.[11]

By the way, this notion that our pathways cannot possibly duplicate those of Lenin and his comrades happens to constitute a central tenet of "Leninist orthodoxy." In 1919 he commented that "each nation is travelling in the same historical direction" but each must follow "very different zigzags and byways." He added that "the more cultured nations are obviously proceeding in a way that differs from that of the less cultured nations. Finland is advancing in a different way. Germany is advancing in a different way." In 1921 he urged yet other comrades to "refrain from copying our tactics but thoroughly vary them and adapt them to the different concrete conditions." He told Italian comrades that principles "must be adapted to the specific conditions of various countries. The revolution in Italy will run a different course from that in Russia. It will start in a different way. How? Neither you nor we know." In 1922 Lenin told comrades in the Communist International that they should not "hang Russian experience in a corner like an icon and pray to it." I should add that this last comment did not—contrary to some misinterpretations—mean that Lenin believed the Russian experience was irrelevant, but rather that it should be critically studied, assimilated, and applied creatively to new and different contexts.[12]

Giving Lenin the attention he deserves involves an approach of critical engagement. To study Lenin's work means actually reading what he had to say in order to understand his thinking. It is important to see not only what he had to say but to see what he did. What was he hoping to do, what did he think he was doing, what was he actually doing—and to what extent was he aware of what he was actually doing? What were the contexts in which all of this was unfolding? What went wrong and what went right? How did his thinking match up with the historical experience of Lenin and his comrades, and how does it match up with our own experience?

Even though there are many questions to answer, I believe there are clearly certain positive qualities of Lenin and the Bolsheviks that are worth learning from. Despite the frequent assertions of critics and even some would-be supporters, it is not the case that Lenin wanted to create an organization that would simply be dominated by him. More than once, a majority of his comrades concluded (sometimes rightly, sometimes not) that he was wrong about one thing or another, and they voted him down—such as in April 1905. In certain contexts, such as whether or not to run some of his polemical articles in the party newspaper, they simply ignored him, to his great chagrin.[13] While Lenin did not particularly enjoy being disagreed with or voted down, and would fight fiercely for positions he believed to be correct, as was the case in April 1905, he favored an organization that functioned like a democratic, cohesive, activist collectivity. In response to a 1921 comment by Adolf Joffe that "the Central Committee—*c'est vous*," Lenin strenuously objected that this was simply not true, elaborating: "The old Central Committee (1919–20) defeated me on one gigantically important question, as you know from the discussion. On organizational and personal questions I have been in a minority countless times. You yourself saw many instances when you were a Central Committee member."[14]

Also worth noting is a point emphasized in Krupskaya's *Reminiscences of Lenin*: "He always, as long as he lived, attached tremendous importance to Party congresses. He held the Party congress to be the highest authority, where all things personal had to be cast aside, where nothing was to be concealed, and everything was to be open and above board. He always took great pains in preparing for Party congresses, and was particularly careful in thinking out his speeches."[15]

Along with this commitment to building a democratic revolutionary organization, I believe there is sufficient scholarship to demonstrate how seriously Lenin absorbed, engaged with, utilized, and developed Marxist theory—not as an abstract intellectual disconnected from the workers' movement, but as a revolutionary intellectual who had become an integral part of the workers' movement. Analysis, political education, program, strategy, and tactics were drawn together by him as a clear, coherent, dynamic totality. And despite inevitable limitations and mistakes, his record as a revolutionary Marxist theorist and political leader adds up to something that is quite impressive and matched by few.

The Bolshevik organization that Lenin was so central in shaping was impressive as well, infused with a relatively high quality of Marxist theory, containing a diverse range of talented and creative activists and serious thinkers who were not afraid to disagree with each other and with Lenin, determined to defend their views, to help test the majority perspectives in practice, and to help make revisions and adjustments as called for, learning through debate and activism and experience. It was a democratic-activist organization that found a way to engage with the actual consciousness and in the real struggles of working-class activists, and to help forge a class-conscious vanguard organization that could provide leadership in practical struggles of the here and now in a manner that helped a layer of class-struggle fighters to lead the revolution of 1917.

Kamenev, his longtime comrade and the first editor of Lenin's collected works, commented that while "the teachings of Lenin as a whole and in all their ramifications are based on the scientific socialism of Karl Marx and Frederick Engels," there is also a new element, which "consists in the adaptation of the basic principles and methods of Marxism to a historical setting and period entirely unknown to Marx."[16]

To do the same thing in adapting the basic principles and methods of Lenin and Bolshevism to our own setting and period, entirely unknown to Lenin and his comrades, strikes me as a challenge that is worth taking up.

Facing Problems

While I am inclined to view very positively the Bolshevik-Leninist experience up through 1917, and to assume that we can draw useful insights and lessons from a critical-minded engagement with that fourteen-year experience, it is also the case that there was a six-year experience after that, before Lenin died, in which what Lars Lih calls "the heroic scenario" failed in the face of disastrous realities. In the pre-1918 scenario, class-conscious workers and their steadfast allies among the poor peasants establish a revolutionary-democratic commune-state that inspires workers' revolutions throughout the world, setting the stage for the development of a global socialist order of the free and the equal. That's the scenario.

"Almost from the very first day of the October Revolution," according to Christopher Read, "Lenin's hopes and expectations for it began to collapse." Perhaps this is overstated, but there is enough truth here to help us understand what Lars Lih tells us: "From 1919 his speeches lose their earlier sharpness and become progressively more unfocused, repetitive, digressive. He becomes halting as he searches for a way to match his ideological scenario with events. A new and unexpected quality appears: Lenin is unsure of himself." Read notes that "Lenin was deeply conscious of the fragility of the forces that had brought him to power, but also of the epochal significance of what was happening," adding that "in the middle of the First World War, at that time of the most massive human bloodletting ever, refinements of morality seemed not only constricting but obscene. A few sacrifices, a moment of ruthlessness, was not only justified but demanded if millions were to be saved at the front and from the worldwide tentacles of imperialist exploitation."[17]

Speaking of the same period, Isaac Deutscher commented many years ago:

> Then comes the great tragedy of the isolation of the Russian Revolution; of its succumbing to incredible, unimaginable destruction, poverty, hunger, and disease as a result of the wars of intervention, the civil wars, and of course the long and exhausting world war which was not of Bolshevik making. As a result of all this, terror was let loose in Russia. Men lost their balance. They lost, even the leaders, the clarity of their thinking and of their minds. They acted under overwhelming and inhuman pressures. I don't undertake to judge them, to blame them or to justify them. I can only see the deep tragedy of this historic process, the result of which was the glorification of violence. But what was to have been a glassful of violence became buckets and buckets full, and then rivers of violence. That is the tragedy of the Russian Revolution.[18]

There is much more to be said about this period, and about what Lenin and his comrades did and failed to do, and about the mistakes and blindspots one can find in the earlier period (up through 1917) that may have contributed to the catastrophe that followed.[19]

Here too, there are lessons to be learned. For some the appropriate lesson is the injunction that we must reject Lenin and all that he stood for. Given the historical realities and our present-day realities, and the outstanding achievement that preceded the catastrophe, I don't think we can afford to do that. It is, however, especially important for us not only to critically sift through Lenin's thought and actions during these tragically violent and authoritarian developments but also to consider the positive ways that he himself sought to overcome and transcend and move beyond the horrors in this final period of his life.

We cannot afford to settle for the superficiality or the morality tales or the dogmatic certainties of sectarianism as we wrestle with the question of what happened in history and with the question of what is to be done. We need to take Lenin more seriously than that, because what the sociologist C. Wright Mills said of Marx is also true of Lenin: "To study his work today, and then come back to our own concerns is to increase our chances of confronting them with useful ideas and solutions."[20]

Chapter Seven
ENDURING LEGACY

Today's remarkable period of world capitalist crisis and global insurgency is causing a growing number of activists to move in revolutionary directions—creating exciting opportunities to help more and more of the rising generation connect with the resources of revolutionary Marxism, vibrantly represented in the lives and ideas of Rosa Luxemburg, Leon Trotsky, and Vladimir Ilyich Lenin. As Lenin argued more than once, a revolutionary movement (that is, a movement that actually proves able to make the kind of democratic socialist revolution that we would like to see) very much needs to be guided by revolutionary theory in order to "get its act together" and help it move in directions that can, in fact, get us "from here to there."

It is startling to find a long-time revolutionary comrade, at this very moment, instead presenting a dismissive attitude toward the ideas of Lenin himself. We find this in an article by Charlie Post, an internationally respected Marxist scholar, in the excellent magazine of the Fourth International, *International Viewpoint* (November 11, 2012). It is quite possible that this involves simply an unintentional misstatement, a formulation stretching just a little too far. Whether or not this is the case, the assertion provides an opportunity for all of us who identify as revolutionary Marxists to think critically about our own tradition, which is a good and useful thing.

The "offending formulation" appears in his review of Lars Lih's valuable biography of Lenin. There is much to agree with in this review, which largely sums up Lih's scholarship both in the short biography *Lenin* and in the massive tome *Lenin Rediscovered*. Of course, one should not get bent out of shape with quibbles over one or another formulation—but in checking on Post's conclusion (suggesting the irrelevance of most of Lenin's political thought), perhaps one should turn back to those "quibbles" for more careful consideration. So let us first turn our attention to the problematical formulation, then to the "quibbles."

In the review's penultimate paragraph, we are informed that "there is little of Lenin's theory—with the exception of *State and Revolution* and *Left-Wing Communism*—that is either original or of enduring value."[1] For those of us who consider ourselves to be Leninists, this is a stunning assertion. It has particular impact coming from one who, like myself, has identified with the Fourth Internationalist tradition of Ernest Mandel, whose politics was inseparable from the perspectives of V. I. Lenin and Leon Trotsky. Stunning or no, the question remains as to whether Post's assertion happens to be right. By sorting through the quibbles, I will work my way to an expression of my own understanding of the answer to that question.

Quibble #1: Mandel's "Luxemburgist" Lenin

For those of us who immersed ourselves in Ernest Mandel's works, listened to his often brilliant talks, and knew him personally as a comrade, I think there might be general agreement that he would probably have insisted that Post's assertion happens to be wrong. Of course, that in itself settles nothing.

Comrade Post covers this base in a footnote: "Ernest Mandel produced a convincing theoretization of the Bolshevik (and early Comintern) practice, based on a theory of consciousness that owes more to Luxemburg than Lenin and Kautsky, in 'The Leninist Theory of Organization: Its Relevance for Today.'"[2] Not surprisingly, in this essay Mandel demonstrates great respect for Luxemburg (especially her "mass strike" conceptualization), but he spends as much time very critically dealing with her 1904 polemic with Lenin.[3] Still, the fact that he draws our attention to Mandel's classic essay on Lenin is to Post's credit, so why quibble over the comment that suggests that Mandel drew his ideas on consciousness from the very admirable Luxemburg?

The reason is that it is a distortion of what Mandel says. Far from giving us a "Luxemburgist" reading of Lenin, it is obvious that Mandel does not limit Lenin's "enduring value" to *State and Revolution* and *Left-Wing Communism*. He embraces much more of Lenin's writing and thinking as he elaborates on the enduring value of the Leninist theory of organization. He tells us that Lenin's conception is a "dialectical unity of three elements: a theory of the present relevance of revolution for the underdeveloped countries in the imperialist epoch (which was later expanded to apply to the entire world in the epoch of the general crisis of capitalism); a theory of the discontinuous and contradictory development of proletarian class consciousness and of its most important stages, which should be differentiated from one another; and a theory of the essence of Marxist theory and its specific relationship to science on the one hand and to proletarian class struggle on the other."

More than thirty years before Lih's *Lenin Rediscovered*, Mandel emphasized that this third key concept, related to the notion that socialist consciousness is something brought into the proletarian class struggle from the outside, "was by no means invented by Lenin but corresponds to a tradition leading from Engels, through Kautsky, to the classical doctrines of the international Social Democracy between 1880 and 1905." And yet, for anyone seriously reading the essay, there is no question that Mandel would not have accepted Post's minimalist characterization of what he had to say about Lenin's thought. Mandel's essay is what it claims to be: a case for the contemporary relevance of Lenin's theory of organization, brilliantly argued and well documented.

Quibble #2:
Lenin as a "Loyal Follower" of Kautsky

In his summary of Lars Lih's invaluable *Lenin Rediscovered*, Post makes very good points while introducing something else to quibble over:

> *Lenin Rediscovered: "What Is to Be Done?" in Context* (Chicago: Haymarket Books, 2008) thoroughly discredits the claims that Lenin, worried about the capacity of workers to make a

revolution, advocated a new form of political organization. Instead, Lenin emerges as a mainstream left-wing European social democrat (the term all pre-1914 socialists used to refer to themselves), *a loyal follower of Karl Kautsky* [emphasis added], the leading theorist of the Second International, and an advocate of building a party like the German Social Democratic Party (SPD) 'under Russian conditions.' Lenin's famous 1902 pamphlet *What Is to Be Done?* was thoroughly unoriginal, embracing the SPD's vision of a fusion of socialism with the worker movement, and prioritizing the struggle for democracy, the "light and air of the worker movement."[4]

The same thing happens as Post summarizes Lih's new biography of Lenin:

> Lenin emerges not as a political innovator, but a quite mainstream pre-1914 left-wing socialist. His nearly religious belief in the capacities of workers and worker leaders to win democracy and socialism shaped his rejection of the "opportunism" (reformism) that led the leaders of European socialism to limit the movement to parliamentary and bureaucratic union activity and support for their "own capitalists" in the First World War. Throughout his political career, Lenin remained *a devoted follower of Kautsky* [emphasis added]—even when Kautsky himself, in Lenin's words, "reneged" on his political commitments during the war. Only in the last years of his life, facing the isolation of the Russian Revolution and the emergence of a conservative bureaucracy in the Soviet state, did Lenin take his first, tentative steps beyond the theoretical and political orthodoxy of the Second International.[5]

To characterize Lenin as "a loyal follower" and "a devoted follower" of Karl Kautsky, and as little more than "a quite mainstream pre-1914 left-wing socialist," strikes me as overstated. Lenin himself never used such terms as "loyal and devoted follower" to describe himself, and there was more to him than that—but why quibble over a few words? After all, as Lih capably demonstrates, Kautsky's Marxism at least up to 1909 was basically consistent with, and certainly influenced, Lenin's own orientation.

What Post makes explicit here are elements that can certainly be found in Lih's account. But there are different ways to read that account. For example, on a panel that I organized at the 2008 Left Forum, when August Nimtz challenged Lih with the argument that Lenin was, independently of Kautsky, immersed in the writings of Marx and Engels, and it was these (not Kautsky) to which he was "loyal" and "devoted," Lih readily agreed. The point that Nimtz emphasized was fully consistent with the points that Ernest Mandel had argued decades earlier—that Lenin did not adhere (in Mandel's words) to "the naive 'belief in the inevitability of progress' à la Bebel and Kautsky that prevailed in the international Social Democracy from the time of Marx's death until the First World War. Lenin's concept of class consciousness was incomparably richer, more contradictory and more dialectical precisely because it was based on a keen grasp of the relevance of the revolution for the present (not 'finally some day' but in the coming years)."[6]

In *The Place of Marxism in History*, Mandel discusses the evolution of Marxism and, while giving appreciative recognition to August Bebel and Karl Kautsky (the "grand old man" of German Social Democracy and "the pope of Marxism" in the Second International, respectively), goes on to insist that it took "a broad international current, embodied essentially by Rosa Luxemburg and the Russian Socialists Lenin and Trotsky, [to] reclaim and revive the Marxist tradition of mass action and revolutionary initiative of the party."[7] He goes on to make an interesting assertion—that up to 1905 "this tradition had been marginalized inside social democracy ... and confined to anarcho-syndicalist and revolutionary-syndicalist circles (in Spain, Britain, Argentina, partially the United States, Italy, and France)."

At least up to the present, Lih does not seem to accept this connection of Lenin with Luxemburg and Trotsky, separate from Kautsky—but, good as he is, that doesn't necessarily mean that Lih is absolutely correct. Post appears to adhere to the interpretation of Lih rather than that of Mandel. Perhaps he and Lih are right—but there is much in the history of the labor and socialist movements that becomes more difficult to sort out if we set aside Mandel's explanation.

It seems to me that activists of today would still be well served by turning to the ideas of Luxemburg, Lenin, and Trotsky, as Mandel urged, with critical minds, to be sure. (Critical thinking was central to the approach of all three.) The fact that each of them was significantly influenced by Kautsky at his best (pre-1910) does not make any of them simply his theoretical clone. Lenin, like Luxemburg and Trotsky, did his own thinking and wrestled creatively with how to apply revolutionary Marxism to his own specific context.

Quibble #3:
There Is No Real "Leninism"?

"To be blunt, there is little of 'Leninism' as a theory—an invention of Bolshevik leaders Zinoviev, Bukharin, and Stalin after Lenin's death in 1924—that remains viable. Lenin was, by his own admission, a Kautskyan—an advocate of the Marxism of the Second International before World War One."

There are three notions intertwined in this sentence, each of them having a certain plausibility. First of all, up to 1914 Lenin did not claim to be "a Leninist" but rather a Marxist who was influenced by Karl Kautsky (even if he never called himself a "Kautskyan"), quite explicitly adhering to the Marxism of the Second International, the world federation of socialist, social-democratic, and labor parties. Second, after the Bolshevik revolution, in the crisis years of the early 1920s (even as Lenin was dying) a Lenin cult was promulgated by a majority of the Russian Communist leadership, and notions of what constituted "Leninism" were put forward by such Bolshevik leaders as Gregory Zinoviev, Nikolai Bukharin, and Joseph Stalin—involving a set of ideas that were not quite the same as what Lenin believed, said, and wrote while he considered himself to be a "Second International Marxist." And third, the "Leninism" concocted by Zinoviev, Bukharin, and Stalin has no more relevance.

The argument that "Leninism" is an artificial construction of the 1920s, after Lenin's death, is not new. In 1977 there appeared in English the seminal essay by outstanding Gramsci editor and scholar, the late Valentino Gerratana—"Stalin, Lenin and 'Leninism.'" Gerratana's essay emphasized that "while he was still alive, Lenin was not regarded as a *source* of authority—even if he possessed considerable personal authority," flowing from the quality of his thought and political practice.[8] Joseph Stalin most successfully and destructively carried out the construction of an artificial "Leninism" *as a source of authority* (which could not be questioned and thereby greatly empowered those claiming to represent it).

Gerratana presents Lenin's thought as qualitatively different than Stalin's authoritative "Leninism." It is complex, laden with insights inseparable from a critical and creative process. His contention—in contrast to Post's—is that one finds a very rich accumulation of political thought and perspectives that are lost in the intellectual superficiality of Stalinism. Developed by Lenin during his lifetime, most of these ideas are gathered in forty-five substantial volumes of his *Collected Works*, although it is certainly not the case that Lenin was uninfluenced by other thinkers, inside and outside of the Second International. While the "Leninism" of closed, finished dogmas was incompatible with Lenin's entire approach to politics, it can be argued that there was a distinctive political approach and body of thought—for the sake of brevity one could refer to a genuine *Leninism*—to which it is worth giving attention.

In our earlier quibbles, we advanced the notion that Lenin's political thought was not simply a carbon copy of Kautsky's. The "Marxism of the Second International," which profoundly influenced Lenin and to which he was organically connected, happened to include the political thought of Rosa Luxemburg, Leon Trotsky, Franz Mehring, David Riazanov, Rudolf Hilferding, and Karl Kautsky at his pre-1910 best, among others (presented in the outstanding volumes edited by Richard B. Day and Daniel Gaido, *Witnesses to Permanent Revolution* and *Discovering Imperialism*).[9] Given the richness of that tradition, it is reasonable to assume that there would be much of interest in Lenin's writings. In point of fact, there is a coherent development of Lenin's political thought leading up to the 1917 revolution in Russia, as well as complex and challenging (if somewhat more problematical) developments of his thought after that revolution. It would be rather odd if, as Post says, "there is little of Lenin's theory . . . that is either original or of enduring value."

While it can be argued that there are problems with the "Lenin-ist" summaries offered by Zinoviev, Bukharin, and Stalin, this does not mean that all efforts to sum up Lenin's ideas (to be found in the writings of Ernest Mandel, Ernst Fischer, Leon Trotsky, Georg Lukács, Antonio Gramsci, and others) are necessarily false.[10] In what follows I will indicate, for what it is worth, what I see as "genuine Leninism." I repeat here points made in my introductory essay to the edited selection of Lenin's writings, *Revolution, Democracy, Socialism.*[11]

Lenin's quite unoriginal starting point (shared with Marx, Kaut-sky, and others) is a belief in the necessary interconnection of socialist theory and practice with the working class and the labor movement. The working class cannot adequately defend its actual interests and overcome its oppression, in his view, without embracing the goal of socialism—an economic system in which the economy is socially owned and democratically controlled in order to meet the needs of all people. Inseparable from this is a *basic understanding of the working class as it is*, which involves a grasp of the diversity and unevenness of working-class experience and consciousness.

This calls for the development of a practical revolutionary ap-proach seeking to connect, in serious ways, with the various sectors and layers of the working class. It involves the understanding that different approaches and goals are required to reach and engage one or another worker, or group or sector or layer of workers. This means thoughtfully utilizing various forms of educational and agitational literature, and developing different kinds of speeches and discus-sions, in order to connect the varieties of working-class experience, and, most important, to help initiate or support various kinds of practical struggles. The more "advanced" or vanguard layers of the working class must be rallied not to narrow and limited goals (in the spirit of "Economism" and "pure and simple trade unionism") but to an expansive sense of solidarity and common cause that has the potential for drawing the class as a whole into the struggle for its collective interests.

This fundamental orientation is the basis for most of what Lenin has to say. It is the basis of other key perspectives that one can find in his writings:

- an understanding of the necessity of working-class political independence in political and social struggles, and the need for its supremacy (or hegemony) if such struggles are to triumph;
- an understanding of the necessity for socialist and working-class support for struggles of all who suffer oppression;
- a coherent conception of organization that is practical, democratic, and revolutionary;
- the development of the united front tactic, in which diverse political forces can work together for common goals, without revolutionary organizations undermining their ability to pose effective revolutionary perspectives to the capitalist status quo;
- an intellectual and practical seriousness (and lack of dogmatism or sectarianism) in utilizing Marxist theory;
- an approach of integrating reform struggles with revolutionary strategy;
- a remarkable understanding of the manner in which democratic struggles flow into socialist revolution;
- a commitment to a worker-peasant alliance;
- a profound analysis of imperialism and nationalism;
- a vibrantly revolutionary internationalist approach.

Lenin, not bent on being "innovative," did not invent all of this, although he was a creative thinker who advanced certain lines of thought—it can be demonstrated—in ways that were different from many others in the Marxist intellectual camp. In any event, he put the elements summarized above together in a manner that had powerful impact in his native Russia and throughout the world. This can, I think, legitimately be termed "Leninism"—so that when Ernest Mandel makes reference to "the Leninist theory of organization," for example, he is not speaking nonsense.

Post versus Post

Some of Post's assertions seem to bump into each other. "Since the Second World War," he tells us, "growing segments of the anti-Stalinist revolutionary Left have rightly rejected Kautsky's belief in the inevitability of socialism as the result of the continued degradation of the working class under capitalism." This rejection means the ideas of the Lenin (who was a "devoted follower of Kautsky") are now pretty much irrelevant. Hence the terrible conclusion: Lenin's ideas have no enduring value.

The Marxism of Lenin, we have already suggested, cannot be reduced to the notion of "the inevitability of socialism as the result of the continued degradation of the working class under capitalism" (nor, if we rely on the work of Lars Lih, among others, can this be advanced as an adequate summary of the Marxism of Kautsky at his best). The Marxism of Lenin is much richer and more complex.

And yet, Post actually goes on to offer ideas that, if taken seriously, raise questions about his whole line of argument. For if it is the case—as Post tells us at the conclusion of his review—that "the practice of the Bolsheviks through 1917 remains relevant" to us today, then it can be insisted that the same may be true of the political thought of Lenin. This is so because it is undeniable that Lenin's political thought was very, very influential in what the Bolsheviks did. The final words in Post's review clinch the case:

> While revolutionaries in the capitalist democracies today live in societies fundamentally different from early 20th century Russia and do not have to create clandestine, illegal organizations, the experience of the fusion of revolutionary socialism with rank and file worker leaders and the creation of workers' political and economic organizations independent of the forces of official reformism (union officials and reformist political leaders) remains of enduring importance for contemporary socialists.

Given his centrality to Russian Bolshevism, then, it would seem that there is much in the political thought of Lenin that is of enduring value. And given his own continued enthusiasm for the Bolshevik tradition, and for revolutionary Marxism in general, one can imagine that comrade Post would encourage activists of today and tomorrow to engage—critically, to be sure—with the ideas of such revolutionaries as Luxemburg, Trotsky . . . and Lenin.

What Is to Be Done?

Post's intellectual scope and energy have generated a challenging body of work that merits close attention. Particularly valuable is his conviction that Marxist theory is alive and relevant to the struggles of our own time. Engaging with new realities and advancing new interpretations, he reflects a broader current of thought in the international Left. In grappling critically with what he offers, we at the same time join him in the collective effort to answer the classical Leninist question (of course, not only a Leninist question): What is to be done?

Previous sections of this critique were written at the beginning of 2012. In December of the same year, a new essay by Post appeared entitled "What Is Left of Leninism?," which seems to present a broader appreciation, and as such is worth commenting on here.[12] Instead of dismissing the very concept of Leninism, Post now tells us that "the enduring legacy of Leninism remains the goal of constructing an independent organization of anti-capitalist organizers and activists who attempt to project a political alternative to the forces of official reformism not only in elections, but in mass, extra-parliamentary social struggles."

It seems to me that this is true as far as it goes, although if that's all there is, it seems to place Lenin slightly to the left of Saul Alinsky. A radical community organizer in the United States from the 1940s through the 1960s, Alinsky wrote a biography of his mentor John L. Lewis (the remarkable leader of the Congress of Industrial Organizations) and set down his own ideas about organizing for social change in the interesting and useful books *Reveille for Radicals* and *Rules for Radicals*—providing a political alternative to the forces of official reformism for organizers and activists, involving extra-parliamentary "grassroots" social struggles, although he did not use the term "anticapitalist."[13] In fact, Lenin wrote much more, said much more, and offers activists and organizers much more than comes through in this minimized "Leninism."

Post is a writer and analyst to take seriously, not least because of his acclaimed and challenging recent work *America's Road to Capitalism*. But in this essay it can be argued that he is attempting to accomplish far too much in far too little space. One section of the essay reviews "The World of Mass Social Democratic Parties, 1890–1914" (a massive topic indeed, which he covers in twelve paragraphs), another turns to "The Rise and Decline of the Communist Parties, 1919–1990" (even more massive, therefore requiring fourteen paragraphs), and he finally considers "The Post–Second World War Revolutionary Left" (seven paragraphs).

These thirty-one "historical" paragraphs are by no means devoid of thoughtful points or interesting ideas—but neither are they an adequate summary of what happened in history, despite the display of scholarly apparatus. For example, the whole twelve hundred–plus pages of John Riddell's edited volume of proceedings of the 1922 World Congress of the Communist International, plus chapters 5 through 23 (four hundred pages) of Pierre Broué's massive work on the German Revolution, plus David Morgan's five hundred pages on *The Socialist Left and the German Revolution* are cited—without specific quotations or page references—to "document" Post's sweeping generalizations of what happened in the early Communist movement from 1919 to 1922. After citing all of this material, Post goes on to assure us that "the Comintern actually undermined the development of the non-Russian parties," a one-sided generalization that is demonstrably false in more than one instance, even though accurate in other instances. Sorting through the different instances and making sense of them is, unfortunately, not a responsibility he chooses to assume.

Post repeats the misleading point made in his review of Lars Lih's Lenin biography: "'Leninism' as a distinct organizational theory and practice was invented during the 'Bolshevization' campaign of 1924–25." But he also restates, in a slightly different way, his earlier "left-Alinskyist" definition: "The rational core of the Leninist organizational practice before 1923 was the rejection of a division of labor between the party and unions and the construction of an organization of revolutionary worker activists independently of the labor and parliamentary officialdom capable of contesting the latter's leadership of the workers' movement." The exact meaning of this overly succinct point is not clear, either in regard to specific historical actualities or in regard to on-the-ground practical politics. It seems to be related to the well-known fact, noted in his brief historical summary, that bureaucratic-conservatism and nonrevolutionary reformism infected the mass workers' movements led by Social Democrats and Stalinists, and that Lenin's thinking was inconsistent with this. This notion plays an important role in the final portion of his essay—the twelve paragraphs he utilizes to examine "The New Left Parties in Europe."

In this section, Post makes passing reference to disappointing developments in Britain and France (and for some reason totally ignores more volatile developments in Spain, Portugal, and especially Greece), focusing instead on the once-promising Party of Communist Refoundation (PRC) in Italy and the fluctuating fortunes of the left party (Die Linke) in Germany. Even here, however, the eight paragraphs he is able to devote to the experiences of the two parties cannot take us very far in understanding what is what. He concludes, however, that "ultimately, two factors will shape the future of these new political formations." Most crucial, he asserts quite plausibly, "is the outcome of extra-parliamentary struggles over austerity and privatization, which will shape the political consciousness and confidence of party militants and broad sectors of the working-class and popular movements." This by itself, of course, will not resolve the problem.

The second key factor, according to Post, gets back to what he sees as "what is left of Leninism." This involves "the relative strength within these parties of the 'militant minority' of workplace and movement activists and the conscious anti-capitalist left, on one side, and, the forces of official reformism on the other." Specifically, "the key will be the revival of the rational core of Leninism—the transcendence of the division of labor between party and unions and movements through the organization of radical and revolutionary activists who attempt to contest the forces of official reformism over the conduct of mass struggle." To clarify what this means, Post puts it "another way," suggesting that "the 'militant minority'" must seek to "transform these parties into organizations contesting the direction of all struggles, electoral and extra-electoral." To clarify further, this would be the opposite of allowing "the union-party officialdom" to "maintain the division between 'politics' (elections) and 'economics' (union struggles)."

Such formulations do not seem to match up with all that Lenin had to say, and all that he tried to do. Nor do they offer a clear orientation for revolutionary activists and organizers of our own time. Perhaps if we engage more seriously than Post is inclined to do with what Lenin wrote about similar realities in his time, we will be able to turn to ours with more to work with. The minimalist and even somewhat dismissive approach to "what is left of Leninism" (and to what Leninism added up to in the first place) does not seem to me particularly fruitful. The actual "Leninism" of Lenin can be a resource for us as we try to figure out what is to be done.

Chapter Eight
LUXEMBURG AND LENIN THROUGH EACH OTHER'S EYES

According to Karl Marx, the liberation of the laboring majority must come about through the democratic activity of that majority. Some people must win others to an understanding of the need for struggle, and to ideas of how best to struggle against oppression. Among those with the knowledge, insight, and courage (who seek to inspire and help more and more people to develop their own capacity for such qualities), there are inevitably different points of view on how to understand the world and how best to change it. So there is a need for democratic discussion and debate, as organizations of revolutionaries seek to understand the complex realities of global capitalism and how to replace capitalism with the political freedom and the economic democracy that Marx and other scientific socialists have associated with the future society.

This is the framework in which we can best understand the relationship of Vladimir Ilyich Lenin and Rosa Luxemburg, two of the greatest revolutionary socialists of the twentieth century. Each had risen to the top rank within the left wing of the international labor movement, in the mass parties that had joined together in the Socialist International, also known as the Second International. Both were brilliant, highly educated, and absolutely committed to the Marxist approach to reality.[1]

There are four broad areas in which they expressed differences with each other: (1) questions of building a revolutionary organization,

(2) the relationship of democracy to socialism, (3) confrontations of nationalism with internationalism, and (4) issues of imperialism and capitalist development. What I will argue here is that there is less irreconcilable contradiction, and greater overlap, than is often acknowledged.

Personal Relationship

Before considering these differences, it is worth considering the personal relationship of these revolutionaries. The two had met in 1901, then had crossed swords polemically in 1904, when Luxemburg lined up temporarily with Lenin's Menshevik opponents in the Russian Social Democratic Labor Party (RSDLP). They actually got to know each other, however, amid the revolutionary workers' insurgencies sweeping through Russia and Eastern Europe in 1905–1906. One of Luxemburg's biographers, Elzbieta Ettinger, tells us that she was impressed "with his exceptional mind, a quality always seductive to her, and with his enormous will power and broad knowledge of the Russian reality. He was erudite, shrewd, and determined. The theorists she knew paled in comparison." At a 1907 conference of the Second International, Luxemburg pointed him out to her friend Clara Zetkin. "Take a good look at him. That is Lenin. Look at the self-willed stubborn head. A real Russian peasant's head with a few faintly Asiatic lines. That man will try to overturn mountains. Perhaps he will be crushed by them. But he will never yield."[2] Another Luxemburg biographer, J. P. Nettl, has elaborated on this, commenting:

> A personal sympathy between Lenin and Rosa Luxemburg—based, like all Lenin's friendships, on mutual respect—was born at this time [in 1906] and was to survive for six years until party differences drowned it once more in the froth of polemics. Even then a spark of personal sympathy always survived the renewed hostilities; though Lenin fell out completely with Leo Jogiches [Luxemburg's close comrade in the Polish movement] and necessarily included Rosa Luxemburg in his onslaught on the 'old' Polish leadership, he never went for her

personally as he did in the case of Jogiches—while she in turn deliberately abstained from any public reply to his attacks.[3]

Hannah Arendt, a knowledgeable political theorist in her own right, in summarizing the findings of Nettl's research, noted that central to "Luxemburg's public and private life" was the fact that she was part of "a peer group" that had crystallized—for her—among revolutionaries in Poland, which represented a much broader phenomenon. Something quite similar was described, for example, by another, lesser-known revolutionary of the same period in the Odessa underground, Eugenia Levitskaya. "Turning in my mind the mass of comrades with whom I had occasion to meet, I cannot recall a single reprehensible, contemptible act, a single deception or lie," she wrote. "There was friction. There were faction differences of opinion. But no more than that. Somehow everyone looked after himself morally, became better and more gentle in that friendly family."

Commenting that Nettl "stresses repeatedly the high moral standards of 'the peer group,'" Arendt emphasized that within this revolutionary peer group "such things as ambition, career, status, and even mere success were under the strictest taboo"—at least when it came to the personal level. On the other hand, they shared a powerful ambition for, as Luxemburg joked, "setting a prairie on fire" to advance the cause of working-class revolution and socialist liberation. Arendt comments that Lenin shared the values of Luxemburg's peer group. More than this, based on Nettl's findings she concludes that "there were few people she respected [as intellectual equals], and Jogiches headed a list on which only the names of Lenin and [Marx's outstanding biographer] Franz Mehring could be inscribed with certainty."[4]

There was also a certain chemistry of their personalities that made possible such a relationship—what Gorky captured in describing Lenin as with the words "he loved fun and when he laughed it was with his whole body," and the often wicked sense of humor that one can also find in Luxemburg's polemics and letters. In 1911, she wrote: "Yesterday Lenin came, and up to today he has been here four times already. I enjoy talking with him, he's clever and well educated, and has such an ugly mug, the kind I like to look at." She commented that her cat Mimi "impressed Lenin tremendously, he said that only in Siberia had he seen such a magnificent creature, that she was a *baskii kot*—a majestic cat. She also flirted with him, rolled on her back and behaved enticingly toward him, but when he tried to approach her she whacked him with a paw and snarled like a tiger."[5]

Mimi's behavior captures something of the relationship between Luxemburg and Lenin—their polemics with each other, and mutual criticisms, could be as sharp and unyielding. The case can be made, however, that neither Lenin nor Luxemburg was invariably correct in these various disputes. More than that, it can be argued that even when wrong about something, each was able to identify important aspects of the truth.

Nationalism and Imperialism

Luxemburg's approach to nationalism is in some ways inferior to Lenin's—she tends toward a full-scale dismissal of it as an obstacle to working-class internationalism, while Lenin is attentive to differences between the nationalism of oppressor nations (involving imperialism and racism, which must be opposed) and the nationalism of the oppressed (involving struggles against imperialism and racism, which should be supported). Yet complex developments in our own time give some credence to Luxemburg's warnings.[6]

There are striking similarities between the ways Lenin and Luxemburg approached issues of imperialism and global capitalist development. Both saw capitalism as inherently expansionistic and violent, and yet there are qualitative differences between Luxemburg's *The Accumulation of Capital* and Lenin's *Imperialism, the Highest Stage of Capitalism*. One of the most obvious differences is that Luxemburg does not see imperialism as the highest stage of capitalism, or as something that arose in the late nineteenth century due to the consolidation of multinational corporations under the influence of finance capital, but as something that has existed as an integral part of capitalism from its very beginning.

While Lenin's work is a popularization of the work of others (J. A. Hobson, Rudolf Hilferding, and Nikolai Bukharin), Luxemburg offers a highly original analysis that is critical of what has been called Marx's "realization theory" in the second volume of Marx's *Capital* (some have argued that she misunderstood what Marx was actually saying and doing in Volume 2). While Lenin tends to see multifaceted dimensions, fluidity, and flexibility in capitalist expansion, Luxemburg believes that there are limits—a necessity for capitalism to expand into noncapitalist territories, which will eventually be used up, leading to crisis and collapse. "She has got into a shocking muddle," Lenin complained. "She has distorted Marx." He expressed satisfaction that various Marxist critics were demolishing her position in ways that he had critiqued the Russian populists in his own massive study of 1899, *The Development of Capitalism in Russia*.[7]

At the same time, even economists inclined to agree with Lenin have insisted that Luxemburg was raising important questions, some insisting that answers she provided are well worth considering. One of her severest critics, the Russian Marxist Nikolai Bukharin, hailed Luxemburg's analysis as "a daring theoretical attempt" and "the deed of a brilliant theoretical intellect." This refers to what Roman Rosdolsky praises as "the valid kernel of her book." Ernest Mandel, agreeing with other critics on what he considers secondary issues, nonetheless argues that "the final balance-sheet on Luxemburg's critique . . . must be a nuanced one. We cannot say baldly that she is right or that she is wrong." While sorting through and judging these particular controversies goes beyond what can be done here, a major section of Luxemburg's masterwork deserves comment—a set of chapters in which she examined, with anthropological sensitivity, the devastating impact of capitalist expansion on the rich variety of the world's peoples and cultures, something that one cannot find in the key works of Hilferding, Lenin, and Bukharin. For Lenin, however, this vivid contribution was yet another negative feature. In his marginal notes in her book, he wrote: "The description of the torture of negroes in South America is noisy, colorful and meaningless. Above all it is 'non-Marxist.'" Almost half a century later, noting the "criticism," Hannah Arendt commented aptly, "but who would deny today that it belonged in a book on imperialism?"[8]

Luxemburg's biographer, J. P. Nettl, observes, however, that Lenin "read *The Accumulation of Capital* in 1913, at a time when his political relations with Rosa Luxemburg were at their worst; his critical notes in the margin of the manuscript indicate that he was out to fault her wherever possible; they abound with exclamations like 'nonsense' and 'funny.'"[9] The underlying point of contention between the two revolutionaries at this time was a new flare-up of disagreements on "the organization question."

Revolutionary Organization and Mass Action

There were, over the years, significant fluctuations in Luxemburg's assessment of Lenin's organizational orientation. In 1904, she wrote a savage critique of *One Step Forward, Two Steps Back*, Lenin's explanation of the Bolshevik/Menshevik split in the RSDLP. She accused Lenin of an ultra-centralist and authoritarian orientation that—seeking to ensure "revolutionary purity"—would result in the creation of an irrelevant sect. In 1905–1906, based on a changed situation (including closer contact with Bolsheviks and Mensheviks in a period of revolutionary upsurge), Luxemburg shifted to a pro-Bolshevik position. By 1907, she was defending Lenin from the same kinds of criticisms (this time advanced by Menshevik luminary George Plekhanov) that she herself had made three years before. By 1911 she more or less agreed with Lenin's overwhelmingly negative assessment with all other elements in the RSDLP.

However, when the Bolsheviks, for all practical purposes, carried out what Luxemburg viewed as a definitive and destructive split in the RSDLP—setting up what was essentially a separate Bolshevik party—Luxemburg (throughout 1912 and 1913) denounced the move and persistently agitated for RSDLP unity. The eruption of World War I in 1914, and the triumph of the Russian Revolution three years later, opened an entirely new phase in Luxemburg's thinking, which included her helping to found the German Communist Party at the start of 1919, when her life was cut short by a right-wing death squad.[10]

While it has been demonstrated that in 1904 Luxemburg distorted Lenin's actual views in her anti-Bolshevik polemic, even here we can find rich insights of value to revolutionary activists. She wrote:

On the one hand, we have the mass; on the other, its historic goal, located outside of existing society. On one hand, we have the day-to-day struggle, on the other, the social revolution. Such are the terms of the dialectical contradiction through which the socialist movement makes its way.

It follows that this movement can best advance by tacking betwixt and between the two dangers by which it is constantly being threatened. One is the loss of its mass character; the other, the abandonment of its goal. One is the danger of sinking back to the condition of a sect; the other, the danger of becoming a movement of bourgeois social reform.[11]

While Lenin was dismissive of Luxemburg's approach—tagging it "the whole notorious organization-as-process theory"—an examination of his own accounts of the evolution of Bolshevism in 1907 and again in 1920 show a keen awareness, after some years of experience, that the development of a revolutionary party is indeed a process.[12] More than this—although many commentators have counterposed a so-called "spontaneist" idolization of mass action by Luxemburg to a centralist idolization of a "vanguard party" by Lenin—a serious examination of their writings reveals that both revolutionaries theorized a dynamic interplay of mass action and organization, often with strikingly similar formulations. In *The Mass Strike, the Trade Union, and the Political Party*, Luxemburg wrote:

> The social democrats are the most enlightened, most class-conscious vanguard of the proletariat. They cannot and dare not wait, in a fatalist fashion, with folded arms for the advent of the "revolutionary situation," to wait for that which, in every spontaneous peoples' movement falls from the clouds. On the contrary, they must now, as always, hasten the development of things and endeavor to accelerate events.[13]

In *What Is to Be Done?* Lenin wrote:

> The spontaneity of the masses demands a high degree of consciousness from us Social-Democrats. The greater the spontaneous upsurge of the masses and the more widespread the

movement, the more rapid, incomparably so, the demand for greater consciousness in the theoretical, political and organizational work of Social-Democracy.[14]

Democracy and Revolution

The relationship of democracy to the struggle for socialism was another contested question between Lenin and Luxemburg, but here also the realities were far more complex and more interesting than is often assumed. We have noted that Luxemburg was not inclined to support the nationalism of the oppressed, particularly their right to national self-determination, in part because this was not a working-class demand but instead was merely a bourgeois-democratic demand, one that threatened to divide the workers and would become irrelevant if a working-class revolution was successful. By 1915, however, Lenin had become insistent on the necessity of fighting for all democratic demands as inseparable from the workers' struggle for socialism. It is worth considering his position at length:

> The proletariat cannot be victorious except through democracy, i.e., by giving full effect to democracy and by linking with each step of its struggle democratic demands formulated in the most resolute terms. . . . We must *combine* the revolutionary struggle against capitalism with a revolutionary program and tactics on all democratic demands: a republic, a militia, the popular election of officials, equal rights for women, the self-determination of nations, etc. While capitalism exists, these demands—all of them—can only be accomplished as an exception, and even then in an incomplete and distorted form. Basing ourselves on the democracy already achieved, and exposing its incompleteness under capitalism, we demand the overthrow of capitalism, the expropriation of the bourgeoisie, as a necessary basis both for the abolition of the poverty of the masses and for the *complete* and *all-round* institution of *all* democratic reforms.[15]

One of the terrible ironies of the Russian Revolution, however, is that once the workers and peasants swept the Bolsheviks into power—based in large measure on this revolutionary-democratic orientation—Russia was overwhelmed by catastrophes: military invasions, a brutalizing civil war, economic collapse brought on by an international capitalist blockade plus the Bolsheviks' own mistakes, famine, and more.

The leaders of the new Communist regime—Lenin, Red Army leader Leon Trotsky, and others—established a one-party dictatorship, and tended to project its authoritarian and ruthless policies as being more than simply extreme emergency measures designed to ensure survival but rather as a pathway to socialism, which would allow the reestablishment of democracy at a future time.

"Socialist democracy does not come as some sort of Christmas present for the worthy people who, in the interim, have loyally supported a handful of socialist dictators," Luxemburg argued. Genuine socialism was inseparable from freedom, and "freedom must always be freedom for those who think differently." She warned: "Without general elections, without unrestricted freedom of press and assembly, without a free struggle of opinion, life dies out in every public institution, becomes a mere semblance of life, in which only the bureaucracy remains as the active element . . . at bottom, then, a clique affair—a dictatorship, to be sure, not the dictatorship of the proletariat but only the dictatorship of a handful of politicians."[16]

On the other hand, Luxemburg also argued that the Russian Revolution would be unable to move forward on the path she was calling for until its desperate isolation was ended—above all by the triumph of socialist workers' revolutions in advanced industrial countries that could come to its assistance, particularly Germany. She added that "whatever a party could offer of courage, revolutionary far-sightedness and consistency in an historic hour, Lenin, Trotsky and all the other comrades have given in good measure." She added that "there is no doubt either . . . that Lenin and Trotsky on their thorny path beset by traps of all kinds, have taken many a decisive step only with the greatest inner hesitation and with the most violent inner opposition."[17]

Luxemburg and a number of her revolutionary comrades in Germany were murdered before they could lead the revolution that she was calling for. Afterward, and after the 1921 publication of her unfinished critique of the Russian Revolution, Lenin offered a glowing evaluation of his contentious comrade, insisting that more than once Rosa Luxemburg was wrong—he enumerated his disagreements— but that "a good old Russian fable" captured what was essential: "Eagles may at times fly lower than hens, but hens can never rise to the height of eagles." He insisted that "in spite of her mistakes she was— and remains for us—an eagle. And not only will Communists all over the world cherish her memory, but her biography and her *complete* works . . . will serve as useful manuals for training many generations of Communists all over the world."[18]

August Thalheimer, a revolutionary who knew and worked with both of them, insisted on the formulation "not Luxemburg *or* Lenin—but Luxemburg *and* Lenin," explaining that "each of them gave . . . what the other did not, and could not, give." One can learn much from their differences, but also from what Thalheimer called the "spiritual bond of these two great revolutionary champions of the working class and their closest comrades in arms."[19]

Chapter Nine
CAUTION: ACTIVISTS USING LENIN

"Read Lenin again—be careful."

—C. Wright Mills

In what follows, I will suggest how the practical politics of Lenin may relate to our time, as of 2012–2013. The perspective I am offering here is specific to the United States. I am familiar with my own country, but I do not have sufficient knowledge of other places to lay out specific proposals for them.

Four underlying ideas help to shape my conception of a revolutionary party: 1) there must be a coming together of socialism and the working class if either is to have a positive future; 2) those of us who think like that need to work together hard and effectively—which means we need to be part of a serious organization—at a certain point, when a significant number of workers are ready, this will be a party; 3) a key function of the revolutionary organization, and eventually the revolutionary party, is to train more and more people in the skills of how to think, how to analyze, how to organize meetings and struggles, how to reach out and help educate and train more and more people in this way; and 4) a key function of the revolutionary organization, and ultimately the revolutionary party, is to act as a democratic/disciplined force in actual workers' struggles in ways that help to advance those struggles—that is the path to socialism.

A serious organization means *not* a social club or affinity group for those who like socialism. It is also *not* a missionary group—appealing from outside the working class, urging people to listen to our socialist ideas, buy our socialist literature, come to our socialist meetings, and join with us in thinking revolutionary thoughts. This can be a way to attract some handfuls of thoughtful people. But some of us have also had enough experience to know that this doesn't work as a means for mobilizing a working-class majority in the effort to replace capitalism with socialism. This leaves us with the question: What *is* a serious socialist organization?

In reaching for an answer, I want to do several things. First, I want to check in with Marx and Engels on what they thought about the revolutionary party and program. Second, I want to draw from the Russian experience—particularly as reflected in what Lenin had to say. Third, I want to sketch aspects of the US experience in building revolutionary movements and parties. Fourth, I want to discuss some fatal illusions that infected the 1960s generation of would-be "Leninists" in the United States. And finally, I want to explore aspects of where we are now—the present-day context in which would-be party-builders in the United States find themselves, and the practical tasks I think make sense in this context.

Checking In with Marx and Engels

The working class, as Marx and Engels defined it, is composed of those who make a living by selling their ability to work (which consists of energy for manual labor, intellectual labor, or both). It is those whose labor creates the goods and services all of us depend on. It also includes family members and others dependent on the paychecks of those who sell their ability to work—and also unemployed and retired workers. It is the creative majority, whose labor creates and sustains the economy on which society depends, those without whom capitalism could not function. This is a force that potentially has the interest and the power to challenge capitalism. If they join together, the workers have the power to bring to birth a new and better world. There are aspects in the dynamics of capitalism that create more and more workers and dynamics that tend to push them in this direction.

According to Marx and Engels, revolutionary socialists, or communists, should not see themselves apart from the actual lives and struggles and movements and organizations of the working class. They are—or should be—an organic part of the working class and the movements and organizations of the workers that struggle for working-class emancipation. At the same time, those of us who are revolutionary socialists have a specific understanding—which we have a responsibility to share with others in our class—of the need for working-class solidarity and of what Marx and Engels called "the historic line of march" that we should also share and help to implement. Those who think and act this way constitute a vanguard layer of the working class. Elements of this vanguard layer—in the course of history—sometimes sought to advance this work by pulling together into organizations affiliated with the International Workingmen's Association, later the Socialist International, and later yet the Communist International.

The "historic line of march" that Marx and Engels referred to is sometimes called a "program." The *Communist Manifesto* advances such a program—that is, an outline of what to do to push back capitalist oppression and to achieve a socialist future. Marx based this program, to a significant degree, on the kinds of struggles he saw working-class activists engaging in.

This program consists of different parts. One involves building organizations of workers at their workplaces—these are known as trade unions—in order to struggle for and compel capitalist employers to pay higher wages, provide better (healthier, safer) working conditions, to agree to a shorter workday (ten hours instead of twelve, eight instead of ten, and so on), and to allow for more dignity on the job. In addition to building trade unions, the *Manifesto* encourages workers to push for reforms (which means improving life in the here and now, before a revolution takes place), which could be fought for by social movements for a shorter workday, for giving all people the right to vote, for women's rights, for an end to child labor, for public schools, for an end to racism, in opposition to war policies, and so on.

In addition to building such trade unions and social movements, Marx advocated the creation of an independent labor party of the working class to struggle for reforms and ultimately to win political power for the working class majority. Marx and Engels called this "winning the battle of democracy," establishing working-class rule politically in order to expand it economically, with a revolutionary transition to socialism. That's the program.

I think the independent labor party was the ultimate revolutionary party Marx and Engels had in mind, but like us they also participated in revolutionary groups (some more formal than others) to help carry out the work up until that party came into being. By the time of the Socialist International, however, in the years from 1889 to 1914, there were a number of such parties that came into being—although, when push came to shove, most of them turned out *not* to be revolutionary after all. An exception was what turned out to be a majority (or Bolshevik) segment of the Russian Socialist Democratic Labor Party, which led the great 1917 revolution that inaugurated the modern Communist movement.

The Russian and US Experience

Of course, it was Lenin's leadership that was a key factor in all of this, and one aspect of that—one of the reasons it is so fruitful to study his writings—is that he not only helped make a revolution, but he played a central role in analyzing and preparing the conditions in which it could be made. As Lars Lih has argued so well, it is not the case that Lenin sought to build a so-called "party of a new type," but it is the case that more insightfully and creatively and consistently than many, he helped to elaborate and apply the organizational principles of the revolutionary party that most Marxists formally adhered to. Central to Lenin, as to Marx, was the notion that the workers' movement and socialism must be merged. With Lenin we also find an alertness to the existence of different working-class layers—a relatively small layer animated by a high degree of experience, commitment, and revolutionary class consciousness, also a broader conscious and activist layer, as well as the less conscious and less active mass of workers (elements of which would be drawn into the more advanced layers over the course of time and struggle). And more than many, Lenin emphasized the need for a high degree of revolutionary activism and discipline in the organization of the working-class vanguard.

This was conceived of largely as self-discipline—and was a discipline related to an organization not only with a revolutionary program, but one which had been able to prove itself in mass struggles, and one organically rooted in the working class. It is worth reminding ourselves of Lenin's argument in *Left-Wing Communism: An Infantile Disorder* that there are three necessary conditions for a genuinely revolutionary party. First is the revolutionary class consciousness of a vanguard layer of the working class. Second is a correct political strategy and tactics on the part of organized revolutionaries. Third is an intimate and sustained contact "with the broadest masses of working people." Without these conditions being met, Lenin tells us, all attempts at a disciplined revolutionary party will "inevitably fall flat and end up in phrase-mongering and clowning."[1]

This gets at one of the key problems facing would-be party-builders in the United States for several decades. For the most part, revolutionary Marxists in the United States today cannot honestly say that we have either the first or the third of these necessary conditions—we have neither a substantial layer of the working class that is revolutionary nor a sustained connection of revolutionary socialists with the broad masses of working people. Yet these things are necessary for a crystallization of what Lenin himself would have considered a serious revolutionary party.

Such class-conscious layers did come into being in the United States in the past—certainly in the period from the American Civil War (1861–1865) down to the period of World War II and just after. Workers' class consciousness involves more than whatever notions happen to be in the minds of various members of the working class at any particular moment. It involves an understanding of the insight that was contained in the constitutional preamble of the American Federation of Labor (AFL) from 1886 to 1955: "A struggle is going on in all the nations of the civilized world, between the oppressors and the oppressed of all countries, a struggle between the capitalist and the laborer, which grows in intensity from year to year, and will work disastrous results to the toiling millions, if they are not combined for mutual protection and benefit."[2] Not all workers have absorbed this insight into their consciousness, but those who have done so can be said to have at least an elementary class consciousness.

Within this context of struggle and organization, a radical workers' subculture flourished, reinforced by fiery speeches, thoughtful analyses, and vivid memoirs such as those gathered in my book *Work and Struggle*. The elementary class-consciousness expressed in the founding preamble of the American Federation of Labor is also reflected in the three best known verses of Ralph Chaplin's labor anthem "Solidarity Forever," the second of which tells us:

> They have taken untold millions that they never toiled to earn,
> But without our brain and muscle not a single wheel can turn.
> We can break their haughty power, gain our freedom when we
>   learn
> That the union makes us strong.[3]

It comes through as well in this ditty from Industrial Workers of the World (IWW) martyr Joe Hill:

> Come all ye toilers that work for wages
> Come from every land,
> Join the fighting band,
> In one union grand,
> Then for the workers we'll make upon this earth a paradise
> When the slaves get wise and organize.[4]

And this, from James Oppenheim, inspired by embattled women textile workers in the Lawrence strike of 1912:

> As we come marching, marching, we bring the greater days.
> The rising of the women means the rising of the race.
> No more the drudge and idler—ten that toil while one reposes,
> But a sharing of life's glories—bread and roses, bread and roses![5]

Also part of this subculture were a variety of novels, short stories, and plays and (by the early decades of the twentieth century) even some motion pictures, not to mention cartoons and drawings and paintings, as well as innumerable picnics and parties and parades. All were part of an anticapitalist counterculture, reflecting and nourishing ideas and standards, insights and values and goals, ways of thinking and pathways of living and acting, that were an integral part of the organized Left over the decades stretching from the Civil War to the Second World War. Often this "subculture" was more like a network of subcultures having very distinctive ethnic attributes, but these different ethnic currents were at various times connected by left-wing political structures (such as the old Knights of Labor, the Socialist Party of Eugene V. Debs, the IWW, the Communist Party, various groups of socialist militants, Trotskyists, anarchists, and others) and also, to an extent, by trade union frameworks—culminating in the 1930s in the remarkable Congress of Industrial Organizations (CIO).

If we examine the decade of what has been called "Labor's Giant Step"—the 1930s—we see a variety of intersecting struggles that were inseparable from, reflected in, and nourished by a broad, amazingly rich and vibrant, left-wing subculture. In addition to several significant socialist and communist formations, there was an array of organizations formed around a variety of issues— groups and coalitions for labor rights and democracy, against war and militarism, against racism and fascism, against poverty and unemployment, and so on. Related to such things were an incredible number of conferences, educational classes and forums, books and pamphlets, newspapers and magazines, fictional literature, songs and poems, plays and paintings, picnics and socials, marches and rallies—all blending together to create an expanding and deepening pool of ideas, sensibilities and human relationships, as well as a sense of solidarity, of insight and understanding. It was, in fact, a subculture that generated and nourished the kind of consciousness necessary for the sustained struggles that brought about a genuine power shift in US society to the benefit of the working-class majority.

But there was a dramatic break in the continuity of this labor-radical tradition in the United States after 1945, due to the realities that resulted from the Second World War, and the social, economic, political, and cultural transformations of the 1950s and 1960s— when such factors as the Cold War, anti-left repression, the military-industrial complex, consumerist culture, and suburbanization became predominant. The organizations associated with the labor movement were similarly transformed—impacted by a complex combination of assaults, co-optations, corruptions, and erosions. The communities, culture, and consciousness of the working class became so different from the mid-1940s to the 1960s that only faded shreds of the old radical labor subculture remained. The youth radicalization of the 1960s developed apart from the organized labor movement, with the new crop of Marxists and socialists relatively isolated from the working-class majority—to the detriment of all concerned (except for the capitalists).

Fatal Illusions

At this point, I want to focus on fatal illusions of the generation of would-be "Leninists" coming into being in the 1960s and 1970s, a phenomenon crystallizing in the United States during the last phases of the youth radicalization that had swept through our country and so much of the world. With the demonstrated inadequacy of the social-democratic and left-libertarian currents dominating the "New Left," many activists gravitated to what they viewed as Leninism—seeking something more cohesive, more disciplined, with a strategic orientation promising to embrace the working-class majority in something that could culminate in a revolutionary transformation. There were different Trotskyist and Maoist incarnations of this, and other incarnations as well. Many of us (I would estimate a few thousand in all) were studying Lenin and others who were identified with some variant of Leninism.

One problem, in my opinion, is that we did not even understand our own class location. If you didn't work in a factory and if, materially, you were relatively well off, and certainly if you were a student, then you were often put in that fuzzy-minded grab bag called the "middle class"—and that's how many of us self-identified, as "middle class," even though five times out of six we were, according to the definition of Marx and Engels, working class. This confusion, I think, was related to general socioeconomic trends, regarding the transformation of the working class, which was at that time beyond our understanding. Given this reality, it is hardly surprising that only a few of us had any connection to the working-class movement—but the nature of the working-class movement (highly deradicalized, with the disintegration of the labor-radical subculture) was also not conducive to positive interaction with such young radicals.

We also failed to understand that what Lenin and his contemporaries had been saying and writing took place in a context in which there were class-conscious layers of the working class, nurtured by a labor-radical subculture and assuming the form of often powerful organizations. This meant that we were unable to understand the actual meaning and implications of what people like Lenin were saying—that is, we were burdened with a stilted understanding of Leninism.

A number of us, nonetheless, went into industry in order to connect with the working class, although our own confusion undoubtedly undermined our effectiveness. The industrial implantations certainly did not mean that we had accomplished the merger of socialism with the working class. Whatever gains were made, many of them were wiped out by developments that we were utterly unprepared for—the decline and elimination of more and more US industry thanks to something that would eventually become known as "globalization."

The long-term economic, social, cultural, and political trends of 1946 through 1976, and then the new developments in the twentieth century's final decades, added up to the utter decomposition of the working class that we would-be "Leninists" had imagined we would somehow connect with. This is not to say that the working class vanished—but it had radically changed in ways that we were unable to comprehend and cope with.

There was also confusion about "identities"—a tendency to separate or even counterpose issues of class from issues of gender, race, ethnicity, sexuality, and so on, as well as from issues having to do with war, the environment, civil liberties, as if all of these were not, in fact, matters that are inseparable from the multifaceted reality that is the working class. This relates to a point made some years ago by a seasoned revolutionary, George Breitman, of the US Socialist Workers Party. In examining the mass radicalization that swept the United States during the 1960s and 1970s, Breitman identified the mighty social movements and the early beginnings of what some have labeled "identity politics" in this illuminating manner: "It is idiotic and insulting to think that the worker responds only to economic issues. He can be radicalized in various ways, over various issues, and he is." Breitman developed this point:

> The radicalization of the worker can begin off the job as well as on. It can begin from the fact that the worker is a woman as well as a man; that the worker is Black or Chicano or a member of some other oppressed minority as well as white; that the worker is a father or mother whose son can be drafted [into the military]; that the worker is young as well as middle-aged or about to retire. If we grasp the fact that the working class is stratified and divided in many ways—the capitalists prefer it that way—then we will be better able to understand how the radicalization will develop among workers and how to intervene more effectively. Those who haven't already learned important lessons from the radicalization of oppressed minorities, youth and women had better hurry up and learn them, because most of the people involved in these radicalizations are workers or come from working-class families.[6]

This perception was entirely consistent with the perspectives of Lenin, of course, who told us that a revolutionary socialist's ideal should be "the tribune of the people, who is able to react to every manifestation of tyranny and oppression, no matter where it appears, no matter what stratum or class of people it affects; who . . . is able to take advantage of every event, however small, in order to set forth before all his socialist convictions and democratic demands, in order to clarify for all and everyone the world-historic significance of the struggle for the emancipation of the proletariat."[7] A failure to comprehend fully the logic traced by Lenin and Breitman contributed to difficulties encountered by many on the US Left in moving beyond their own small, rarified political universes.

In any event, to a very large extent, our would-be "Leninist" organizations became precisely what Lenin had warned against—

without an intimate and sustained contact "with the broadest masses of working people," our attempts at a disciplined revolutionary party were destined to "inevitably fall flat and end up in phrase-mongering and clowning."

Where We Are

I want to fast-forward to the present. Despite dramatic changes, capitalism continues to exist in ways that continue to make the fundamental perspectives of Marx and Lenin relevant to our situation in the United States. But we need to look thoughtfully at present-day realities to see how this is so.

We have, for a matter of decades now, been enduring a multi-faceted assault from the capitalist class that has taken a variety of forms. One of the purposes of "globalization" and the myriad of technical innovations, it seems clear to some of us, has been to erode and disintegrate centers of working-class power in the advanced capitalist nations—industrial heartlands that had provided the basis for the power of the industrial unions that in the 1930s and 1950s had forced a power shift, bringing great benefits to the working class, partly at the expense of the big business corporations that dominate our economy.

We have seen a decomposition of that working class, and its re-composition as a more deskilled, lower-income, non-unionized, largely service-sector proletariat—with remaining union strength shifting mostly from the private sector to the public sector (the opposite of what once had been the case). This has been accompanied by a cultural and political assault—a well-financed and brilliantly orchestrated effort to blunt, fragment, disorient, and marginalize working-class consciousness.

One aspect of this has been the creation of a phony-populist and highly popular Fox News universe, supplemented by a tidal wave of right-wing talk-radio honchos and the manufacture of the so-called tea party movement defending big business interests with a rhetoric that plays on fears and prejudices and confusion existing among large sectors of the working class. Related to this is the initiation of so-called "culture wars" around issues of fundamentalist

Christianity, anti-abortion bigotry, hostility to feminism, homopho-
bia, gun culture, anti-immigrant bias, and so on.

Politically, especially since 1980, there have been waves of increasingly right-wing capitalist campaigns, and largely Republican
Party policies but also Democratic Party policies, which have
brought us union-busting, tax cuts for the rich, deregulation and
privatization, the gutting of social programs, and so on. This was
also related to a deepened commitment to renew and secure a global
"American Century" through war and sweeping trade agreements.

But reality trumps hype, and the unraveling of US military adventures, the rise of substantial global rivals to US economic power,
and the surprise appearance of multiple crises in the capitalist economy could not be explained away by conservative pundits and politicians. This combined with a longer-standing reality: income levels
and working conditions and living conditions that over the years
had been deteriorating, while the profits and wealth of the upper
crust were visibly growing by leaps and bounds.

There is not sufficient class consciousness for a majority of the
working class even to say that they are working class. Most are not
rich and are not poor, so they have been persuaded to refer to themselves as "middle class"—but they are working class nonetheless, and
growing layers of them have been experiencing a deepening disillusionment and a rising discontent. More and more of them have been
entertaining relatively radical ideas, despite their mixed consciousness.

This experience has been contributing to the recomposition of
elements and variants of what amounts to a labor-radical subculture.
More and more people who are part of the recomposed working class
are being pushed down and kicked around, and such things generate
a radicalizing consciousness. This has even had the effect of pushing
the organized labor movement in the United States, the trade unions,
in a leftward direction. There is a willingness to work with open left-
ists and to consider militant tactics in ways that would have been
unimaginable a few decades back. The rebirth and recomposition of
what amounts to a new manifestation of a labor-radical subculture is
nurtured by unions, community groups, and leftist collectives. It is
overflowing on the Internet, is advanced through alternative radio,
permeates comedy, music, and graphic novels, and pokes through in

various corners of our popular culture and even in the mainstream—in widely read works of fiction, television, film, and more.

This reality resulted in Barak Obama talking a more radical line (when he was running for president in 2008) than any mainstream candidate has done in the United States since I have been alive. His rhetoric was only a couple of steps away from that of a class-struggle socialist, and he was talking this way not because he believed in it or hoped to implement it—God forbid!—but because he believed that this would help generate a popular enthusiasm to get him elected president of the United States. This shows how far radicalized class consciousness has come in the United States. But we have to look at the other side of the ledger. Some white workers still voted against him because he is black, while other workers of various racial and ethnic backgrounds voted for him because they really, really, really believed that he was on their side. Both of these realities demonstrate the continued limitations of class consciousness in the United States. We can find the same mixed reality in the struggles of the Wisconsin working class, which coalesced in an amazing mass strike and extended labor occupation of the state capitol, but which then gave way to the promises and lures of inadequate Democratic Party politicians who led the movement down to defeat.

The radicalization and militancy within the working class continue to manifest themselves in important ways, although they have some distance to go before they cohere into the kind of working-class consciousness we need to push back our oppressors. In my native Pittsburgh this has been very clear in the local turnout for recent protests against the G-20 summit in our city, in the support for the Occupy movement that pits the interests of the 99 percent against the immense power of the wealthy 1 percent, and in the fightback against efforts to gut our public transportation system. It seems very clear to me that we are in an incredibly fluid situation, with great opportunities and potential for the recomposition of a conscious working-class Left in our country. I would like to offer an insightful comment on this by the seasoned journalist Chris Hedges, who for a number of years was an international correspondent for the *New York Times*:

The engine of all protest movements rests, finally, not in the hands of the protesters but the ruling class. If the ruling class responds rationally to the grievances and injustices that drive people into the streets, as it did during the New Deal, if it institutes jobs programs for the poor and the young, a prolongation of unemployment benefits (which hundreds of thousands of Americans have just lost), improved Medicare for all, infrastructure projects, a moratorium on foreclosures and bank repossessions, and a forgiveness of student debt, then a mass movement can be diluted. Under a rational ruling class, one that responds to the demands of the citizenry, the energy in the street can be channeled back into the mainstream. But once the system calcifies as a servant of the interests of the corporate elites, as has happened in the United States, formal political power thwarts justice rather than advances it.

Our dying corporate class, corrupt, engorged on obscene profits and indifferent to human suffering, is the guarantee that the mass movement will expand and flourish. No one knows when. No one knows how. The future movement may not resemble Occupy. It may not even bear the name Occupy. But it will come. I have seen this before. And we should use this time to prepare, to educate ourselves about the best ways to fight back, to learn from our mistakes, as many Occupiers are doing in New York, Washington, D.C., Philadelphia and other cities. There are dark and turbulent days ahead. There are powerful and frightening forces of hate, backed by corporate money, that will seek to hijack public rage and frustration to create a culture of fear. It is not certain we will win. But it is certain this is not over.[8]

I think what Hedges says is pretty much on target. Veterans of Occupy, and supporters, are still here, are thinking and evaluating their experience, and are seeking ways to move forward. In Pittsburgh, since leaving the encampment at "People's Park" (formerly and currently "Mellon Park"), some of the most serious elements have flowed into a sort of "Community-Labor Occupy" though the names are *Pittsburghers for Public Transit* and the United Steel Workers union's broadly conceived *Fight Back Pittsburgh*. Through these and other formations, the struggle seems likely to continue and deepen.

This brings us to the tasks facing revolutionary socialists in the United States. I want to begin with two of the things that I believe we should *not* do.

What Not to Do

Imagine a group of half a dozen or a dozen young activists who believe they have the Correct Program and that they are building the genuine nucleus of a Revolutionary Vanguard Party. Imagine that they make a point of throwing themselves into the struggle against major cuts in their city's public transit system, and that they also go down, during the Occupy Wall Street movement, to the related Occupy site in their city to talk to activists there about socialism. So far, so good.

But then imagine that they did not actually participate in the Occupy movement—that instead they went down to lecture to it, to sell their literature, and to try to recruit away from that struggle. They view it as a non–working class, essentially petty-bourgeois enterprise mired in the chaos of ideological confusion. And they are partly right—in the Occupy movement there was a chaos of ideological confusion: a chaos of anarchist and left-reformist and radical-Christian and free-market libertarian and revolutionary socialist and idiosyncratic personal notions swirled around in the incredibly animated debates and the discussions.

But I would argue that the class composition of the occupiers—when we strip away the conceptual fuzziness of "middle classness"—was essentially working class. Occupy was hated by members of the working class who inhabited the Fox News universe, but a majority of the working class approved of their message of challenging the megawealthy 1 percent and standing up for the 99 percent. Major sectors of the organized labor movement stood up for, and materially helped, the Occupy movement, certainly in Pittsburgh.

But the sterling class-struggle socialists, in all the magnificence of their tiny little group, decide to stand aside. They become irrelevant to the Occupy movement, and unsuccessful in their missionary work, so they finally stop bothering with it. Imagine, also, that in a slightly different way, they also draw back from the transit struggle in which they had played such an important role. After selling pamphlets and magazines containing socialist discussions of the transit struggle, after working to recruit transit activists to their own specific projects, after new forces (including some from the Occupy movement) came into the struggle, and at the moment when push was coming to shove in the transit struggle, imagine that they decide they need to pull back in order to focus on consolidating their own members and organization. There are groups that have functioned in pretty much this way. It is unlikely that such a mode of operation can result in a genuinely revolutionary party.

In reaction against such sectarian small-group politics, there are some who have advanced a "unity" recipe. This is premised on a recognition that all of us adhere, in various ways, to the same basic principles (as codified, for example, in the *Communist Manifesto*) and that—in the amazing new period that is opening up before us, behind us, and all around us—now is the time for a unified socialist organization of several thousand people working together, as opposed to the bits and pieces of such an organization competing with each other, brandishing separate newspapers, organizing separate educational conferences, promoting separate projects, articulating separate political lines.

But it is not clear that an attempt to merge into a single group would be a fruitful expenditure of one's time—because it may not yield the positive results its proponents imagine. Imagine throwing one's self into intensive unity discussions and negotiations with those who are in the small sectarian group just described. Multiply that times ten—with some of the other groups considering socialism as a goal that can be achieved by working in the Democratic Party, or as a goal consistent with the oppressive regime of North Korea, or in some cases as a goal that can probably not really be achieved, or in other cases as a goal that will be achieved through following their own particular, rigidly worked-out game plan.

Even if we were able to create such a unified organization, encompassing all of these tendencies, it is not clear that the result would be worth much. It could turn out to be a big multifactional sect that is not able to play an effective role in the actual struggles of our time, or to present a coherent perspective and a hospitable atmosphere for the radicalizing layers of the working class that are just about ready to embrace socialism as part of their evolving class consciousness.

What to Do

So what should we be doing instead to advance the goal of building a revolutionary party in the United States? First of all, we must recognize that the most we can do at this moment is to help create the preconditions for such a party. Things may be different in ten years or even five years—but that is the situation now.

To advance this, the primary thing is to be immersed in the actual struggles of our time—the Occupy movement, the transit struggle, opposition to war and racism, the ongoing class struggle for economic justice, and more. As part of this immersion, we must learn and learn more, help advance the struggle to the best of our abilities, and (when we are able) to teach—teach how to do things, how to strategize, how to function, how to analyze a situation (using socialist perspectives and Marxist ideas in a way that is open and yet comprehensible to others).

Related to this, of course, we need to help share and develop Marxist theory, and a Marxist understanding of history, in ways that can be helpful to people in comprehending and advancing the struggles of today. Both things together—the immersion in struggles and the engagement with socialist theory and education—are essential, in my opinion.

To advance both of these tasks, I think it helps to be part of a Marxist organization that is committed to doing both, an organization that understands clearly that it is not *the* Vanguard but instead that it is part of a process, a process of creating the preconditions for the emergence of a revolutionary party that will encompass activists from a number of organizations (and people who are members of no organization and in some cases not even activists yet).

The kind of organization that I would be part of should, in my opinion, avoid hothouse efforts to create The Revolutionary Party. Instead, it should focus on being immersed in, helping, and learning from the actual struggles of our time, and both in that context of struggle and also transcending that context, give attention to using and teaching and developing socialist consciousness and Marxist theory.

We should go out of our way to work with others, especially taking seriously any common work we can carry out with other socialists—and anarchists too, some of whom are fine and principled revolutionary activists. In some cases, we will simply be doing good work together in a transit struggle or Occupy action or union effort. In some cases we will be able to establish more formal united front efforts. And with it all, I think, we should reach for an increase of discussion, comradely debate, friendships, and more.

And the "more than friendship" I have in mind refers not to love affairs (although I imagine there may be some of those, and that's okay), but involves seeing all of this as preparing conditions out of which a revolutionary party can emerge—representing an evolving and broad vanguard layer of the working class.

There is another aspect of this party-building perspective that needs to be raised. A genuinely revolutionary party cannot simply be a collection of "jolly good fellows" who have gotten to know each other during an accumulation of struggles. We need to be united around a program—an understanding of where we are, where we want to end up, and how to get from here to there. We do have a basic program in the *Communist Manifesto*, of course, but we need to have a sense of how this applies to twenty-first-century realities and of how we need to be applying this to US conditions of our time. These will need to emerge from hard work—involving especially learning from our struggles but also through some research and study, and from debates and discussions with our various comrades in struggle. Such a process of developing our program will need to evolve as part of the general process of preparing the conditions for the revolutionary party.

In trying to advance this complex and incredibly important process of building a revolutionary party, it seems to me that it is useful to compare notes with comrades in different contexts, with different experiences, with different insights and notions. We need to keep thinking, keep learning from our experiences and from each other, and keep engaging in outreach and struggles and creative efforts to reach more people, drawing more people into this molecular process of composing a vanguard layer for revolutionary struggle, providing the social basis and needed experience for a revolutionary party capable of bringing the fundamental, life-affirming changes we genuinely need.

Chapter Ten
LENINISM IS UNFINISHED

A tragic development has unfolded on the British Left—the destructive crisis of that country's Socialist Workers Party (SWP). People have been hurt and humiliated, the organizational measures taken (and not taken) have aroused fierce controversy, there have been expulsions and resignations, after a narrow vote at a party congress there has been an unsuccessful internal ban on further discussion of the matter, and serious damage has been done to one of the most important organizations on the global revolutionary left.

A public intervention in the discussion by the SWP's most prominent theorist, Alex Callinicos, has posed a key question—in part as a defense of the decisions implemented by the leadership of his organization—as the title of his article: "Is Leninism Finished?" Responding to him, a US socialist blogger, Louis Proyect, has affirmed: "Leninism Is Finished."[1] The question and answer would seem to have great significance for revolutionaries of all lands.

The British SWP

The scandal and subsequent organizational developments and measures within the SWP, together generating the crisis, have been discussed at length and in depth by others. Some of the Internet discussion is saturated with voyeuristic speculations, rumor-mongering, and sectarian gloating far removed from serious, genuinely progressive, or revolutionary politics. Some of it, coming from members of the SWP, has been informative and thoughtful. Anyone with access to the Internet can easily read it all, if they have the time and the inclination. Since both Callinicos and Proyect cite an article by Owen Jones, a left-wing columnist in the pages of the *Independent*, I will allow him to summarize what seems to have happened:

> The largest far-left organisation in Britain, the Socialist Workers Party, is currently imploding in the aftermath of a shocking internal scandal. After a leading figure was accused of raping a member, the party set up a "court" staffed with senior party members, which exonerated him. "Creeping feminism" has been flung around as a political insult. Prominent members, such as authors China Miéville and Richard Seymour, have publicly assailed their party's leadership. Activists are reported to be in open rebellion at their autocratic leadership, or are simply deserting *en masse*.
>
> This might all sound parochial, the obscure goings-on out on the fringes of Britain's marginal revolutionary left. But the SWP has long punched above its weight. It formed the basis of the organisation behind the Stop the War Coalition, for example, which—almost exactly a decade ago—mobilised up to two million people to take to the streets against the impending Iraqi bloodbath. Even as they repelled other activists with sectarianism and aggressive recruitment drives, they helped drive crucial movements such as Unite Against Fascism, which recently organised a huge demonstration in Walthamstow that humiliated the racist English Defence League. Thousands hungry for an alternative to the disaster of neo-liberalism have entered the SWP's ranks over the years—many, sadly, to end up burnt out and demoralised.[2]

The first paragraph tells us that the SWP is "imploding," which is really not clear as of this writing [January 2013], but to say that it is currently *wracked by crisis* is to state the obvious. Nor is it necessary to take sides in regard to the charge of "sectarianism and aggressive recruitment drives" (and also to the assertion that many SWPers "end up burnt out and demoralized"). All the more impressive, in the face of these criticisms, is the acknowledgement that "the SWP has long punched above its weight" with a capacity to organize impressive struggles and to mobilize thousands and even millions is something that cannot be said about most left-wing groups in Britain or the United States, and Callinicos makes the obvious point:

> What our critics dislike most about us—how we organise ourselves—is crucial to our ability, as Jones puts it, to punch above our weight. Our version of democratic centralism comes down to two things. First, decisions must be debated fully, but once they have been taken, by majority vote, they are binding on all members. This is necessary if we are to test our ideas in action.
>
> Secondly, to ensure that these decisions are implemented and that the SWP intervenes effectively in the struggle, a strong political leadership, directly accountable to the annual conference, campaigns within the organisation to give a clear direction to our party's work. It is this model of democratic centralism that has allowed us to concentrate our forces on key objectives, and thereby to build so effectively the various united fronts we have supported.

In fact, there is an overly expansive aspect to Callinicos's definition of democratic centralism—a point to which we will need to return. But there does seem to be some correlation between the way the SWP seeks to organize itself (consciously drawing on the Leninist tradition) and its political effectiveness.

Is Leninism Finished?

Louis Proyect has long wrestled with the question of revolutionary organization, driven to do so in large measure because of his own traumas (shared by others, including myself) in the SWP of the United States over a quarter of a century back. The political traditions of the US SWP, and its crisis of the 1980s (and consequent implosion) are not exactly the same as the traditions and crisis of the British SWP—but there are certainly parallels.[3] Proyect focuses his attention on these for the purpose of making what he hopes will be useful generalizations for the Left as a whole. Yet there seems to be a serious contradiction in the line of argument that he puts forward.

Early in his article, Proyect tells us that former SWPer Peter Camejo especially influenced him:

> After he began figuring out that the party he had belonged to for decades was on a suicidal sectarian path, he took a leave of absence to go to Venezuela and read Lenin with fresh eyes. This was one of the first things he told me over the phone: "Louis, we have to drop the democratic centralism stuff." That is what he got out of reading Lenin. I was convinced that he was right and spent the better part of the thirty years following our phone conversation spreading that message to the left.

The contradiction is that for much of his article, Proyect insists that Lenin's own organizational thinking (including on the matter of democratic centralism) is consistent with the thinking of Proyect himself, not with the thinking of Callinicos and others whom he accuses of following in the footsteps of Gregory Zinoviev and Leon Trotsky. Callinicos's conceptions, he insists, are rooted not in Lenin but in "the Zinovievist Comintern of the 1920s, which Trotsky adopted as a model." But this means a more appropriate title for his essay would be: "Cominternism Is Dead, Long Live Genuine Leninism!"[4]

It may be, however, that Proyect's position is similar to that of Charlie Post, who argues that there was nothing in Lenin's thinking to distinguish him from Karl Kautsky (of pre-1914 vintage), and that "Leninism" is an invention of Zinoviev and other leaders of the Comintern of the 1920s.[5]

Among the many problems with this, however, is the fact that the 1920s Communist International of Zinoviev and Trotsky was also the Comintern of Lenin himself. (There is also a reality highlighted by the immense, very rich contributions of John Riddell and others, that there was much more of value in the early Communist International than one would be led to believe by superficial attacks on "Zinovievism.") There is no question that other comrades in the pre-1914 Socialist International—particularly George Plekhanov and Karl Kautsky—profoundly influenced Lenin. But his thought cannot be reduced to that. Nor did his thinking stop in 1914. In fact, the 1921 Comintern theses "The Organizational Structure of the Communist Parties, the Methods and Content of Their Work" were put forward at Lenin's insistence. Not only did Lenin help to shape the theses (which included a substantial emphasis on democratic centralism), he also defended them after they were adopted.[6]

Apparently to present a Lenin more consistent with political points he wishes to stress, Proyect chooses to leave this and much else out of his account of the history of the Bolsheviks. Yet a fairly selective reading of Lars Lih's contributions cannot render more than a fragmentary understanding of Lenin, Bolshevism, and the Russian Revolution. This is not to deny an important point that Proyect makes: "Lenin sought nothing more than to create a party based on the German social democracy in Russia. There was never any intention to build a new kind of party, even during the most furious battles with the Mensheviks who after all (as Lih convincingly makes the case) were simply a faction of the same broad party that Lenin belonged to."

In elaborating on this, however, Proyect tends to play fast and loose with the historical evidence in order to "prove" that Lenin himself was no "Leninist" (when, as we shall see, Lenin actually *was* an approximation of what we would call a "Leninist"). Such dilution results in the loss of ideas and historical experiences that we really cannot afford to lose. It is unfortunate that a selective utilization of John Reed's classic *Ten Days That Shook the World* serves to push aside, for all practical purposes, what is presented in Trotsky's classic *History of the Russian Revolution*. Consider the complex and dynamic notion that Trotsky advances in his preface:

> The masses go into a revolution not with a prepared plan of social reconstruction but with a sharp feeling that they cannot endure the old régime. Only the guiding layers of a class have a political program, and even this still requires the test of events, and the approval of the masses. . . . Only on the basis of a study of political processes in the masses themselves, can we understand the rôle of parties and leaders, whom we least of all are inclined to ignore. They constitute not an independent, but nevertheless a very important, element in the process. Without a guiding organisation, the energy of the masses

would dissipate like steam not enclosed in a piston-box. But nevertheless what moves things is not the piston or the box, but the steam.[7]

We need to wrestle with the meaning of this dialectical passage if, as revolutionary activists, we are to make our way through the no-less-dynamic complexities of our own time. Proyect presents as the "essence" of Lenin's approach the fact that he and other Bolsheviks could publicly argue against each other and openly vote in opposite ways. But this draws us away from the Leninist "essence" that Trotsky points us to. This is especially unfortunate because it can obscure the positive contribution Proyect makes in his article.

Revolutionary Vanguard and Mass Struggle

Proyect argues that revolutionary socialist organizations must stop giving in to a fatal sectarian temptation, the false vision that *they* are the "revolutionary vanguard," or perhaps *the nucleus* of the revolutionary vanguard party of the future. Even in its less pathological variants, he warns, revolutionary socialist groups can thereby create for themselves a vanguardist "glass ceiling." The problem is that "the group sees itself as the nucleus of the future revolutionary party no matter how much lip service is given to fusing with other groups during a prerevolutionary period, etc." At some point the perceived necessity of preserving and advancing the group's special role as "nucleus" will nurture fatally sectarian dynamics within the group and between that group and other forces.

In criticizing the relatively healthy pre-crisis British SWP and the relatively healthy pre-1980 US SWP, Proyect makes the point that "it would be virtually impossible for SWP members in Britain to take a position on Cuba identical to the American SWP's and *vice versa*." He tellingly adds that this is "a moot point since most members become indoctrinated through lectures and classes after joining the groups and tend to toe the line, often responding to peer pressure and the faith that their party leaders must know what is right." To the extent that he is right (as I know he is about the US SWP and suspect he may be about the British SWP), this suggests an issue that defenders of any kind of "Leninism" (and of political-organizational coherence in general) must wrestle with.

No serious socialist group can afford to abandon the education of its members around theory and history ("indoctrination") in the form of lectures and classes. Nor can any human group abolish "peer pressure." But what healthy countervailing tendencies can be nourished that will help overcome the negative tendencies to which Proyect usefully directs our attention?

Proyect tells a story from the late 1960s of his discussion with an older veteran of the Trotskyist movement when both were members of the SWP. After a Maoist friend had challenged him, the young recruit asked what the SWP's program was. The old-timer "waved his hand in the direction of our bookstore and replied, 'It's all there.'" It is interesting to consider Proyect's interpretation of this—that it "meant having positions on everything from WWII to Kronstadt. Becoming a 'cadre' meant learning the positions embodied in over a hundred pamphlets and books and defending them in public." This was, in fact, the conception of many (not all) comrades of that time—but there is another, quite different way of understanding the old comrade's comment.

It is not the case that SWP bookstores were simply stocked with pamphlets and books outlining positions on everything from the Second World War to the Kronstadt uprising of 1921. Rather, they contained a rich array of material—accounts of labor struggles, antiracist struggles, women's liberation struggles, the history of the revolutionary movement, writings by Marx and Engels, Rosa Luxemburg, Lenin and Trotsky, Isaac Deutscher, Ernest Mandel, Che Guevara, Malcolm X (in some cases, also Simone de Beauvoir, Kate Millett, Sheila Rowbotham), as well as some of the most creative thinkers in the SWP—not simply James P. Cannon (worth reading despite the criticisms made of him), but people like George Breitman and Joseph Hansen who developed insights and innovative formulations incompatible with any closed "orthodoxy." To say "it's all there" could be seen as reference not to a closed system of Truth, but to a rich and multifaceted tradition, an approach that is rigorous but also open, critical-minded, and revolutionary, with theory and analysis rooted in the actual mass struggles of one's own time. This may not be what that particular old comrade meant, but I did know some old comrades who happened to think this way.

The proposed political orientation that emerges from Proyect's piece could be stated, I think, with four basic and interrelated points.

1. There is a revolutionary vanguard layer that is part of the working class (broadly defined) and of the workers' movement. This layer consists of those who have more information, analyses, organizing know-how, a sense of how to get from the oppressive "here" to the more desirable "there," and a greater conscious political passion than the majority. It has the capacity to connect with and help radicalize and mobilize growing sectors of that working-class majority. But this vanguard is multifaceted, not concentrated in a single organization, and some who are part of it are not necessarily in *any* revolutionary organization.

2. Only through the coordinated efforts of different components of this broad vanguard layer will it become possible to mobilize tens of thousands, hundreds of thousands, and millions of people in serious challenges to the capitalist status quo, which should be the primary goal of revolutionaries today.[8]

3. Mass action coordinated by the broad vanguard layer obviously must go parallel with—and is inseparable from—efforts to nurture revolutionary consciousness within more and more of the working class as a whole. Various groups and individuals can and should feel free to develop theoretical perspectives, share their ideas, disagree with each other, engage in debates, and so on, while continuing to collaborate closely in building the mass struggles. This is the pathway to revolution.

4. If one or another segment of this broad vanguard layer—under the banner of some spurious "Leninism"—seeks to dominate the broader effort at the expense of other segments, the result would be fragmentation and defeat. Along with this, the program of the *Communist Manifesto* should be the decisive element in the programmatic orientation of these unified vanguard elements. There is no need for "programmatic agreement" on such historical matters as analyses of the 1921 Kronstadt rebellion, or the Second World War, or the nature of the former Soviet Union.

This approach, which I think Proyect is advancing, makes sense to me. It projects the seasoning and tempering, through mass struggle, of substantial layers of activists who are part of the broad working-class vanguard, helping prepare the social base and organizational experience that are preconditions for the crystallization of a genuine revolutionary working-class party, or the practical equivalent of that party.

Owen Jones similarly seems to get it right when he argues for:

> A broad network that unites progressive opponents of the [neo-liberal] Coalition. That means those in Labour who want a proper alternative to Tory austerity, Greens, independent lefties, but also those who would not otherwise identify as political, but who are furious and frustrated. In the past two years of traipsing around the country, speaking to students, workers, unemployed and disabled people, I've met thousands who want to do something with their anger.

A broad left front, agreeing on certain basic programmatic principles, he continues:

> Could link together workers facing falling wages while their tax credits are cut; unemployed people demonised by a cynical media and political establishment; crusaders against the mass tax avoidance of the wealthy; sick and disabled people having basic support stripped away; campaigners against crippling cuts to our public services; young people facing a future of debt, joblessness and falling living standards; and trade unions standing their ground in the onslaught against workers' rights.

The way Alex Callincos dismisses this seems odd to me. "This sounds very nice but is quite misleading," he tells us, "since Jones is an increasingly high profile member of the Labour Party." He then goes on to repeat the traditional SWP critique of the British Labor Party, counterposing this to the tradition that the SWP is attempting to continue: "Started by Karl Marx and Friedrich Engels, this tradition reached its highpoint in the Russian Revolution of October 1917, when the Bolshevik Party led the first and still the only successful working class revolution. Leon Trotsky, who with Vladimir Lenin headed the Bolsheviks in October 1917, then fought the degeneration of the revolution with the rise of Stalin's tyranny between the mid-1920s and the early 1930s." All of which is fine—*and could be quite consistent with responding positively to the left front for working-class mass action that Jones is proposing.* It seems obvious to me that the SWP could make powerful contributions to the process being projected here.

If instead of seeing the revolutionary vanguard and its organization(s) as being forged through actual mass struggles, however, one quite simply sees the Socialist Workers Party as the one, true, already-existing revolutionary vanguard organization making its way through a morass of flawed competitors, then perhaps one can afford to be dismissive. Is that what Callinicos actually believes? If so, then the parallels Proyect is drawing between the two SWPs and his warning about a "vanguardist glass ceiling" may be appropriate.

Boundaries of Democratic Centralism

If something approximating a revolutionary vanguard party, with good politics and a mass base, can actually be forged by different currents joining together in the class struggle, then the question is posed as to how such a formation can hold together and be an effective force for the advance of the working class and the revolutionary cause. And this brings us back to the question of democratic centralism.

Regarding democratic centralism, particularly what this meant for Lenin and what it should mean for us, it seems to me that Proyect veers off the path of historical accuracy and political logic, while Callinicos traps himself in a problematical formulation that may be related to the present crisis of the British SWP.

Here is how Proyect explains the meaning of Lenin's conception of democratic centralism and relates it to our own time:

[According to John Reed's *Ten Days That Shook the World*, in a 1917 public discussion on freedom of the press for capitalist newspapers] Lenin and Riazanov debated at a mass meeting and then voted against each other. This was normal Bolshevik functioning. All discipline meant was a [parliamentary] deputy voting according to instructions from the party's central committee, etc. For example, if Alex Callinicos was elected to Parliament and instructed to vote against funding the war in Iraq, and then voted for funding, the party would be entitled to expel him.

This very narrow interpretation, however, is not the way the Mensheviks (Lenin's factional adversaries in the Russian Social Democratic Labor Party) understood democratic centralism—and they were the first ones to introduce the term into the Russian revolutionary movement. The term involved much more for them than simply control over parliamentary delegates. According to their resolution of November 1905, "decisions of the guiding collectives are binding on the members of those organizations of which the collective is the organ. Actions affecting the organization as a whole ... must be decided upon by all members of the organization. Decisions of lower level organizations must not be implemented if they contradict decisions of higher organizations." The Bolsheviks fully accepted the term. In a 1906 discussion, Lenin explained: "The principle of democratic centralism and autonomy for local Party organizations implies universal and full *freedom to criticize* so long as this does not disturb the unity of a definite action; it rules out *all* criticism which disrupts or makes difficult the *unity* of an action decided by the Party."[9]

At this point, it is time for us to turn our attention back to the formulation of Callinicos that we questioned earlier—that "our version of democratic centralism" involves two key points: 1) "decisions must be debated fully, but once the vote has been taken, by majority vote, they are binding on all members," and 2) "a strong political leadership, directly accountable to the annual congress, campaigns within the organization to give a clear direction to our party's work." This two-point definition is different from the way Lenin and his comrades defined the term. Missing in what they put forward is the emphasis on "a strong political leadership ... giving clear direction to our party's work." But also missing is the broad insistence that "decisions" as such "are binding on all members."

In fact, Lenin was absolutely resistant to the efforts of some of his Menshevik comrades to establish "limits within which decisions of Party congresses may be criticized." As he stressed:

> In a revolutionary epoch like the present, all theoretical errors and tactical deviations of the Party are most ruthlessly criticized by experience itself, which enlightens and educates the working class with unprecedented rapidity. At such a time, the duty of every Social Democrat is to strive to ensure that the ideological struggle within the Party on questions of theory and tactics is conducted as openly, widely and freely as possible, but that on no account does it disturb or hamper the unity of revolutionary action of the Social-Democratic proletariat. . . .
>
> We are profoundly convinced that the workers' Social-Democratic organizations must be united, but in these united organizations there must be wide and free discussion of Party questions, free comradely criticism and assessment of events in Party life.[10]

Lenin went on to argue that "criticism within the *principles* of the Party Program must be quite free, . . . not only at Party meetings, but also at public meetings."[11]

One might expect a change in the way Lenin and his comrades discussed the concept of democratic centralism in the 1921 organizational resolution on organization—but the section of that document dealing explicitly with democratic centralism contains nothing to contradict what Lenin was saying in 1906. In fact, the document contains warnings regarding efforts by Communist Party leaderships to go too far in the direction of centralization. "Centralization in the Communist Party does not mean formal, mechanical centralization, but the *centralization of Communist activity*, i.e., the creation of a leadership that is strong and effective and at the same time flexible," the document explained. It elaborated: "Formal or mechanical centralization would mean the centralization of 'power' in the hands of the Party bureaucracy, allowing it *to dominate* the other members of the Party or the revolutionary proletarian masses outside the Party."[12]

Freedom of discussion, unity of action remains the shorthand definition of Lenin's understanding of democratic centralism. The creation of an inclusive, diverse, yet cohesive democratic collectivity of activists is something precious and necessary that serious revolutionaries must continue to reach for. It is not clear that the world can be changed without that.

Unfinished Leninism

As a serious Marxist theorist and educator, Alex Callinicos, in explaining the SWP commitment to the Leninist tradition, asks: "What does continuing a tradition mean?" He answers quite aptly that "genuinely carrying on a tradition requires its continuous creative renewal." This dovetails with points made by the organizational resolution that Lenin helped to prepare for the 1921 congress of the Communist International:

> There is no absolute form of organization which is correct for all Communists Parties at all times. The conditions of the proletarian class struggle are constantly changing, and so the proletarian vanguard has always to be looking for effective forms of organization. Equally, each Party must develop its own special forms of organization to meet the particular historically determined conditions within the country.[13]

Both the 1921 resolution and Callinicos's article, each in their own way, make the point that there has not arisen some qualitatively new form of organization—whether reformist or "movementist" or anarchist or syndicalist—that makes unnecessary the kind of revolutionary organization that Lenin sought to build. We will need something like that kind of organization in order to challenge capitalism effectively and to replace it with socialism. Some of the formulations Callinicos advances seem to indicate such an organization already exists in the form of the British SWP. To question whether that organization is actually *the* party of the revolutionary vanguard (as opposed as an element of the future organization that has yet to be forged) does not eliminate the underlying point: the centrality of revolutionary organization.

If there is truly the need for such a revolutionary organization—that is inclusive, diverse, democratic, and cohesive—then it seems clear that Leninism is far from "finished" in any sense of the word. It is something that is needed; it still has relevance. More than this, the organizational forms and norms associated with Leninism must be applied creatively and flexibly, continually adapting to the shifting political, social, cultural realities faced by revolutionaries. These forms and norms must never become a final, finished, closed system—they are necessarily open, fluid, unfinished. In seeking to accomplish what the Bolsheviks accomplished but to do it better, we need to engage with the *praxis* (thought and practical experience) of Lenin and his comrades, making use of it in facing our own realities. Much work remains to be done—the struggle continues.

Chapter Eleven
LENINISM FOR DANGEROUS TIMES

How can we move from capitalism's violent oppressiveness to the economic democracy, the genuine freedom, the socialism that we desire? This question was central to the life and work of V. I. Lenin. In exploring that, I want to spin my remarks around quotations from Georg Lukács, plus an old American Trotskyist, Lenin himself, and a couple of young British activists.

In 1924 Lenin died, several years after the brilliant intellectual Lukács had committed himself to the cause of working-class revolution and socialism. As a leader of the Hungarian Communist Party seeking to apply Karl Marx's ideas to the struggles of the workers and the oppressed, Lukács emphasized that Lenin's thought was infused by a sense of "the actuality of revolution," which would be essential in establishing (as Lukács put it) "firm guide-lines for all questions on the daily agenda, whether they were political or economic, involved theory or tactics, agitation or organization."[1] That is to say, Lenin was concerned in all of his political thinking and activity with the question of what must be done—actually, in the real world—for the workers to take power. Not rhetorically or theoretically, but *in fact*, to figure out what it would take and then to do exactly that.

Our purpose—as revolutionary socialists—is not simply to persuade people that socialism could be so much better than capitalism. Our purpose is not simply to protest, and organize protests, against capitalist injustice. Our purpose is not simply to organize struggles to bring about improvements under capitalism. Our purpose is not simply to interpret history and current events (or anything else) from a revolutionary socialist standpoint. Our primary purpose is to overturn existing power relationships, and to put political power into the hands of an organized, class-conscious working class (the class that we are part of, the class of the laboring majority), which is the key to establishing a socialist democracy. If we fail to do that, then our future—in my opinion—is suggested by that brilliant film *Children of Men* and by Rosa Luxemburg's prediction of a downward slide into barbarism as the alternative to socialism.

Now I want to tell you something about my friend Morris Lewit, who died at the age of ninety-five in 1998. It meant a lot to me to know him—a revolutionary working-class intellectual and activist who never gave up, who helped to make history and never turned away from his commitments and principles. He was born in the Russian Empire (in what is now known as Belarus) in 1903, the same year as the birth of Bolshevism, and he was a teenage participant in the Russian Revolution, the Bolshevik Revolution, and the Russian civil war, who in 1920 fled from the murderous onslaught of anti-Semitic and anticommunist White Armies that were funded by the governments of Britain, France, and the United States to crush the revolution. He found passage on a ship carrying immigrants to the United States, and on the ship he met a vivacious teenage Bolshevik activist named Sylvia Bleeker. They loved each other and became lifelong companions, members of the early Communist movement in the United States, immersed in trade union struggles, and by 1930—in reaction against the lethal infection in the Communist movement of Stalinist tyranny—members of the American Trotskyist movement. There is much more to be said about this tough but gentle man and his companion, class-struggle militants throughout the tumultuous 1930s and beyond. But here it is enough to note that in the 1940s, when the central leaders of the Socialist Workers Party (SWP) were imprisoned because of the organization's anti-imperialist position during the Second World War, Morris was chosen to be acting National Secretary of the SWP. In that capacity, under the party name of "Morris Stein," he said something that has been more than once been attacked as representing a negative quality in the Trotskyist tradition.[2] Before looking at that, I want to share other things he said at the same time, words that fit in with the Lukács notion of "the actuality of revolution."

In his 1944 remarks, Morris commented that "history has imposed on us a great mission, the mission of liberating humanity from the rotten putrid capitalist system." In his opinion "this fight is the only fight worth the sacrifice of one's freedom and even of one's life," and for him it involved "a responsibility that demanded that differences be resolved in the democratic way by majority vote rather than by the method of factional struggle, personal recriminations, et cetera." For Morris, this included a "spirit of collective leadership where the collectivity gives greater strength and greater wisdom to each individual." He added that "our revolutionary program and policy is best served by a party of democratic centralism," which he defined in the traditional Trotskyist manner as "centralism in action; fullest democracy in the internal life of the organization." He emphasized that "our movement must be imbued with the comradeship of people who are in the life-and-death struggle for a common cause."[3]

But now we come to the presumably poisonous aspect of Morris's remarks, in which he described the Socialist Workers Party of the United States in this way: "We can tolerate no rivals. The working class, to make a revolution can do it through only one party and one program. . . . We are monopolists in politics and we operate like monopolists. Either through merger or irreconcilable struggle. We have proved this by the whole history of our movement."[4] Before judging this statement, we need to understand its meaning. The history of the US Trotskyist movement involved decisions to merge with, not compete with, other revolutionary socialist forces on the left—the American Workers Party headed by A. J. Muste in the mid-1930s and the left wing of the Socialist Party in the late 1930s. There were also "irreconcilable struggles" against the authoritarian Stalinism dominating the Communist Party and against the thoroughgoing social-democratic reformism dominating the nonrevolutionary remnants of the Socialist Party. There was also the very sharp struggle with the split-off from the SWP led by Max Shachtman, although in 1947 there was, in fact, the prospect of a merger. That prospect was closed off by growing differences over the question of Cold War anticommunism and by the Shachtman group's gradual reformist trajectory.

Still, one can raise the question as to whether the Stein position was totally wrong. Should there be competing revolutionary socialist groups or is the merger of the different revolutionary groups preferable? On the other hand, can there be a merger of socialists who are revolutionary with socialists who are against revolution? Can there be a merger of socialists who insist on democracy with socialists who shrug it off? Can there be a merger of socialists who are anti-imperialist with socialists who are aligned with imperialism? Or is there a need for irreconcilable struggle of revolutionary socialists with those who are against democracy, those who are opposed to revolution, those who are aligned with imperialism? This suggests that there is a different way of understanding the Morris Stein remarks than that advanced by his critics.

But also Morris was speaking at a certain historical moment. The United States in 1944 had just come out of the great class struggles of the 1930s, and it was on the eve of a new wave of class-struggle militancy that would burst forth at the end of the Second World War. There was the significant layer of socialist and semi-socialist elements in the Congress of Industrial Organizations (CIO), and the Communist Party was at its numerical high point. All of this provided a certain context for the Morris Stein remarks. One can argue whether or not those remarks were the best ones to make or believe in the 1940s, but the orientation made little sense when I joined Morris's party in the quite different context of the 1970s. Those of us in that later period couldn't even understand the meaning of the Leninist concepts that had developed in that earlier context, although we read Lenin and considered ourselves Leninists. When I was in my twenties, as a member of the SWP back in the 1970s, I believed that the Left was divided up into three pieces: first, those who were the revolutionary vanguard—which meant those of us already in the SWP; second, those who were either our allies or contacts; and third, our opponents. We had a monopoly on Revolutionary Truth.

And when it first became clear to me that things began going terribly wrong in the SWP, as inevitably they did back in the early 1980s, I initially felt the darkest despair: if the revolutionary party, humanity's only hope, was fatally flawed, then there could be no real possibility of a socialist future. But as I turned (at the urging of an older comrade, George Breitman) to the study of the actual history of the Russian workers' movement in which Lenin and his comrades built an effective revolutionary party, I realized that many of us who considered ourselves Leninists suffered from a fundamental misunderstanding.

The revolutionary vanguard is not those who claim to be building a revolutionary vanguard party under the banner of Lenin. The vanguard is a broad layer of the working class that has a significant degree of class consciousness, that has some understanding of capitalism and the need to go beyond it, with some accumulated experience and commitment in the struggle against oppression and exploitation. Only when an organization has a significant membership base in this layer can it be considered a revolutionary vanguard party.

And that brings us to the Lenin quote. This can be found at the start of the second chapter in *Left-Wing Communism: An Infantile Disorder* where Lenin argues that there are three necessary conditions for a genuinely revolutionary party. First is the revolutionary class consciousness of a vanguard layer of the working class. Second is a correct political strategy and tactics on the part of organized revolutionaries. Third is an intimate and sustained contact "with the broadest masses of working people." Without these conditions being met, Lenin tells us, all attempts at a disciplined revolutionary party will "inevitably fall flat and end up in phrase-mongering and clowning."[5]

The class-conscious layers of the radicalizing working class prevalent in the early twentieth century and in the 1930s and 1940s did not exist, except as battered shreds and disconnected threads in the years of Cold War anticommunism and relative affluence that I grew up in and became politically active in. The organizations that claimed to be Leninist parties consequently tended to end up mired in phrase-mongering and clowning, which—far from sustaining contact with the broadest masses of working people—created little revolutionary universes. They believed they were repositories of Revolutionary Truth, and this made them dogmatic and rigid, with hostility and contempt for other left-wing groups that were very much like themselves. Organizational discipline in even the best of the groups had a dual function. On the one hand, it could quite positively enable relatively small groups to make outstanding contributions in mass movements against war, for racial justice, for women's liberation, and so on. But it also served to keep the membership of the organization in line, with an uncritical loyalty to the group's version of Revolutionary Truth, and to the group's leadership that oversaw the way that Truth was applied.

One problem with the Morris Stein "monopolist" formulation is that whatever validity it had was historically specific. For many years we have lived in a very different world than the one existing in the mid-1940s. Capitalism still exists, imperialism still exists, the working class still exists, as do the exploitation and oppression and crises that capitalism inevitably generates. But at the same time, all of these things are incredibly different. The working class of the 1940s is long gone, as is the working-class movement of that time. Both our own recomposed working class and the crisis-ridden, fluidly decomposing and recomposing working-class *movement* of our time bear little resemblance to what existed when Morris Stein forty-one years old.

The reality we face now and the way that Leninist ideas apply to that reality deserve much more consideration than I have time to offer here. But I want to conclude with a few thoughts that hopefully will be helpful. First of all, the turn capitalism has taken over the past few decades has knocked the stuffing out of our class, has ridden roughshod over its organizations and communities, has driven down its quality of life. More than this, there has been a proletarianization process engulfing and embracing many occupations and social layers once considered "middle class," while at the same time technology and globalization have eroded the industries that were once at the heart of working-class employment, replacing them with jobs that pay less and are less secure. And all of this has contributed to a slow-moving, contradictory, but intensifying radicalization process, and out of this process have been emerging new struggles, new forms of struggle, and a still-evolving crystallization of a new, diverse vanguard layer of the working class.

The possibilities now exist for the coming together of the kind of revolutionary party that Lenin spoke of. This means that no such party yet exists, and that no unified nucleus or core group of such a party exists—and none can yet exist until there is the crystallization of a radical working-class subculture capable of sustaining a class-conscious vanguard layer of a size substantial enough, in turn, to sustain the kind of genuine revolutionary party described by Lenin. My prediction and firm belief is that the core group, the nucleus, of such a party will be composed of activists who are currently in a number of different revolutionary groups, plus activists who are in no revolutionary group at all, plus some people who at this moment are neither revolutionaries nor activists—but who will become so in future struggles.

The responsibility of any revolutionary group worth its salt will be to help create the preconditions necessary for the emergence of such a party. One aspect of this will involve communicating to more and more people a socialist understanding of what is happening in our society and our world, and doing this in words and ways that will make sense to them. This means we must also develop a clearer comprehension of that reality. Related to this is the need to help define and initiate struggles, or join in already existing struggles, to win improvements in the here and now for more and more sectors of the working class and the oppressed.

And this brings me to the final quote, from authors of an imperfect but important book entitled *Beyond Capitalism?* that blends experience (for example) from the Occupy movement with Marxist insights. In that book, Luke Cooper and Simon Hardy say this: "The creation of new forms of political organization which draw upon the spirit of the social movements, rekindle grassroots trade union organization, and embolden participation of wider sections of society in social mobilizations is an orientation on which the success of the left ultimately depends." They elaborate on "the need to regroup the left in new political formations that provide a space for strategic thinking, that allow different strategies to co-exist in a certain tension, while also creating the conditions for unity and action." They explain that this should not be seen "as an excuse to avoid reflective, strategic discussion but as a starting-point through which we can move towards a greater degree of genuine unity."[6]

I think it is important for our different groups of the socialist Left *not* to rush into hothouse efforts to forge some premature organizational unity. Instead we should focus on working together in real, practical struggles, with an eye toward possible unity, but with a focus on the actual struggles. Those struggles are the necessary, transformative precondition for possible unity. The only fruitful unity will come on the basis of joint action in such real, practical struggles. If such unity is achieved, the result might be a democratic, durable, well-run organization of several thousand, with full-time organizers and new technologies being utilized to enable more and more people to become activist cadres working together to build local struggles, as well as advancing left-wing educational and cultural work, throughout the country. Such an organization could do a lot to lay the groundwork and create the possibility for the kind of revolutionary party we need.

Moving Forward to Build a Mass Socialist Movement

I very much appreciate Luke Cooper's excellent response to my "Getting Our Priorities Straight." It maps out much of the common ground between us, and it offers food for thought for those wanting to move forward to build the mass socialist movement that now appears to be a possibility. Given that agreement, and the fact that some of this simply needs to be lived through more before we can find additional things to say that are useful, I feel little need to "answer" him. But I do want to offer a few thoughts regarding my defense of Morris Stein, and related matters, in a way that I think addresses some questions posed for us as we seek to move forward together.

The Poetry of Dialectics

It seems to me that things move forward in part through the interpenetration of contradictory elements, and that sometimes there are different meanings embedded in one and the same thing—which constitutes one of the "laws" of poetry as well as dialectics, and of life itself. What Morris Stein (Lewit) said in 1944 he would not have said twenty years later, when the context within which he lived had radically altered, and it certainly was not the kind of thing he was saying in the 1980s and early 1990s when I knew him. To say such things in the later contexts would have been false, and in important ways to say "we are monopolists in politics" was false in 1944 as well. But to grasp the meaning these words had for Morris and his comrades we must give attention to the experience and context shaping that formulation.

The insights we can get from such contextualization may help us understand and deal more adequately with the challenges we face as revolutionary activists today and tomorrow. The seeming plausibility of what Morris said (which can only be grasped by daring to reach for its partial truth) highlights the nature of the experience that caused revolutionary socialists (in this case within the Trotskyist tradition) to view—correctly, in my opinion—the bankruptcy of Stalinism and social democracy even back then. It highlights the qualitative difference between the years when, through the tumultuous struggles of the 1930s, there had been a consolidation of a vanguard layer of the working class and our own time when such a layer is still in the process of recomposing. And it highlights the seriousness with which Morris and his comrades took themselves, which I still believe to be one of their exemplary qualities.

The kind of projections that Morris articulated in 1944 made sense (reflected elements of truth) given the possibilities and tasks of the moment: fighting hard to win the vanguard layer of the working class to the revolutionary program, which would open the way for socialist revolution.

From the different standpoint, however, of being aware of *contradictory qualities* among the Stalinists, among the social democrats, and among disparate others on the Left, and also from the standpoint of relating to *positive elements* among those contradictory qualities, the projections and formulations of the SWP in 1944 made less sense.

Related to this, in regard to how realities actually turned out, the formulations also made less sense than it seemed to the comrades at that time. Knowing what we know now, we can argue that the 1944 formulations—especially the "we are monopolists in politics" phrases—were quite simply wrong. The proof of this is the demonstrated dead-end sectarianism of groups that have continued to believe in and articulate that standpoint.

Beyond "Monopolism"

On the other hand, in the changed circumstances of the 1950s, Morris and his comrades were inclined toward the very different formulations of SWP leader James P. Cannon, as they explored possibilities of regroupment on the left. Consider these very non-monopolist remarks of Cannon at a meeting of diverse socialists in 1958:

> Socialists of different tendencies have begun to think of each other as comrades. Free discussion and fraternization, and sentiment for united action and regroupment of all the scattered forces, are the order of the day for us now everywhere. I say that's a good day for us and for our cause—the cause of American socialism.
>
> It doesn't bother me at all that, in a meeting such as ours, we have some criticism of each other; and that some things are said by one speaker that another can't fully endorse—that's not the significant thing about this great meeting tonight. The significant thing is that socialists of different tendencies stand together here on the same platform and urge united action against the capitalist class. . . .
>
> I want to turn the clock back to the good old days of solidarity and cooperation in practical action against the common enemy. Fraternal cooperation and solidarity in practical action do not exclude differences of opinion, do not exclude discussion and debate as we go along. There is no socialist life without free discussion of differences. But while we discuss our differences, we should also remember what we have in common as socialists, and act together in support of it.[7]

These remarks have, in my opinion, even more relevance in our present context than they did in the context that generated them fifty-five years ago.

There is one other point that must be made, however. The belief at the core of the 1944 comments of Morris Stein, and at the core of Cannon's 1946 remarks on "The American Theses" (which projected the Socialist Workers Party giving leadership to the "Coming

American Revolution") contributed to the survival of the SWP as a revolutionary element into the 1960s and 1970s.[8]

I was not recruited to revolutionary Marxist politics by the followers of Felix Morrow and Albert Goldman, who had abandoned revolutionary politics by the 1960s. I was not recruited by what remained of Max Shachtman's organization (although a left-wing split-off from it did influence me positively), nor was I recruited by the group around Bert Cochran that left the SWP in the 1950s but had disappeared by the early 1960s. All of these had important things to say, offered compelling insights, contained admirable people, made genuine contributions. But none of them survived as an organized force, with revolutionary perspectives intact and some credibility, capable of recruiting and helping to politically train the person that I was in the 1960s and 1970s. The SWP did survive as such a force, and it was able to grow and play a very positive role before succumbing to the contradictions that I have analyzed elsewhere.

What We Believe In

The convictions that Morris Stein expressed in 1944, and that Cannon expressed in defense of the "Theses on the American Revolution" in 1946, involved a belief in the need for and the possibility of a revolution in our society and our time, and also a belief in one's self and one's organization as elements that could be essential in bringing such revolution into being.

During a factional dispute in the early 1950s, with a current of incredibly fine, capable, and intelligent people led by Bert Cochran, Cannon argued that one of the characteristics of the opposition, nonetheless, was an element of demoralization, a loss of belief in this rock-hard revolutionary conviction. "They don't 'feel' that way," he commented, "and nobody can talk them out of the way they do feel." He went on to make an argument that was perhaps not entirely fair or balanced, but not entirely devoid of truth: "There is a line in the document of the Cochranites that sneers at the 1946 SWP convention and at the 'Theses on the American Revolution' adopted there. It says: 'We were children of destiny, at least in our own minds.' In that derision of the party's aspiration, the whole pessimistic, capitulatory ideology of Cochranism is contained."[9]

I do think there is something to this. I have seen it in many who went through the same negative SWP experience in the United States that I did in the 1980s, and who are inclined to move from having a sense of humor about it all (a good thing) to no longer being able to take any of it seriously (a bad thing, in my opinion). Whole organizations can be afflicted with this. There is so much intellectual modesty and humility (and "sophistication"), and lack of actual belief in revolutionary ideas and convictions, that the entire organization can be in a perpetual mode of brooding and drift, with a great deal of joking about revolutionary ideas and aspirations and little sense that we are capable of really changing the world. And some are incapable of even trying to be part of an organization, instead using the Internet as a substitute for real-world politics.

I think there are a number of instances when traumas of one kind or another shake good people out of organizations to which we were deeply committed, making them susceptible to such dynamics.

Yet ours is an amazing time, in which political and social and economic crises have generated a spreading and deepening radical ferment. The opportunities for revolutionary activism and growth are great. The possibilities of revolutionary socialist unity are very real. We must not be afraid to believe in ourselves as revolutionaries, and in our revolutionary aspirations and ideas. We must draw upon as many resources as we can, negative but also positive lessons from past comrades, as we attempt—in this wondrous new context—to move forward, and forward again, to realize the goal of building a mass socialist movement that can truly create a better world.

Chapter Twelve

ORGANIZING FOR TWENTY-FIRST-CENTURY SOCIALISM:
THE HISTORY AND FUTURE OF LENINISM

Keynote Presentation at Symposium on "Organizing for Twenty-First Century Socialism" in Sydney, Australia, June 8–9, 2013

Leninism is worth talking about not only for understanding some of what happened in history but also for helping change the world in the here and now of the early twenty-first century. I want to explain what I mean by the term *Leninism*, then touch on several historical controversies that may shed light on how to make use of this tradition in our ongoing political work. This will be followed by thoughts on ways to apply and contribute to the Leninist tradition in our practical efforts for the coming period.

In this particular period of radicalization and ferment, as activists are engaged in sorting through their own experiences, gathering more information about the realities related to those experiences, and engaging with the ideas and examples of revolutionaries who preceded us, a serious engagement with the Leninist tradition will be unavoidable.

That is not because this long-dead revolutionary can tell us all we need to know about building an organization, a movement, and a set of struggles capable of making a revolution. Lenin and his comrades lived in a very different time, functioned within a political, technological, and cultural context that was dramatically different from ours, and also Lenin got important things wrong—making mistakes that, unlike us, he can no longer learn from.[1]

Serious engagement with Leninism is unavoidable for serious activists because Lenin and his comrades developed an incredibly rich body of thought and experience as they faced the oppression and destructiveness and violence of capitalism, and this thought and experience had a powerful impact—for a time—in helping the workers and the oppressed to win important victories. Capitalism continues to exist, the working class continues to exist, various forms of capitalist oppression and destructiveness and violence continue to exist. That is really what the Occupy movement, the Arab spring, the anti-austerity rebellions, and the other insurgencies of our time are all about. So it makes sense to consider what the Leninist tradition may offer.[2]

Leninism's Meaning and Value

It has become common among some on the left to contrast Lenin's own thinking to what has come to be known as "Leninism." I don't accept that.

How can we best understand "Leninism"? In Joseph Stalin's influential 1924 classic, *The Foundations of Leninism*, we are told that "Leninism is Marxism in the era of imperialism and the proletarian revolution"—suggesting that if you wish to be a genuine Marxist, you cannot question but only embrace Lenin's ideas. This totalistic formulation is worth contrasting with the quite different formulations of three other prominent comrades of Lenin: Nikolai Bukharin, Gregory Zinoviev, and Leon Trotsky. In his valuable biography of Stalin, Robert C. Tucker indicates that Bukharin and Zinoviev refer to Leninism as Lenin's *retrieval* of Marx's revolutionary orientation or his *application* of Marx's ideas to Russian realities. Trotsky goes so far as to warn that—as Tucker paraphrases it—"a dogmatization of Lenin was contrary to the essentially non-doctrinaire, innovative, and critical-minded spirit of Leninism." In contrast, Stalin's "Leninism is Marxism" formulation presents Lenin's thought as the One True Marxism that could not be questioned. His 1924 booklet provides a condensed systematization that was "catechistic in style and authoritarian in tone," as Tucker aptly notes.[3]

Related to this, it is worth recalling a very fine 1977 essay entitled "Stalin, Lenin and 'Leninism'" by the late Valentino Gerratana (an outstanding scholar who did important work on the Italian Marxist Antonio Gramsci), who emphasized that "while he was still alive, Lenin was not regarded as a *source* of authority—even if he possessed considerable personal authority," flowing from the quality of his thought and political practice. The construction of an artificial "Leninism" *as a source of authority* (which could not be questioned, and thereby greatly empowered those claiming to represent it) was carried out most successfully and destructively by Stalin, whose dictatorship destroyed Leninism under the banner of Leninism, to paraphrase what one of his fiercest critics, dissident communist M. N. Riutin, wrote in the early 1930s.[4] Gerratana reflected:

> The reduction of Lenin's thought to a systematic, *concentrated* form, and the construction of a finished theoretical system, involved not only the exclusion of everything that was considered accidental to the development of his thought, but also the separation of the end-result from the process that generated it— from the oscillations, approximations, mistakes and corrections essential to the process itself. Moreover, it should be realized that the process remained incomplete, and was cut short at a moment of profound intellectual tension, when Lenin was searching with difficulty for a new way forward. Thus the whole project of his successors [who constructed this artificial "Leninism"] was from the start based on a mystification.[5]

Lenin was influenced by other thinkers. He was very much a part of what Lars Lih has called "the best of Second International Marxism." The so-called "Leninism" of closed, finished dogmas was incompatible with Lenin's entire approach to politics. But it can be argued that he helped generate a distinctive political approach and body of thought—for the sake of brevity one could refer to a genuine *Leninism*—to which it is worth giving attention.

Lenin's quite unoriginal starting point (shared with Karl Marx, Karl Kautsky, Rosa Luxemburg, and others) is a belief in the necessary interconnection of socialist theory and practice with the working class and labor movement. The working class cannot adequately defend its actual interests and overcome its oppression, in his view, without embracing the goal of socialism—an economic system in which the economy is socially owned and democratically controlled in order to meet the needs of all people.

This fundamental orientation is the basis for most of what Lenin has to say, which taken together constitutes what Marcel Liebman once called the "Leninism" of Lenin. The scope of his political thought is something I attempted to convey in my collection of his writings in *Revolution, Democracy, Socialism*. It embraces various aspects of the labor movement: class consciousness and culture, trade unions, social movements for reforms, the relationship of reform to revolution, electoral struggles, dynamics of party-building, united front coalitions, class alliances (especially the worker-peasant alliance), the interplay of democratic and socialist struggles, questions of nationalism and imperialism, ways of utilizing Marxist theory, and more.[6]

At certain points, Lenin's utilization of Marxism was different from some of what passed for Marxism among a majority of the world's socialists by 1919, when the Communist International was formed. What distinguished Lenin's Bolsheviks from many others is a refusal to make certain compromises, either with capitalist politicians or labor bureaucracies, and a determination to follow through to the end the implications of the revolutionary Marxist orientation as expressed in Lenin's writings. This suggests that there was a decisive element of difference, when all was said and done, between the kind of party that Kautsky was a member of in Germany and the kind of party that Lenin and his comrades were building in Russia. At the same time, as Neil Harding, Lars Lih, August Nimtz, and others have emphasized, Lenin's thought can most fruitfully be understood in continuity with that of Marx. As the reformist Eduard Bernstein once put it: "Do you know? Marx had a strong Bolshevik streak!"[7]

Lenin's Comrades

Another key point is that Lenin's ideas and practical political efforts cannot adequately be comprehended outside of the context of his comrades and cothinkers. It goes against the grain of Lenin's own method, and against what actually happened in history, to present Lenin not as one among a diverse collection of capable comrades, but as the one authoritative representative of True Marxism. While one can make a strong case that Lenin was the first among equals, it is quite simply wrong to be dismissive of his comrades as a collection of "yes men" and "yes women" or as an inadequate bunch who never measured up. A problem of many (though hardly all) of us in the Trotskyist tradition is a tendency to view other prominent Bolsheviks, aside from Lenin and Trotsky, simply as bunglers—they got it wrong, they misunderstood, they failed to remain true to the brilliance of their would-be mentor.

To think that a revolution can really be understood in that way, and to think that an effective revolutionary organization can be built according to such a model, is highly problematical.

Two of the favorite whipping boys for those wishing to elevate Lenin above his followers are Gregory Zinoviev and Lev Kamenev. Lars Lih has the distinction of being in the vanguard of those inclined to push back against the dismissal of these two close comrades of Lenin. His defense of Zinoviev is worth reading. While hardly uncritical, Lih writes: "Two comments by [prominent Bolshevik Anatoly] Lunacharsky seem to me to hit the right note: he called Zinoviev 'a person who had a profound understanding of the essence of Bolshevism' and one who was 'romantically' devoted to the party. I will present Zinoviev as someone who was under the spell of the Leninist drama of hegemony, but with a decidedly populist bent."[8]

Lih tells us that in the Soviet Republic in the early 1920s Zinoviev was insisting that "there should be a party reorganization to get cells closer to the factory floor. Party democracy—especially in the sense of free discussion—should be intensified as the basic means of party education." He adds (based on a critical examination of Zinoviev's writings): "My impression is that Zinoviev was genuinely concerned about the problems faced by ordinary people." Regarding his influence in the Comintern, Lih writes:

> Zinoviev's emphasis on the concept of hegemony makes one think of Antonio Gramsci. As a foreign communist, Gramsci would have dealt more with Zinoviev than with any other Bolshevik leader and must have been influenced by his particular understanding of Leninism. Certainly it would have been satisfyingly ironic if the despised Zinoviev turned out ultimately to have more enduring intellectual influence (via his talented pupil Gramsci) than any other top Bolshevik.[9]

I would argue that enduring intellectual influence can more rightly be credited to Lenin himself, and also to Leon Trotsky. Nor is this to suggest that Zinoviev was free from serious faults, some of which have been highlighted by revolutionaries who worked with him—Alfred Rosmer, Victor Serge, Angelica Balabanoff, and others. This was especially manifest in some of his functioning in the Communist International—in which he sought what turned out to be damaging shortcuts, sometimes resorted to dishonest and high-handed measures, helped to initiate a slanderous and destructive anti-Trotsky campaign, and launched a so-called "Bolshevization" campaign moving in the direction of a super-centralized Communist International in which decisions were made and orders enforced from Moscow, the seat of the Comintern—sometimes in later years referred to critically as "Cominternism" (for example, in James P. Cannon's 1953 speech "Internationalism and the SWP") and sometimes more recently as "Zinovievism." Cannon commented: "After the degeneration of the Russian party and the emergence of Stalinism, the centralism of the Comintern—which Trotsky and Lenin had handled like a two-edged sword, which they didn't want to swing carelessly—became in the hands of Stalin an instrument for suppressing all independent thought throughout the movement." Yet Zinoviev was the transitional figure in this negative development, especially when—closely aligned with Stalin from 1922 to 1926—he helped to develop an increasingly undemocratic theory and practice of "Leninism" that was soon turned against Zinoviev himself when he began to disagree with and resist the way Stalin's policies were unfolding.[10]

But Lih's emphasis on the need to take Zinoviev seriously as a revolutionary seems to me well placed, nonetheless. Lih also takes up the cudgels on behalf of Lev Kamenev, the target of Lenin's critique of a presumably ossified "Old Bolshevism" in 1917, for example in "The Ironic Triumph of Old Bolshevism: The Debates of April 1917 in Context" in the journal *Russian History* a couple of years back. Lars challenges the standard account of Lenin—against Kamenev's "old Bolshevik" objections—reorienting the Bolshevik party in preparation for the October Revolution, writing that "Kamenev seems to think he won the debate with Lenin in April 1917," and Lars suggests that Kamenev was right.[11] One need not agree fully with this reinterpretation of the April 1917 debate in order to appreciate Lih's positive contribution.

A partial dissent might be constructed by making reference to the memoirs of an eyewitness, Lenin's close comrade and devoted companion Nadezhda Krupskaya, a shrewd revolutionary in her own right. In her *Reminiscences of Lenin*, Krupskaya quotes Lenin to indicate his outlook in early 1917: "Without a doubt, this coming revolution can only be a proletarian revolution, and in an even more profound sense of the word: a proletarian socialist revolution. This coming revolution will show in an even greater degree, on the one hand, that only grim battles, only civil wars, can free humanity from the yoke of capital; on the other hand, that only class-conscious proletarians can and will give leadership to the vast majority of the exploited."[12]

Krupskaya described the presentation of the April Theses this way: "Lenin expounded his views as to what had to be done in a number of theses. In these theses he weighed the situation, and clearly set forth the aims that had to be striven for and the ways that had to be followed to attain them. The comrades were somewhat taken aback for the moment. Many of them thought that Ilyich was presenting the case in much too blunt a manner, and that it was too early yet to speak of a socialist revolution." She notes that Lenin's theses were published in the Bolshevik paper *Pravda*, followed by a polemic from Kamenev "in which he dissociated himself from these theses. Kamenev's article stated that they were the expression of

Lenin's personal views, which neither *Pravda* nor the Bureau of the Central Committee shared. It was not these theses of Lenin's that the Bolshevik delegates had accepted, but those of the Central Committee Bureau, Kamenev alleged."[13]

Krupskaya concluded: "A struggle started within the Bolshevik organization. It did not last long." Within a week, Lenin's position was upheld by the Bolshevik majority. This account is similar to what one finds in the accounts of other eyewitnesses—the Mensheviks Nikolai Sukhanov and Raphael Abramovitch, the Menshevik-turned-Bolshevik Alexandra Kollontai, and the Bolshevik-turned-Menshevik W. S. Woytinsky.[14]

There are three extremely important facts that emerge, however, in Lars Lih's account. First of all, Lenin did not feel bound by some rigid notion of "democratic centralism" to refrain from expressing his own views if they happened to be in contradiction to those of the formal leadership of the revolutionary party to which he belonged. For Lenin, revolutionary principles always trump organizational harmony, and this was an element essential to his conception of democratic centralism and revolutionary organization.

Second, an open debate between comrades in the pages of the party newspaper was by no means alien to the Leninism of the early Bolsheviks. Elsewhere Lih quotes from a 1925 history of the Bolshevik party written by a veteran Bolshevik organizer, Vladimir Nevsky, who tells us that democratic centralism represented "complete democracy," explaining that in 1917 "the organization of the Bolsheviks lived fully the life of a genuine proletarian democratic organization," with "free discussion, a lively exchange of opinions," taking place in "the absence of any bureaucratic attitude to getting things done—in a word, the active participation of emphatically all members in the affairs of the organization."[15]

Third is that the "Old Bolshevism" that Kamenev defended had been a collectively developed orientation, the common position of Lenin and the Bolshevik comrades with whom he now disagreed. Both the Bolshevik and Menshevik wings of Russian socialism had seen Russia's revolution as a "bourgeois-democratic"—preliminary to the future transition to socialism. But in 1917 no less than before, the politics of all Bolsheviks was grounded in a militantly class-struggle orientation distinct from the worker-capitalist alliance position of the Mensheviks, projecting an uncompromising worker-peasant alliance. This common ground between "Old Bolshevism" and the April Theses, rooted in the collectively developed politics over a period of years (not the blinding revolutionary authority of the Unquestioned Leader), is what made it relatively easy for Lenin to win the debate so quickly in 1917.

Communist International

There is another aspect of Leninism, often raised as a truly negative feature to be avoided by serious activists of today. That is the extreme, intolerant sectarianism purported to be at the very heart of the Communist International that Lenin and his comrades established, of which Gregory Zinoviev was the president in its early years. Sometimes critics of the form Leninism took beginning in the mid-1920s denounce it as "Zinovievism" (which we have already noted), but there is a tendency to extend this to the historical moment of the Comintern's earliest days. Some of what is being denounced, however, can more fairly be laid at Lenin's door—in particular the Twenty-One Conditions for affiliation to the Communist International.

Adopted at the 1920 Second Congress of the Comintern, this document began with an important explanation. The initial popularity of the Russian Revolution and the Communist International, among radicalizing workers of various countries, attracted some parties that were not actually in agreement with the revolutionary Marxist program of the new International, particularly some still led by reformist or semi-reformist leaders closely associated with the Second International. This meant that the Comintern "is in danger of being diluted by vacillating and irresolute groups that have not yet broken from the ideology of the Second International." This ideology had led to a general capitulation to the imperialist slaughter of World War I and the suppression of revolutionaries within the various organizations.

The incredibly strict conditions designed to prevent the possibility of such reformist dilution explicitly excluded any consideration of membership in the Comintern for well-known reformist socialists, insisting that Communist principles and organizational perspectives be strictly adhered to, with no organizational ties to the parties and trade unions associated with the Second International being permitted.

Some critics utilized this to dismiss Lenin and the Comintern as authoritarian and destructive. Such an ahistorical approach, however, not only ignores the historically specific context that caused the adoption of the Twenty-One Points but urges us to dismiss the efforts of countless revolutionaries who made the early Communist International a living reality. A serious examination of the immense, multivolume work on that entity by John Riddell and his colleagues, which includes considerable contributions on overcoming sectarianism, building united fronts, and so on, suggests the shallowness of such an approach.

This is not to insist that all aspects of the Twenty-One Conditions must be accepted or that any of them are beyond criticism. In order to begin a serious critique, however, it also makes sense to take seriously the reasons given for their adoption—reasons that at that particular moment in history may have had greater validity than some critics allow.

This brings us to a final point in this initial portion of my remarks. We are incredibly far from the specific realities of the Communist International or of the Socialist International or even of Karl Marx's International Workingmen's Association. In some ways we are far ahead of any of these—but in very important ways, socialists from these first three workers' internationals were far in advance of us. There is much to learn from the Leninist tradition. But one must use it critically and creatively for it to make sense in our own particular context and time period. That happens to be central to the method of Lenin.

Internationalism in Our Own Time

I will now turn, in the second half of my remarks, to thoughts on how we can utilize and contribute to the Leninist tradition as we struggle for socialism in the twenty-first century.

I gave a presentation in London last year on my thoughts regarding what I think it will take to engage fruitfully in the process of building a revolutionary party in the United States. What I said then still makes sense to me, but one of the comrades there made an excellent criticism. My comments involved an immersion in the specific realities in the United States—and I still think that what we do must be grounded in the local actualities and national specifics that we are part of. But she pointed out that the international dimension was largely missing, and I had to agree with her that this was a serious weakness. There were references to opposing war and imperialism, but that was about it.

For serious Marxists, however, internationalism has always involved more than that—and it has also involved much more than simply rhetorical solidarity with the struggles of the workers and oppressed of all lands. It especially means grounding our nationally specific politics in an understanding of what is happening with capitalism as a global system, and in creative interaction with sisters and brothers fighting against oppression and for economic justice throughout the world. Struggles, gains, and setbacks in one place impact struggles in other places. Important lessons learned here can provide incredibly useful lessons elsewhere. Experiences of those who struggle in other lands can not only inspire us but provide invaluable insights about what we might do next in our own contexts. This was true in the time of Lenin, as reflected, for example, in the amazing multivolume retrieval of material on the early Communist International that John Riddell and his coworkers have been making available to us. If anything, it is even more true in our much-vaunted age of globalization, in which working-class organizing and solidarity across borders will undoubtedly provide the key to winning strategies in both our short-term and long-term efforts to push back capitalist tyranny, and finally to end it.

Australian revolutionaries have been making cutting-edge contributions to the development of such internationalism, through conferences like this, and especially through the outstanding service provided online with *Links, the International Journal of Socialist Renewal*. The World Social Forum, at least in its earlier years, was also part of this global radicalization process. Vital contributions have also come from the dramatic proliferation of worldwide information sharing and communication through the Internet. Serious revolutionary groups in all countries, it seems to me, need to find ways to advance such virtual and face-to-face engagement, to strengthen the cooperative process of advancing our interrelated liberation struggles. Revolutionary internationalism must be more than a slogan, it should involve a collaboration and activities that are central to our efforts.

From Small Groups to Mass Parties

Many revolutionaries are faced with the challenge of how small socialist groups can give way to mass socialist parties and movements. A number of us have concluded that it is a fatal mistake for a small group to see itself as the nucleus or the embryo of a mass revolutionary party. Such a party will, in fact, be formed by the coming together of elements from a number of groups, as well as a number of people not presently in any group, and even more who do not presently think of themselves as socialists at all. It will crystallize through innumerable experiences and struggles, blending together with a broad labor-radical subculture of ideas, discussions, and creative activities. The creation of a genuine revolutionary party consistent with Lenin's own orientation can only come about on the basis of a substantial portion of a broad, class-conscious, vanguard layer of the working class. One of our primary jobs, as revolutionary socialists, is to do all that we can—through mass struggles, through socialist education, through working with others—to contribute to the crystallization of such a vanguard layer, a layer that will be the basis for a mass revolutionary party.

It is obviously important for existing small groups of socialists to work together, as much as they can, to advance this process—a process that will cause them to go out of existence by merging into the larger revolutionary party-to-be. Sometimes there is such a substantial overlap in the basic principles of the different groups that it makes sense for them to become a single, larger group as they work to help create the preconditions for a genuine mass revolutionary party. Sometimes there are obstacles that make such fusions unlikely or impossible—there may be fundamental disagreements around the process or desirability of creating a mass revolutionary party, there may be fundamental disagreements on how to relate to capitalist political forces, there may be fundamental disagreements around the relation of democracy to socialism. Such fundamental disagreements might mean that organizational unity is not in the cards—but there could still be the basis for, and the desirability of, what Lenin once called "fighting unity" and what are sometimes referred to as united fronts.[16]

In the midst of the 1905 revolutionary upsurge in Russia, Lenin argued against a call for all the different revolutionary groups to submerge their differences and unite in a single group. "In the interests of the revolution," he wrote, "our ideal should by no means be that all parties, all trends and all shades of opinion fuse in a revolutionary chaos." He referred to other "hasty and half-baked experiments" in such unity, seeking to "lump together the most heterogeneous elements" that achieved little more than "mutual friction and bitter disappointment." On the other hand, if diverse groups focus on how to advance a specific struggle around democratic rights or economic justice—agreeing to disagree on points of difference while cooperating to achieve a meaningful immediate aim—much can be achieved. As long as fundamental differences exist, Lenin insisted, "we shall inevitably have to march separately, but we can strike together more than once, and particularly now" amid the revolutionary insurgency.[17] History also shows us that, to the extent that practical experience eliminates fundamental differences, it becomes possible for different forces to come together into a single organization, with very positive results. This was the case at certain points in revolutionary Russia and in many other instances.

It appears that circumstances in Australia today may be contributing to some groups going beyond simply a "fighting unity" toward the achievement of an organizational unity that could greatly strengthen the efforts of revolutionary socialists. This experience is very exciting, and it is being watched and will provide invaluable lessons for revolutionaries in other countries.

Principled Flexibility

Related to this, it is worth noting another essential element in Lenin's methodology—the way he combined an insistence on the clarity of basic principles (those of revolutionary Marxism) with what might be called a principled flexibility. More than one person, including severe critics who knew him well among the Mensheviks, was struck by his extreme disinclination to make a show of his own knowledge, and by his deep desire to learn from others—especially fellow revolutionary activists, workers, and peasants. He understood that one must be able to listen and learn from those one wishes to teach, and that the development of knowledge is interactive and collective. He even learned from political opponents—the British liberal J. A. Hobson powerfully influenced his book *Imperialism: the Highest Stage of Capitalism*, anarchists influenced his classic *The State and Revolution*, the populists of the Socialist Revolutionary Party influenced him enough to cause him to steal their agrarian program of land to the peasants, and during the revolutionary upsurge of 1905 he scolded some Bolshevik comrades more drawn to revolutionary rhetoric than to practical workers' struggles, saying: "Take a lesson from the Mensheviks, for Christ's sake!"[18]

In more than one way, Lenin's theoretical approach was not a closed system but rather what can be called an open Marxism. He called it a guide to action, emphasizing that reality is always much more complex, vibrant, and multicolored than theory can ever be, and that theory must continually be developed and renewed through the engagement with actual political struggle and experience. That is the kind of Marxism we need in order to comprehend the rapidly evolving capitalism of our time, and the multifaceted and fluid realities of working-class life and experience. This involves dramatic shifts and fluctuations in regard to working-class occupations and the labor process, and the proletarianization of large swaths of the labor force not traditionally perceived of as "working class." It also involves the interplay of class with ethnicity, race, gender, religion, culture, and more. Lenin's approach helps to orient us to the amazing dynamics of globalization, and to understand that issues often perceived as "identity politics" are inseparable from class politics. This comes through in the famous passage in *What Is to Be Done?*, which is worth reminding ourselves of again and again:

> The Social-Democrat's ideal should not be the trade union secretary, but *the tribune of the people*, who is able to react to

every manifestation of tyranny and oppression, no matter where it appears, no matter what stratum or class of the people it affects; who is able to generalise all these manifestations and produce a single picture of police violence and capitalist exploitation; who is able to take advantage of every event, however small, in order to set forth *before all* his socialist convictions and his democratic demands, in order to clarify for *all* and everyone the world-historic significance of the struggle for the emancipation of the proletariat.[19]

This remains as true now as it was a hundred years ago.

The Centrality of Democracy

It also dovetails with the centrality of democracy to the working-class struggle for socialism that Lenin was emphasizing two years before the Bolshevik Revolution. It is also worth quoting at length, because it helps to define what we must be doing today in the struggle for socialism in our own century:

> The proletariat cannot be victorious except through democracy, i.e., by giving full effect to democracy and by linking with each step of its struggle democratic demands formulated in the most resolute terms. . . . We must *combine* the revolutionary struggle against capitalism with a revolutionary programme and tactics on all democratic demands: a republic, a militia, the popular election of officials, equal rights for women, the self-determination of nations, etc. While capitalism exists, these demands— all of them—can only be accomplished as an exception, and even then in an incomplete and distorted form. Basing ourselves on the democracy already achieved, and exposing its incompleteness under capitalism, we demand the overthrow of capitalism, the expropriation of the bourgeoisie, as a necessary basis both for the abolition of the poverty of the masses and for the *complete* and *all-round* institution of *all* democratic reforms. Some of these reforms will be started before the overthrow of the bourgeoisie, others *in the course* of that overthrow, and still others after it. The social revolution is not a single battle but a

period covering a series of battles over all sorts of problems of economic and democratic reform, which are consummated only by the expropriation of the bourgeoisie. It is for the sake of this final aim that we must formulate *every one* of our democratic demands in a consistently revolutionary way. It is quite conceivable that the workers of some particular country will overthrow the bourgeoisie *before* even a single fundamental democratic reform has been fully achieved. It is, however, quite inconceivable that the proletariat, as a historical class, will be able to defeat the bourgeoisie, unless it is prepared for that by being educated in the spirit of the most consistent and resolutely revolutionary democracy.[20]

The centrality of democracy in the struggle for socialism applies not only in the social and political struggles within society but also in the internal structure and practice of the socialist organization itself. In my book *Lenin and the Revolutionary Party* and in other places, I have written a great deal on the actual meaning and practice of the concept of "democratic centralism"—what Lenin defined as full freedom of discussion and unity in action, and others have written about as well. It has been documented that the Bolshevik organization had a considerable degree of internal democracy. We have already noted here how this changed dramatically under the rule of Joseph Stalin. That was a disastrous development largely rooted in the devastation and isolation of Soviet Russia in the midst of the civil war years, combined with the extreme economic backwardness and poverty of the Russian economy. This resulted in what were supposed to be emergency measures that, in fact, became permanent—which eliminated any genuine democracy in the Soviet Union, and also eliminated genuine internal democracy in all communist parties controlled by the Stalin leadership.

Internal Culture and Cadre Development

What we have found even among all too many anti-Stalinist organizations committed to revolutionary socialism are—in the name of Leninism and "democratic centralism"—practices that cut across the possibility of the kind of internal democracy that seems to have existed, historically, in Lenin's organization. Such internal democracy is one feature that made it possible for the Bolsheviks to be the kind of revolutionary force that triumphed in 1917. One of the reasons for the disappointing absence of that kind of democracy in many relatively small socialist groups in later years may have to do with a flaw in their self-conception. Some function more or less as sects, creating their own political universe that involves a self-conception that they constitute the "revolutionary vanguard" (or the politically correct nucleus around which a vanguard must form). The hope for the future is often seen as preserving the authority and ideological purity of this precious organization. This can engender ideological and organizational rigidities that distort the way that democratic centralism (particularly "full freedom of discussion") might be understood and practiced.

If our self-conception is that we do not yet have a revolutionary party (not even in embryo), and that our purpose is to help create the preconditions that might make the emergence of such a party possible, this could encourage a different kind of internal practice, in some ways matching the way we would be dealing with those outside of our group. A primary goal would be to generate more and more thought, experience, and creativity among one's comrades and others, as activists are working together in order to bring into being a force that can successfully challenge capitalism. There are indications, in fact, that such an extended pre-party process—even in underground conditions—existed through the 1890s and early 1900s among Marxist-oriented revolutionaries, creating a subculture that nurtured a genuine internal democracy as the Russian Social Democratic Labor Party (and its Bolshevik faction) finally took shape.

One of the revolutionaries-in-the-making from that time, Eugenia Levitskaya, later reminisced: "Turning over in my mind the mass of comrades with whom I had occasion to meet, I cannot recall a single reprehensible, contemptible act, a single deception or lie. There was friction. There were factional differences of opinion. But no more than that. Somehow everyone looked after himself morally, became better and more gentle in that friendly family." (This sense of things can be found in a different context many years later, when the veteran revolutionary James P. Cannon commented: "The true art of being a socialist consists in anticipating the socialist future; in not waiting for its actual realization, but in striving here and now, insofar as the circumstances of class society permit, to live like a socialist; to live under capitalism according to the higher standards of a socialist future.") A vibrant elaboration of this comradely subculture among Russian revolutionaries comes through in Maxim Gorky's novel of 1906, entitled *Mother*: "The purest in heart, the finest in mind are moving against evil and trampling falsehood underfoot." A central figure in this subculture, Lenin wrote in *What Is to Be Done?* about the organizational ideal of 1902 as "a close and compact body of comrades in which complete, mutual confidence prevails." Even amid the fierce polemical controversies among the Russian Communists in 1920, Lenin quoted Trotsky—with whom he was then in sharp disagreement—that "ideological struggle within the Party does not mean mutual ostracism but mutual influence."[21]

One of the most important elements in this subculture, I think, should be an inclusiveness that persistently and insistently works to overcome, in the revolutionary organization, the divisive oppressions of racism, sexism, heterosexism, and other destructive dynamics blighting human relationships in the larger society. At times this may generate painful tensions and conflicts. Scrupulously democratic process, combined with considerable thoughtfulness and sensitivity, will be needed to help maintain balance and cohesion as the organization works frankly and seriously toward fruitful results.

Such a general subculture contributes to the realization of a primary task for any revolutionary organization worth its salt—the development of durable cadres. By this term *cadre* I am referring to experienced activists, educated in political theory, analytically oriented, with practical organizational skills, who are able to attract new and train new members of the revolutionary organization, and also to contribute to expanding efforts in broader movements for social change. This means knowing something of the history of the class struggle and of broad liberation struggles, knowing the economic and political realities of society, knowing how to size up a situation, knowing how to interact with others to help communicate that knowledge to them, knowing how to organize meetings and political actions. Such qualities need to be developed among increasing numbers of people. The proliferation of such durable cadres is essential for all the life-giving struggles leading up to the possibility of socialist revolution.

Taking Power to Bring About Socialism

Lenin's thought, as Marxist philosopher Georg Lukács emphasized nine decades back, was infused by a sense of "the actuality of revolution," which would be essential in establishing (as Lukács put it) "firm guide-lines for all questions on the daily agenda, whether they were political or economic, involved theory or tactics, agitation or organization."[22] That is to say, Lenin was concerned in all of his political thinking and activity with the question of what it would take—actually—to take power. Not rhetorically or theoretically, but *in fact*, and then to do exactly that. Everything else we do politically must be geared to realizing that primary purpose.

I want to conclude with two additional notions on what may need to be done by a revolutionary party that really intends to implement the revolutionary-democratic approach for bringing about socialism that we saw Lenin laying out in the long quotation about democratic struggles offered a few minutes ago in this presentation. One notion has to do with ways that practical struggles in the here and now can be integrated into a strategy for the working class to take power. The other notion involves defining a bit more specifically what the socialism we are struggling for would look like, in order to help guide the practical struggles of today and tomorrow.

The "Old Bolshevik" strategic orientation that Lenin developed with his comrades involved the notion that a worker-peasant alliance would bring about the democratic revolution that would overthrow monarchist oppression and clear the way for an effective struggle for socialism. This was popularized into political agitation and mobilization around three demands: (1) an eight-hour workday for workers, (2) land redistribution for the peasants, and (3) a constituent assembly to establish a democratic republic. These came to be known as "the three whales of Bolshevism"—based on the popular Russian folktale that the world is balanced on the backs of three whales.[23]

What are the "three whales" of your own revolutionary perspective in Australia and ours in the United States? What is the strategic orientation that could bring the working class to power in society today, and how can this be expressed in popular and practical struggles in the here and now, in a way that can capture the imaginations of masses of people? Finding answers to such questions is a challenge facing revolutionary socialists of each and every country in the twenty-first century.

Other guidelines for the practical struggles of today and tomorrow need to be provided by the question of what the socialism we are struggling for would actually look like. It has become a tradition for Marxists to scoff, proudly and indignantly, that we cannot provide "utopian blueprints" of the future society, and there is validity to this. But it seems to me that present-day realities are eroding that validity.

For decades we have been treated to the spectacle of parties claiming to be socialist coming to power (or at least being voted into office) and then—in contradiction to their stated goals—carrying out so-called realistic policies designed to salvage and maintain one or another version of actually existing capitalism. In some cases, this is combined with implementing welfare-state social reforms; in other cases, it is combined with slashing previously implemented welfare-state reforms. Do we intend to do better than that? If so, we need to figure out how, and be able explain that to those whose mass support will be needed to make it so.[24]

If there is an alternative to the present impasse of capitalism, and to capitalism itself, we need to be able to say—quite specifically—what that would look like and, with at least some key specifics, how it would be done. It would involve a society free from poverty and unemployment, with decent education and health care and housing for all, with a secure economic infrastructure (including mass transit systems), and the elimination of air and water pollution, and of the destructive use of our natural resources. It would involve liberty and justice for all, with the free development of each person being the condition for the free development of all. This would involve an economic democracy, to ensure that society's economic resources would be utilized to make these proposed changes a reality.

Such things can be explained in ways that highlight how they can actually be carried out, based on real-world specifics. This can, in turn, provide the basis for immediate struggles—struggles whose beginning is in our present-day capitalist society, but whose end will take us beyond that framework to the future of genuine democracy and freedom. The socialism that we want can be embedded in the struggles of today and the victories of tomorrow. Some may see this approach as being somewhat akin to Leon Trotsky's "Transitional Program," although in the *Communist Manifesto* Marx and Engels seem to have sketched a similar approach, suggesting:

> In the beginning, this cannot be effected except by means of despotic inroads on the rights of property, and on the conditions of bourgeois production; by means of measures, therefore, which appear economically insufficient and untenable, but which, in the course of the movement, outstrip themselves, necessitate further inroads upon the old social order, and are unavoidable as a means of entirely revolutionizing the mode of production.[25]

The challenge for us is to get increasingly specific and practical about the socialist alternative to capitalism, building organizations and movements that can develop mass consciousness and mass struggles capable of bringing about that alternative. That's the point of what we're doing—the actuality of revolution, the culmination of what so many of us, so many of our brothers and sisters, have been struggling for over so many years, a socialist future to be created in the twenty-first century.

NOTES

Chapter Three: TRAVESTIES, STATUES, AND LAUGHTER

1. Tom Stoppard, *Travesties* (New York: Grove Press, 1975, 1993), 60. One could say that there is another serious political revolutionary in the play—Lenin's wife and comrade, Nadezhda Krupskaya—though her function in the play is basically to recount what Lenin thought and did.

2. On the recent revival at Princeton, see www.mccarter.org/travesties /index.html, and the post-performance panel discussion, www.mccarter.org/travesties/pages/conversation.html. On the other plays, see Tom Stoppard, *The Coast of Utopia* (New York: Grove Press, 2007); Tom Stoppard, *Rock 'n' Roll* (New York: Grove Press, 2007).

3. Edmund Wilson, *To the Finland Station: A Study in the Writing and Acting of History* (New York: Farrar, Straus and Giroux, 1972), 458.

4. Maxim Gorky, "V. I. Lenin," in *Lenin and Gorky: Letters, Reminiscences, Articles* (Moscow: Progress Publishers, 1973), 255, 271 (with a slight modification in translation). For fierce criticism of Lenin and his comrades, see Maxim Gorky, *Untimely Thoughts: Essays on Revolution, Culture, and the Bolsheviks, 1917–1918* (New Haven, CT: Yale University Press, 1995).

5. Angelica Balabanoff, *Impressions of Lenin* (Ann Arbor: University of Michigan Press, 1964), 149. (A slight modification in translation was made here.)

6. Two recent and excellent accounts of Marx and his ideas can be found in Mary Gabriel, *Love and Capital: Karl and Jenny Marx and the Birth of a Revolution* (New York: Little Brown and Co., 2011) and Terry Eagleton, *Why Marx Was Right* (New Haven, CT: Yale University Press, 2011). An early documented account of the Russian Revolution and Civil War, more or less corroborated by later scholarship, can be found in William Henry Chamberlin's 1935 work *The Russian Revolution, 191–1921*, 2 vols. (Princeton, NJ: University of Princeton Press, 1987).

Early journalistic accounts of Stalin's tyranny, more or less corroborated by later scholarship, can be found in William Chamberlin, *Russia's Iron Age* (Boston: Little Brown and Co., 1934) and Eugene Lyons, *Assignment in Utopia* (New York: Harcourt, Brace and Co., 1937).

7.   *Tom Stoppard in Conversation*, ed. Paul Delaney (Ann Arbor: University of Michigan Press, 1994), 64; Andrei Codrescu, *The Posthuman Dada Guide: Tzara and Lenin Play Chess* (Princeton, NJ: Princeton University Press, 2009), 14, 186, 187, 188; the journalistic comment that Codrescu challenges can be found in Arthur Ransome, *Russia in 1919* (New York: B. W. Huebsch, 1919), 122. A challenge to the view that "Lenin perverted Marxism" can be found in Lars Lih, *Lenin Rediscovered: "What Is to Be Done?" in Context* (Chicago: Haymarket Books, 2009) and Neil Harding, *Lenin's Political Thought: Theory and Practice in the Democratic and Socialist Revolutions* (Chicago: Haymarket Books, 2009). Challenges to the conceptualization of Lenin as a mass murderer can be found in Moshe Lewin, *Russia/USSR/Russia: The Drive and Drift of a Superstate* (New York: Pantheon, 1995) and Moshe Lewin, *The Soviet Century* (London: Verso, 2005). Of course, any head of state in time of war (including Winston Churchill, Franklin D. Roosevelt, and others) can be characterized as a mass murderer, though it is not clear that this is Codrescu's meaning.

8.   Robert Conquest, *The Great Terror: A Reassessment* (New York: Oxford University Press, 1990), 251; Hannah Arendt quoted in Elisabeth Young-Bruehl, *Hannah Arendt: For Love of the World* (New Haven, CT: Yale University Press, 1982), 411; Whittaker Chambers, "The End of a Dark Age Ushers in New Dangers," *Life*, April 30, 1956, reprinted in *Ghosts on the Roof, Selected Essays*, ed. Terry Teachout (New Brunswick, NJ: Transaction Publishers, 1996), 280. Similar points emerge in a classic anthology of informed anticommunist writings, *Verdict of Three Decades: From the Literature of Individual Revolt Against Soviet Communism: 1917–1950*, ed. Julien Steinberg (New York: Duell, Sloan and Pearce, 1950), and in the study by George F. Kennan, scholarly and acute US Ambassador to Soviet Russia in the time of Stalin: *Russia and the West Under Lenin and Stalin* (New York: New American Library, 1962). For much information relevant to these questions, see the magisterial study by Arno J. Mayer, *The Furies: Violence and Terror in the French and Russian Revolutions* (Princeton, NJ: Princeton University Press, 2000). Indispensible are two volumes by Robert C. Tucker—*Stalin as Revolutionary: 1879–1929* (New York: W. W. Norton, 1992) and *Stalin in Power: The Revolution From Above, 1928–1941* (New York: W. W. Norton, 1992). Also see Paul Le Blanc, *Marx, Lenin and the Revolutionary Experience: Studies of Communism and Radicalism*

in the Age of Globalization (New York: Routledge, 2006) from which some of the material in this discussion is drawn.

9. Stefan T. Possony, *Lenin: The Compulsive Revolutionary* (Chicago: Henry Regnery Co., 1964), vii, 392. A more recent study consistent with this is Helen Rappaport, *Conspirator: Lenin in Exile* (New York: Basic Books, 2010), interweaving considerable research with political hostility and personal denigration. For what strike me as more reliable biographies, see Ronald W. Clark, *Lenin: A Biography* (New York: Harper and Row, 1988), and Lars T. Lih, *Lenin* (London: Reaktion, 2011).

10. A classic articulation of the conservative outlook can be found in Russell Kirk, *The Conservative Mind: From Burke to Eliot* (Chicago: Henry Regnery Co., 1960). On Possony's elitism and racism, see Nathaniel Weyl and Stefan Possony, *The Geography of Intellect* (Chicago: Henry Regnery Co., 1963), 144, 147, 266, 267, 268, 271, 288, 289.

11. Leon Trotsky, *On Lenin* (London: George G. Harrap and Co., 1971), 166–67; Kennan, *Russia and the West Under Lenin and Stalin,* 243.

12. Carter Elwood, *The Non-Geometric Lenin: Essays on the Development of the Bolshevik Party 1910–1914* (London: Anthem Press, 2011), xiv, xvii, xviii.

13. Isaac Don Levine, *The Man Lenin* (New York: Thomas Seltzer, 1924), 13, 36, 157, 160, 176.

14. Ibid., 179, 192, 193. For more on Lenin's personal life, see Tamara Deutscher, *Not by Politics Alone: The Other Lenin* (London: George Allen and Unwin, 1973).

15. John Fleming, *Stoppard's Theatre: Finding Order Amid Chaos* (Austin: University of Texas Press, 2001), 118, 119; Max Eastman, *Artists in Uniform: A Study of Literature and Bureaucratism* (New York: Octogon Press, 1972),146; Robert C. Tucker, ed., *The Lenin Anthology* (New York: W. W. Norton, 1975), 148.

16. Vladimir Ilyich Lenin, *On Culture and Cultural Revolution* (Honolulu, HI: University Press of the Pacific, 2001), 247, 233, 234.

17. Gorky, *Untimely Thoughts,* 268; Trotsky, *On Lenin,* 165; Anatoly Lunacharsky, *Revolutionary Silhouettes* (New York: Hill and Wang, 1967), 41; Clare Sheridan, *Mayfair to Moscow—Clare Sheridan's Diary* (New York: Boni and Liveright, 1921), 120.

18. Kennan, *Russia and the West Under Lenin and Stalin,* 244.

19. For more on Lenin's perspectives, see V. I. Lenin, *Revolution, Democracy, Socialism: Selected Writings,* ed. Paul Le Blanc (London: Pluto Press, 2008) and Paul Le Blanc, *Lenin and the Revolutionary Party* (Amherst, NY: Humanity Books, 1993). Also see the slideshow on Lenin (along with slideshows on Marxism, Leon, Trotsky, and Rosa Luxemburg): http://getpoliticalnow.com/political-lives/.

20. See for example, the reportage and reflections of BBC journalist Paul Mason, *Why It's Kicking Off Everywhere: The New Global Revolutions* (London: Verso, 2012).

21. For example, Stoppard makes fun (appropriately) of Lenin's desperate but sometimes absurd schemes for getting back into Russia as the anti-tsarist revolution is unfolding—and at one point, in an attempt to develop a disguise, he puts on a curly blond wig. It might make sense, and be more in character, for Lenin and Krupskaya themselves to burst into laughter (joining in the audience's mirth) at such silliness.

Chapter Four: STILL KICKING: LENIN AND HIS BIOGRAPHERS

1. Christopher Read, *Lenin: A Revolutionary Life* (London/New York: Routledge, 2005), 284; Hannah Arendt, *On Revolution* (London: Penguin Books, 1990), 65.

2. Some of the debate can be found online though *Links: International Journal of Socialist Renewal*, http://links.org.au/taxonomy/term/665.

3. Robert Service, *Lenin: A Political Life*, vol. 3 (Bloomington, IN: University of Indiana Press, 1995), 323; Robert Service, *Lenin: A Biography* (Cambridge, MA: Harvard University Press, 2000), 493.

4. Helen Rappaport, *Conspirator: Lenin in Exile* (New York: Basic Books, 2010), ix, 217–18, 219, 221, 306, 355.

5. Carter Elwood, *The Non-Geometric Lenin: Essays on the Development of the Bolshevik Party 1910–1914* (London/New York: Anthem Press, 2011).

6. This new point, along with much else, is challenged in a fine and appreciative review by Lars Lih, "The Non-Geometric Elwood," *Canadian Slavonic Papers/Revue canadienne des slavistes* 74, nos. 1–2, March–June/mars–juin, 2012, 45–73.

7. Katy Turton, *Forgotten Lives: The Role of Lenin's Sisters in the Russian Revolution, 1864–1937* (London/New York: Palgrave Macmillan, 2007), 2, 4, 19–23, 26, 27.

8. Philip Pomper, *Lenin's Brother: The Origins of the October Revolution* (New York: W. W. Norton, 2010), 205, 206, 207.

9. Beryl Williams, *Lenin* (Harlow, UK: Longman, 2000), 205–06.

10. James D. White, *Lenin: The Practice and Theory of Revolution* (Houndmills, UK: Palgrave, 2001), 202.

11. The outstanding work on Lenin and religion is Roland Boer, *Lenin, Religion and Theology* (New York: Palgrave Macmillan, 2013).

12. Read, *Lenin: A Revolutionary Life*, 171.

13. Ibid., 29. Something akin to this notion emerged in the later writings of one of the most important witnesses of and participants in the history we are studying, Victor Serge (who does not, however, simply reject the Bolshevik-Leninist ideals to which he committed much of his

life). See, for example, the new and restored edition of his rich and illuminating *Memoirs of a Revolutionary* (New York: New York Review of Books, 2012), 155–58, and one of his last articles, "The Socialist Imperative," *Partisan Review* 14, no. 5 (September–October, 1947). Also see Susan Weissman, *Victor Serge: The Course Is Set on Hope* (London: Verso, 2001), 47–49, 267–77.

14. Read, *Lenin: A Revolutionary Life*, 59, 61, 62, 63.
15. Ibid., 128, 207, 234.
16. Ibid., 66, 73, 146, 148, 87, 190.
17. Ibid., 78, 93, 190–91.
18. Ibid., 148, 168, 169.
19. Ibid., 146, 225.
20. Ibid., 174.
21. V. I. Lenin, *Revolution, Democracy, Socialism, Selected Writings*, ed. Paul Le Blanc (London: Pluto Press, 2008), 279–80.
22. Read, *Lenin: A Revolutionary Life*, 208.
23. Ibid., 200, 251.
24. Ibid., 291, 288.
25. Lars Lih, *Lenin* (London: Reaktion, 2011), 13.
26. Ibid., 203, 205.
27. Ibid., 13.
28. D. S. Mirsky, *Lenin* (London: Holme Press, 1931), 192; Paul Le Blanc, "Lenin's Marxism," *Platypus Review*, May 2011 (http://platypus1917.org/2011/05/05/lenin%E2%80%99s-marxism); Le Blanc, *Lenin and the Revolutionary Party*; David Riazanov, *Karl Marx and Friedrich Engels: An Introduction to Their Lives and Work* (New York: Monthly Review Press, 1974); August H. Nimtz, Jr., *Marx and Engels: Their Contribution to the Democratic Breakthrough* (Albany, NY: State University of New York Press, 2000). August Nimtz, in a critical review of Lih's *Lenin Rediscovered*, "A Return to Lenin—But Without Marx and Engels?," *Science & Society*, October 2009, argues that Lenin's primary inspiration was Marx, not Kautsky. The seeming distance between Nimtz and Lih narrowed as their *agreement* on the primacy of Marx (not Kautsky) for Lenin became clear, and with their agreement that after 1914 Lenin continued to respect the pre-1910 Kautsky.
29. Lih, *Lenin*, 13, 15.
30. Read, *Lenin: A Revolutionary Life*, 291.

Chapter Five: LENIN AND REVOLUTIONARY DEMOCRACY

1. Paul Le Blanc, "Introduction: Ten Reasons for Not Reading Lenin," in *Revolution, Democracy, Socialism*, 63, 65. Examples of the anti-Lenin interpretation can be found in Bertram D. Wolfe, *Lenin and the Twen-*

tieth Century (Stanford, CA: Hoover Institution, 1984); Leonard Schapiro, *The Communist Party of the Soviet Union* (New York: Vintage Books, 1960); Richard Pipes, *The Russian Revolution* (New York: Alfred A Knopf, 1991). Also see an early salvo in the current scholarly critique of this interpretation in Lars T. Lih, "How a Founding Document Was Found, or One Hundred Years of Lenin's What Is to Be Done?" *Kritika: Explorations in Russian and Eurasian History* 4, no. 1 (Winter 2003): 5–49.

2. Paul Le Blanc, *Marx, Lenin, and the Revolutionary Experience: Studies of Communism and Radicalism in the Age of Globalization* (New York: Routledge, 2006).

3. John Reed, *Ten Days That Shook the World* (New York: Signet Books, 1967), 114.

4. N. K. Krupskaya, *Reminiscences of Lenin* (New York: International Publishers, 1979), 96, 205, 211, 229.

5. Reed, *Ten Days*, 256.

6. N. N. Sukhanov, *The Russian Revolution 1917: A Personal Record* (Princeton, NJ: Princeton University Press, 1984), 279–80, 289.

7. Albert Rhys Williams, *Lenin: The Man and His Work* (New York: Scott and Seltzer, 1919), 45, 48; Albert Rhys Williams, *Journey into Revolution: Petrograd, 1917–1918* (Chicago: Quadrangle Books, 1969), 51, 62.

8. N. Bukharin and E. Preobrazhensky, *The ABC of Communism* (Harmondsworth, UK: Penguin Books, 1969), 63, 65.

9. Gregory Zinoviev, *History of the Bolshevik Party from the Beginnings to February 1917: A Popular Outline* (London: New Park Publications, 1973), 78.

10. V. I. Lenin, "Urgent Tasks of Our Movement," in *Collected Works*, vol. 4 (Moscow: Progress Publishers, 1972), 370–71.

11. Lars Lih, *Lenin Rediscovered: "What Is to Be Done?" in Context* (Leiden/Boston: Brill, 2006).

12. Max Eastman, *Marx, Lenin and the Science of Revolution* (London: George Allen & Unwin, 1926), 159–60. Compare this to Eric Hobsbawm's more recent reflection in *The Age of Extremes: A History of the World, 1914–1991* (New York: Vintage Books, 1996), 76: "The force of the movements for world revolution lay in the communist form of organization, Lenin's 'party of a new type,' a formidable innovation of twentieth-century social engineering, comparable to the invention of Christian monastic and other orders of the Middle Ages. It gave even small organizations disproportionate effectiveness because the party could command extraordinary devotion and self-sacrifice from its members, more than military discipline and cohesiveness, and a total concentration on carrying out party decisions at all costs." He adds

that the success of such organizations, as revolutionary parties, "depends on what happens among the masses."

13. Soma Marik, *Reinterrogating the Classical Marxist Discourses of Revolutionary Democracy* (Delhi, India: Aakar, 2008), 289.

14. J. Arch Getty and Oleg V. Naumov, *The Road to Terror: Stalin and the Self-Destruction of the Bolsheviks, 1932–1939* (New Haven, CT: Yale University Press, 1999), 11.

15. Williams, *Journey into Revolution*, 326–27; Robert C. Tucker, *Stalin in Power: The Revolution from Above, 1928–1941* (New York: W. W. Norton, 1992), 8, 65.

16. Alan Adler, ed., *Theses, Resolutions and Manifestos of the First Four Congresses of the Third International* (London: Ink Links, 1980), 235.

17. See, for example, Leon Trotsky, *History of the Russian Revolution*, Three Volumes in One (New York: Simon and Schuster, 1936). A survey of later social history consistent with such an analytical narrative can be found in Ronald G. Suny, "Toward a Social History of the October Revolution," *American Historical Review* 88, no. 1 (February 1983). A fine piece of recent scholarship, Kevin Murphy's *Revolution and Counterrevolution: Class Struggle in a Moscow Metal Factory* (New York: Berghahn Books, 2005), extends this mode of analysis into the post-revolutionary period.

18. An important, if one-sided, contribution on this tragic evolution can be found in Simon Pirani, *The Russian Revolution in Retreat, 1920–24: Soviet Workers and the New Communist Elite* (London: Routledge, 2008), but also see Paul Le Blanc, "Bolshevism and Revolutionary Democracy," *New Politics*, Winter 2009.

19. Isaac Steinberg, *Spiridonova: Revolutionary Terrorist* (Freeport, NY: Books for Libraries Press, 1971), 235–36. For detailed documentation, see George Leggett, *The Cheka: Lenin's Political Police* (Oxford: Clarendon Press, 1981).

20. Albert Rhys Williams, *Through the Russian Revolution* (New York: Monthly Review Press, 1967), 276–77, 278.

21. Victor Serge, *Memoirs of a Revolutionary* (London: Writers and Readers, 1984), 132–33.

22. Lenin's comments are gathered together in Paul Le Blanc, *From Marx to Gramsci: A Reader in Revolutionary Marxist Politics* (Amherst, NY: Humanity Books, 1996), 59; and Paul Le Blanc, *Lenin and the Revolutionary Party* (Amherst, NY: Humanity Books, 1993), 341–42.

23. Leon Trotsky, "The New Course," in *The Challenge of the Left Opposition, 1923–25*, ed. Naomi Allen (New York: Pathfinder Press, 1975), 127, 134–35.

24. Victor Serge, *Year One of the Russian Revolution* (Chicago: Holt, Rinehart and Winston, 1972), 60–61.

25. Getty and Naumov, *The Road to Terror*, 8.
26. Leon Trotsky, "What Next?" in *The Struggle Against Fascism in Germany*, ed. George Breitman and Merry Maisel (New York: Pathfinder Press, 1971), 213.
27. Paul Le Blanc, *Marx, Lenin, and the Revolutionary Experience: Studies of Communism and Radicalism in the Age of Globalization* (New York: Routledge, 2006), 133–34. Also see Sobhanlal Datta Gupta, ed., *The Ryutin Platform: Stalin and the Crisis of the Proletarian Dictatorship, Platform of the "Union of Marxists-Leninists"* (Kolkata, India: Seribaan, 2010).
28. Moshe Lewin, *The Soviet Century* (London: Verso, 2005), 308.
29. Michal Reiman, *The Birth of Stalinism: The USSR on the Eve of the "Second Revolution"* (Bloomington, IN: Indiana University Press, 1987), 119.
30. Roy Medvedev, *Let History Judge: The Origins and Consequences of Stalinism*, Revised Edition (New York: Columbia University Press, 1989); Vadim Z. Rogovin, *1937, Stalin's Year of Terror* (Oak Park, MI: Mehring Books, 1998) and *Stalin's Terror of 1937-1938: Political Genocide in the USSR* (Oak Park, MI: Mehring Books, 2009); Wendy Z. Goldman, *Terror and Democracy in the Age of Stalin: The Social Dynamics of Repression* (Cambridge: Cambridge University Press, 2007).
31. On "Western Marxism," see Perry Anderson, *Considerations on Western Marxism* (London: Verso, 1979). Gramsci's political writings and prison notebooks up to the 1930s stand together with four works stretching from 1923 to 1929 by Lukács as outstanding additions to an authentic Leninism. For Gramsci, see *Selections from Political Writings 1910–1920* (New York: International Publishers, 1977), *Selections from Political Writings 1921–1926* (New York: International Publishers, 1978), and *Selections from the Prison Notebooks* (New York: International Publishers, 1971); for Lukács, see *History and Class Consciousness: Studies in Marxist Dialectics* (Cambridge, MA: MIT Press, 1971), *Lenin: A Study in the Unity of His Thought* (Cambridge, MA: MIT Press, 1971), *A Defence of "History and Class Consciousness"—Tailism and the Dialectic* (London Verso, 2000), and "Blum Theses, 1928–1929," in *Tactics and Ethics: Political Essays, 1919–1929* (New York: Harper and Row, 1973). The works of Trotsky also fit into this category—a valuable survey can be found in Kunal Chattopadhyay, *The Marxism of Leon Trotsky* (Kolkata, India: Progressive Publishers, 2006). An immense if imperfect chronicle can be found in Robert J. Alexander, *International Trotskyism 1929–1985: A Documented Analysis of the Movement* (Durham, NC: Duke University Press, 1991), but also see the Encyclopedia of Trotskyism On-Line (http://www.marxists.org/history/etol/index.htm) and Bill Dunn and Hugo Radice, eds., *100 Years of Permanent Revolu-*

tion, Results and Prospects (London: Pluto Press, 2006).

32. This is discussed further in Paul Le Blanc, "Lenin's Return," *WorkingUSA: The Journal of Labor and Society* 10, no. 3 (August 2007): 273–85.

Chapter Six: THE GREAT LENIN DEBATE OF 2012

1. See Paul Le Blanc, "Lenin's Return," and also my introductory essay "Ten Reasons for Not Reading Lenin," in *V. I. Lenin: Revolution, Democracy, Socialism; Selected Writings*, ed. Paul Le Blanc (London: Pluto Press, 2008), 3–80.

2. Most of the relevant material in the debate can be found through *Links: International Journal of Socialist Renewal*, http://links.org.au/taxonomy/term/665.

3. Despite problems in Pham's methodology, he usefully drew attention to the fact that Lenin did not have the intention, in 1912, of creating the "party of a new type" attributed to him by many—for example, P. N. Pospelov et al., *Lenin: A Biography* (Moscow: Progress Publishers, 1965), 82, 189–91, and Bertram D. Wolfe, "A Party of a New Type," in *Lenin and the Twentieth Century: A Bertram D. Wolfe Retrospective*, ed. Lennard D. Gerson (Stanford: Hoover Institution Press, 1984), 12–41.

4. Material relevant to this can be found in: Paul Le Blanc, *From Marx to Gramsci* (Atlantic Highlands, NJ: Humanities Press, 1996), especially 2–23; Isaac Deutscher, "Marxism in Our Time," in *Marxism in Our Time* (San Francisco: Ramparts Press, 1971), 15–30; Victor Kiernan, "History," in *Marx: The First Hundred Years*, ed. David McLellan (Oxford, UK: Fontana Paperbacks, 1983), 57–102; Eric Hobsbawm, "Marx and History," *New Left Review* 1, no.143 (January–February 1984); Ernest Mandel, *The Place of Marxism in History* (Atlantic Highlands, NJ: Humanities Press, 1996); Terry Eagleton, *Why Marx Was Right* (New Haven, CT: Yale University Press, 2011).

5. For interesting and informative discussions on the discipline of history, see: Edward Hallet Carr, *What Is History?* (New York: Vintage Books, 1961); Richard J. Evans, *In Defense of History* (New York: W. W. Norton, 2000); Alex Callinicos, *Theories and Narratives: Reflections on the Philosophy of History* (Durham, NC: Duke University Press, 1995).

6. See extensive discussion and documentation in Paul Le Blanc, "The Lenin Wars: Over a Cliff with Lars Lih," *Links*, February 12, 2012, http://links.org.au/node/2752.

7. Lars Lih, "A Faction Is Not a Party," *Weekly Worker*, May 3, 2012, http://www.cpgb.org.uk/article.php?article_id=1004820; for the article on 1912, see Paul Le Blanc, "The Birth of the Bolshevik Party in 1912," *Links*, April 17, 2012, http://links.org.au/node/2832.

8.   Christopher Read, *Lenin: A Revolutionary Life* (London/New York: Routledge, 2005), 78.

9.   Rosa Luxemburg, "Credo: On the State of Russian Social Democracy," in *The Rosa Luxemburg Reader*, Peter Hudis and Kevin Anderson, eds. (New York: Monthly Review Press, 2004), 269, 272, 273.

10.   Lars Lih, "Bolshevism and Revolutionary Social Democracy," *Weekly Worker* 917, June 7, 2012, http://www.cpgb.org.uk/article.php?article _id=1004864.

11.   These points are made in Paul Le Blanc, *Lenin and the Revolutionary Party* (Amherst, NY: Humanity Books, 1996), 360, 372.

12.   Read, *Lenin: A Revolutionary Life*, 226. A faulty interpretation of this last quote, in my opinion, is presented in Paul Kellogg, "Leninism: It's Not What You Think," *Links: International Journal of Socialist Renewal*, http://links.org.au/node/1407, which has Lenin dismissing a presumably bungled and dogmatic text on party organizational principles, allegedly adopted by the Communist International due to the highhandedness of Gregory Zinoviev, a document that, we are told, Lenin himself had no hand in writing. In fact, Lenin actively assisted Otto Kuusinen in the drafting of the document and was very supportive of it— see Aino Kuusinen, *The Rings of Destiny: Inside Soviet Russia from Lenin to Brezhnev* (New York: William Morrow and Co., 1974), 37, and Lenin's letters to Otto Kuusinen and Wilhelm Koenen in *Collected Works*, vol. 42 (Moscow: Progress Publishers, 1971), 316–19, and to Gregory Zinoviev in *Collected Works*, vol. 45 (Moscow: Progress Publishers, Publishers), 185–86. Also see John Riddell, ed., *Toward the United Front: Proceedings of the Fourth Congress of the Communist International, 1922* (Leiden/Boston: Brill, 2012), 303–305. My own quite different interpretation of the material Kellogg deals with can be found in *Lenin and the Revolutionary Party*, 316–17.

13.   Carter Elwood, "Lenin and *Pravda*, 1912–1914," in Carter Elwood, *The Non-Geometric Lenin: Essays on the Development of the Bolshevik Party 1910–1914* (London/New York: Anthem Press, 2011), 37–55. For a fine review of this volume, see Lars T. Lih, "The Non-Geometric Elwood," *Canadian Slavonic Papers/Revue canadienne des slavistes* 54, nos. 1–2, March–June/mars–juin, 2012, 45–73.

14.   Quoted in Robert C. Tucker, *Stalin as Revolutionary 1879–1929* (New York: W. W. Norton, 1978), 51.

15.   N. K. Krupskaya, *Reminiscences of Lenin* (New York: International Publishers, 1970), 89.

16.   Kamenev quoted in Le Blanc, *Lenin and the Revolutionary Party*, 19.

17.   Lars Lih, *Lenin* (London Reaktion, 2011), 188; Read, *Lenin: A Revolutionary Life*, 208.

18. Isaac Deutscher, "Marxism and Nonviolence," in *Marxism in Our Time*, 86. Also see Read, *Lenin: A Revolutionary Life*, 246–55, and Arno J. Mayer, *The Furies: Violence and Terror in the French and Russian Revolutions* (Princeton, NJ: Princeton University Press, 2002).

19. Among sources useful for this effort are: Alexander Rabinowitch, *The Bolsheviks in Power: The First Year of Soviet Rule in Petrograd* (New York: W. W. Norton, 2007); Victor Serge, *Memoirs of a Revolutionary* (London: Writers and Readers, 1984), especially 70–243; the somewhat counterposed studies of Simon Pirani, *The Russian Revolution in Retreat, 1920–24* (New York: Routledge, 2008) and Kevin Murphy, *Revolution and Counterrevolution: Class Struggle in a Moscow Metal Factory* (Chicago: Haymarket Books, 2007); Moshe Lewin, *Lenin's Last Struggle* (New York: Vintage Books, 1970); V. I. Lenin, *Lenin's Final Fight, Speeches and Writings 1922–23*, ed. George Fyson (New York: Pathfinder Press, 1995).

20. C. Wright Mills, *The Marxists* (New York: Dell Publishing Co., 1962), 35.

Chapter Seven: ENDURING LEGACY

1. Charles Post, "Lenin Reconsidered," *International Viewpoint*, November 3, 2011, http://www.internationalviewpoint.org/spip.php?article2361. Available on ESSF (article 23384), "Lenin Reconsidered," http://www.europe-solidaire.org/spip.php?article23384.

2. Ibid.

3. Ernest Mandel, "The Leninist Theory of Organization: Its Relevance for Today," in *Revolutionary Marxism and Social Reality in the 20th Century: Collected Essays*, ed. Steve Bloom (Atlantic Highlands, NJ: Humanities Press, 1994); also see the online version at http://www.marxists.org/archive/mandel/196x/leninism/index.htm.

4. Post, "Lenin Reconsidered."

5. Ibid.

6. Mandel, "The Leninist Theory of Organization," in *Revolutionary Marxism and Social Reality*, Bloom, 91.

7. Ernest Mandel, *The Place of Marxism in History* (Atlantic Highlands, NJ: Humanities Press, 1996); also see online version at http://www.marxists.org/archive/mandel/19xx/marx-hist/index.htm.

8. Valentino Gerratana, "Stalin, Lenin and 'Leninism,'" *New Left Review* 101, May–June 1977, newleftreview.org/I/103/valentine-gerrantna-stalin-lenin-and-leninism.

9. Richard B. Day and Daniel Gaido, eds., *Witnesses to Permanent Revolution: The Documentary Record* (Chicago: Haymarket Books, 2011) and Richard B. Day and Daniel F. Gaido, eds. *Discovering Imperialism:*

Social Democracy to World War I (Chicago: Haymarket Books, 2012).

10. Relevant texts from Mandel can be found in endnotes 2 and 5 above. On others, see: Ernst Fischer and Franz Marek, *The Essential Lenin* (New York: Seabury Press, 1972); Antonio Gramsci, "Leader" (1924), in *Selections from Political Writings 1921–26*, ed. by Quinton Hoare (New York: International Publishers, 1978); Antonio Gramsci, "The Modern Prince," in *Selections from the Prison Notebooks*, ed. by Quintin Hoare and Geoffrey Nowell Smith (New York: International Publishers, 1971); Georg Lukács, *Lenin: A Study in the Unity of His Thought*, 2nd edition (London: Verso, 2009); Leon Trotsky, *Writings from Exile*, ed. by Kunal Chattopadhyay and Paul Le Blanc (London: Pluto Press).

11. Vladimir Ilyich Lenin, *Revolution, Democracy, Socialism: Selected Writings*, ed. Paul Le Blanc (London: Pluto Press, 2008), 59–61.

12. Charles Post, "What Is Left of Leninism? New European Left Parties in Historical Perspective," *Socialist Register 2013: The Question of Strategy*, ed. Leo Panitch, Gregory Albo, and Vivek Chibber (New York: Monthly Review Press, 2012).

13. Saul Alinsky, *Rules for Radicals: A Pragmatic Primer for Realistic Radicals* (New York: Vintage, 1989).

Chapter Eight: LUXEMBURG AND LENIN THROUGH EACH OTHER'S EYES

1. For background on Marx and Marxism consistent with what is presented here, see: Phil Gasper, Karl Marx and Frederick Engels, *The Communist Manifesto: A Road Map to History's Most Important Political Document* (Chicago: Haymarket Books, 2005); Paul Le Blanc, *From Marx to Gramsci* (Amherst, NY: Humanity Books, 1996); Terry Eagleton, *Why Marx Was Right* (New Haven, CT: Yale University Press, 2011); August Nimtz, *Marx and Engels: Their Contribution to the Democratic Breakthrough* (Albany: State University of New York Press, 2000).

2. Elzbieta Ettinger, *Rosa Luxemburg: A Life* (Boston: Beacon Press, 1988), 137, 168; Zetkin's recollection of Luxemburg's remarks in Ronald W. Clark, *Lenin: A Biography* (New York: HarperCollins, 1990), 135.

3. J. P. Nettl, *Rosa Luxemburg*, vol. 1 (New York: Oxford University Press, 1966), 357.

4. Hannah Arendt, "Rosa Luxemburg, 1870–1919," in *Men in Dark Times* (New York: Harcourt, Brace and World, 1968), 41, 43, 44, 45, 54. Levitskaya quoted in Leon Trotsky, *Stalin: An Appraisal of a Man and His Influence* (New York: Stein and Day, 1967), 54.

5. Gorky quoted in Clark, *Lenin: A Biography*, 135; Georg Adler, Peter Hudis, Annelies Laschitza, eds., *The Letters of Rosa Luxemburg* (London: Verso, 2011), 298.

6. See Rosa Luxemburg, *The National Question, Selected Writings*, ed. Horace B. Davis (New York: Monthly Review Press, 1976); Michael Löwy, *Fatherland or Mother Earth? Essays on the National Question* (London: Pluto Press, 1998); and Omar Dahbour and Michelene R. Ishay, eds., *The Nationalism Reader* (Amherst, NY: Humanity Books, 1995), especially 198–214, 322–72.

7. Rosa Luxemburg, *The Accumulation of Capital* (London: Routledge, 2003); V. I. Lenin, *Imperialism, the Highest Stage of Capitalism—A Popular Outline* (New York: International Publishers, 1974); V. I. Lenin, Letter to L. B. Kamenev (March 1913), *Collected Works*, vol. 35 (Moscow: Progress Publishers, 1973), 94. See discussion by Paul Frölich, *Rosa Luxemburg* (Chicago: Haymarket Books, 2010), 150–63, and in Nettl, *Rosa Luxemburg*, vol. 2, 828–41.

8. Nikolai Bukharin, *Imperialism and the Accumulation of Capital*, in Kenneth J. Tarbuck, ed., *The Accumulation of Capital—An Anti-Critique by Rosa Luxemburg and Imperialism and the Accumulation of Capital by Nikolai Bukharin* (New York: Monthly Review Press, 1972), 268; Roman Rosdolsky, *The Making of Marx's "Capital,"* 2 vols. (London: Pluto Press, 1989), 72; Ernest Mandel, "Introduction," in Marx, *Capital, Volume Two*, 68. For two lucid and succinct efforts to draw together the various components of Marx's three-volume work, seeking to demonstrate (in contrast to Luxemburg) that they form a coherent and satisfactory whole, see Ben Fine and Alredo Saad-Filho, *Marx's Capital*, 5th ed. (London: Pluto Press, 2010) and Michael Heinrich, *An Introduction to the Three Volumes of Karl Marx's Capital* (New York: Monthly Review Press, 2012). Lenin's marginal notes to *The Accumulation of Capital* are quoted in Nettl, *Rosa Luxemburg*, vol. 2, 533; Arendt, "Rosa Luxemburg, 1870–1919," 40.

9. Nettl, *Rosa Luxemburg*, vol. 2, 532.

10. On the Bolshevik split, see Paul Le Blanc, "The Birth of the Bolshevik Party in 1912," *Links, International Journal of Socialist Renewal*, April 17, 2012, http://links.org.au/node/2832. On Luxemburg's critical reaction, see Rosa Luxemburg, "Credo: On the State of Russian Social Democracy," in *The Rosa Luxemburg Reader* Peter Hudis and Kevin Anderson, eds. (New York: Monthly Review Press, 2004), 266–80.

11. Rosa Luxemburg, "Organizational Question of Social Democracy," in *Rosa Luxemburg Speaks*, Mary-Alice Waters, ed. (New York: Pathfinder Press, 1970), 128–29. On flaws in Luxemburg's analysis (and the considerable common ground existing between her approach and Lenin's), see Paul Le Blanc, "Luxemburg and Lenin on Organization," in *Rosa Luxemburg, Reflections and Writings*, Paul Le Blanc, ed. (Amherst, NY: Humanity Books, 1999), 81–102, and Paul Le Blanc, *Lenin and the*

Revolutionary Party (Amherst, NY: Humanity Books, 1993), 79–87.

12. The criticism of Luxemburg can be found in V. I. Lenin, "Fine Words: Butter No Parsnips," *Collected Works*, vol. 8 (Moscow: Progress Publishers, 1962), 61. Lenin's own discussion of "organization-as-process" can be found in "Preface to the Collection *Twelve Years*" (1908) in *Collected Works*, vol. 13 (Moscow: Progress Publishers, 1972), 94–113, and *Left-Wing Communism: An Infantile Disorder* (1920), in V. I. Lenin, *Revolution, Democracy, Socialism, Selected Writings*, ed. Paul Le Blanc (London: Pluto Press, 2008), 305–12.

13. Rosa Luxemburg, *The Mass Strike, the Political Party, and the Trade Unions* in *Rosa Luxemburg Speaks*, 200.

14. V. I. Lenin, *What Is to Be Done?*, in *Revolution, Democracy, Socialism*, 138.

15. V. I. Lenin, "The Revolutionary Proletariat and the Right of Nations to Self-Determination," in *Revolution, Democracy, Socialism*, 233–34.

16. Rosa Luxemburg, "The Russian Revolution," in *Rosa Luxemburg Speaks*, 389, 391, 394.

17. Ibid., 369, 375.

18. V. I. Lenin, "Notes of a Publicist," *Collected Works*, Vol. 33 (Moscow: Progress Publishers, 1973), 210. It is worth noting that Lenin was of the opinion that the platform of the Communist International should be based on the program of the Russian Communist Party and also on the program written for the Spartacus League by Rosa Luxemburg. See Gerda and Hermann Weber, *Lenin: Life and Works* (London: Macmillan Press, 1980), 154.

19. August Thalheimer, "Rosa Luxemburg or Lenin" (1930), Marxist Internet Archive, http://www.marxists.org/archive/thalheimer/works/rosa.htm. Also see Helen C. Scott and Paul Le Blanc, "Introduction to Rosa Luxemburg," in *Socialism or Barbarism: The Selected Writings of Rosa Luxemburg*, ed. Paul Le Blanc and Helen C. Scott (London: Pluto Press, 2010), 3–35.

Chapter Nine: CAUTION: ACTIVISTS USING LENIN

1. V. I. Lenin, *Revolution, Democracy, Socialism: Selected Writings*, ed. Paul Le Blanc (London: Pluto Press, 2008), 306.

2. See Paul Le Blanc, *Work and Struggle: Voices from U.S. Labor Radicalism* (New York: Routledge, 2011), 33.

3. There are many places that these lyrics can be found, including online at Wikipedia, http://en.wikipedia.org/wiki/Solidarity_Forever.

4. Quoted in Le Blanc, *Work and Struggle*, 39.

5. Ibid.

6. George Breitman, "The Current Radicalization Compared with Those

of the Past," in *Towards an American Socialist Revolution: A Strategy for the 1970s*, ed. Jack Barnes, George Breitman, Derrick Morrson, Barry Sheppard, Mary-Alice Waters (New York: Pathfinder Press, 1970), 101. Also see Anthony Marcus, ed., *Malcolm X and the Third American Revolution: Selected Writings of George Breitman* (Amherst, NY: Humanity Books, 2005).

7.   The quote is from *What Is to Be Done?* See Lenin, *Revolution, Democracy, Socialism*, 143.

8.   Chris Hedges, "Occupy Wall Street Will Be Back," *Truthdig*, June 18, 2012, http://www.truthdig.com/report/item/occupy_will_be_back_20120618/.

Chapter Ten: LENINISM IS UNFINISHED

1.   Alex Callinicos, "Is Leninism Finished?" *Socialist Review*, January, 2013, http://www.socialistreview.org.uk/article.php?articlenumber =12210, and Louis Proyect, "Leninism Is Finished: A Reply to Alex Callinicos," *Unrepentant Marxist*, January 28, 2013, http://louisproyect .wordpress.com/2013/01/28/leninism-is-finished-a-reply-to-alex -callinicos.

2.   Owen Jones, "British Politics Urgently Needs a New Force—a Movement on the Left to Counter Capitalism's Crisis," *Independent*, January 20, 2013, http://www.independent.co.uk/voices/comment/british -politics-urgently-needs-a-new-force—a-movement-on-the-left-to -counter-capitalisms-crisis-8459099.html.

3.   For a massively documented account of the US SWP experience in the 1980s, see Sarah Lovell, ed., *The Struggle Inside the Socialist Workers Party, 1979–1983*, http://www.marxists.org/history/etol/document/fit /struggleindex.htm and Paul Le Blanc, ed., *Revolutionary Principles and Working-Class Democracy*, http://www.marxists.org/history/etol /document/fit/revprinindex.htm, especially my introductory essay to the latter, "Leninism in the United States and the Decline of the Socialist Workers Party," http://www.marxists.org/history/etol/document /fit/leninismus.htm.

4.   In fact, a day later Proyect posted a communication from some dissident SWPers that approximates such formulations, in a response to Callinicos entitled "Is Zinovievism Finished?" *Unrepentant Marxist*, January 29, 2013, and which concludes: "The time for Leninism to be tried is now long overdue."

5.   Charles Post, "Lenin Reconsidered" (review of Lars Lih's *Lenin*), *International Viewpoint*, November 3, 2011, http://www.international-alviewpoint.org/spip.php?article2361. It seems to me that this is challenged by a serious examination of Lenin's thought—for example,

in V. I. Lenin, *Revolution, Democracy, Socialism: Selected Writings*, ed. Paul Le Blanc (London: Pluto Press, 2008). For a response to Post, see "The Enduring Value of Lenin's Political Thought," *Europe Solidaire Sans Frontières*, February 8, 2012, http://www.europe-solidaire.org /spip.php?article24495.

6. I touch on this in footnote 12 of my essay "The Great Lenin Debate— History and Politics," *Links*, September 1, 2012, criticizing an interpretation by an excellent comrade, Paul Kellogg, which led to a clarifying interchange between myself and Kellogg that provided substantial documentation—see http://links.org.au/node/3011#comments.

7. Leon Trotsky, "Preface," in *The History of the Russian Revolution*, Marxist Internet Archive, http://www.marxists.org/archive/trotsky/1930 /hrr/ch00.htm.

8. Proyect sees this as being related to the experience of SYRIZA in Greece. The meaning of SYRIZA is a focus of debate on the revolutionary left—see the presentation of Strathis Kouvalakis, "On Tasks Facing SYRIZA," *Links*, December 10, 2012, http://links.org.au /node/3145, and Nikos Tamvlakis, "Could SYRIZA Become a 'New PASOK'?" *International Viewpoint*, November 26, 2012, http://www .internationalviewpoint.org/spip.php?article2807.

9. Quoted in Paul Le Blanc, *Lenin and the Revolutionary Party* (Amherst, NY: Humanity Books, 1993), 128, 130. The Menshevik quote is taken from Ralph Carter Elwood, ed., *Resolutions and Decisions of the Communist Party of the Soviet Union, Vol. 1: The Russian Social Democratic Labor Party, 1898–October 1917* (Toronto: University of Toronto, 1974), 93– 94. The Lenin quote is from Lenin's *Collected Works*, Vol. 10, 442–43.

10. Le Blanc, *Lenin and the Revolutionary Party*, 130; Lenin, *Collected Works*, vol. 10, 310–11.

11. Le Blanc, *Lenin and the Revolutionary Party*, 131; Lenin, *Collected Works*, vol. 10, 442–43.

12. "The Organizational Structure of the Communist Parties, the Methods and Content of Their Work: Theses," in Adler, ed., *Theses, Resolutions and Manifestos of the First Four Congresses of the Third International* (London: Ink Links, 1980), 235.

13. Ibid., 234.

Chapter Eleven: LENINISM FOR DANGEROUS TIMES

1. Georg Lukács, *Lenin: A Study on the Unity of His Thought* (London: Verso, 2009), 13.

2. The remarkable stories of Morris Lewit and his companion Sylvia Bleecker are told in Michael Steven Smith and Paul Le Blanc, "Morris Lewit: Pioneer Leader of American Trotskyism (1903-1998)," and

Frank Lovell, "Sylvia Bleecker (1901-1988): Union Organizer, Socialist Agitator, and Lifelong Trotskyist,"in Paul Le Blanc and Thomas
Barrett, eds., *Revolutionary Labor Socialist: The Life, Ideas, and Comrades
of Frank Lovell* (Union City, NJ: Smyrna Press, 2000), 272-301,

3. M. Stein, "Organization Report," *The Party Builder*, vol. I, no. 3, December 1944, 13, 14; M. Stein, "The Organization Methods and Practices of Our Party," *Internal Bulletin*, vol. 6, no. 9, October 1944, 23.

4. M. Stein, "The Internal Party Situation, (Report Delivered at National
Convention, November 16-19, 1944)," *Internal Bulletin*, vol. 6, no. 13,
December 1944, 10–11. Different intrerpretations have been touched
on by Alan Wald and myself in George Breitman, Paul Le Blanc, and
Alan Wald, *Trotskyism in the United States: Historical Essays and Recon-
siderations* (Atlantic Highlands, NJ: Humanities Press, 1996), xi, 280.

5. V. I. Lenin, "Left-Wing Communism, An Infantile Disorder," in *Revolution, Democracy, Socialism: Selected Writings*, ed. Paul Le Blanc (London: Pluto Press, 2008), 306.

6. Luke Cooper and Simon Hardy, *Beyond Capitalism? The Future of Radical Politics* (London: Zero Books, 2012), 152, 160.

7. James P. Cannon, "Socialist Electoral Policy (1958)," in *Speeches for Socialism* (New York: Pathfinder Press, 1971), 337, 338-339.

8. James P. Cannon, "Theses on the American Revolution" and "Report
on 'The American Theses,'" in *The Struggle for the "American Century,"*
ed. by Les Evans (New York: Pathfinder Press, 1977), 289–18.

9. James P. Cannon, "Trade Unionists and Revolutionists," in *Speeches to
the Party* (New York: Pathfinder Press, 1973), 59, 64.

Chapter Twelve: THE HISTORY AND FUTURE OF LENINISM

1. See Paul Le Blanc, "Ten Reasons for Not Reading Lenin," in V. I.
Lenin, *Revolution, Democracy, Socialism: Selected Essays*, ed. Paul Le
Blanc (London: Pluto Press, 2008), 3–80.

2. Two valuable discussions of current realities can be found in: Paul
Mason, *Why It's Still Kicking Off Everywhere: The New Global Revolu-
tions* (London: Verso, 2013); Luke Cooper and Simon Hardy, *Beyond
Capitalism? The Future of Radical Politics* (Winchester, UK: Zero
Books, 2012).

3. J. V. Stalin, *The Foundations of Leninism* in Stalin, *Problems of Leninism*
(Peking: Foreign Languages Press, 1976), 3; also see Stalin Internet
Archive, http://www.marxists.org/reference/archive/stalin/works/1924
/foundations-leninism/introduction.htm. Robert C. Tucker, *Stalin as
Revolutionary 1879–1929* (New York: W. W. Norton, 1974), 313–29.

4. Riutin quoted in Paul Le Blanc, *Marx, Lenin and the Revolutionary
Experience: Studies of Communism and Radicalism in the Age of Global-*

ization (New York: Routledge, 2006), 133–34; Sobhanlal Datta Gupta, ed., *The Ryutin Platform, Stalin and the Crisis of Proletarian Dictatorship: Platform of the "Union of Marxists-Leninists"* (Kolkata, India: Seribaan Books, 2010), 138.

5.   Valentino Gerratana, "Stalin, Lenin and 'Leninism,'" *New Left Review* 1, no. 103, May–June 1977, newleftreview.org/I/103/valentine-gerratana -stalin-lenin-and-leninism.

6.   Le Blanc, "Ten Reasons for Not Reading Lenin," in Lenin, *Revolution, Democracy, Socialism,* 60–61.

7.   Quoted in Sidney Hook, *Towards the Understanding of Karl Marx* (New York: John Day Co., 1933), 43.

8.   Lars T. Lih, "Zinoviev: Populist Leninist," in Ben Lewis and Lars T. Lih, eds., *Zinoviev and Martov: Head to Head in Halle* (London: November Publications, 2011), 40. For Luncharsky's pen portrait, see *Revolutionary Silhouettes* (New York: Hill and Wang, 1968), 75–82.

9.   Lih, 58, 59. Lih's connection of Gramsci's thought with that of Zinoviev deserves critical scrutiny, but is partly corroborated in Gramsci's 1926 letter to Palmiro Togliatti in which he asserts: "Comrades Zinoviev, Trotsky, and Kamenev have made powerful contributions toward educating us for the Revolution. At times they have corrected us energetically and severely; they have been our teachers." The quote can be found in John M. Cammett, *Antonio Gramsci and the Origins of Italian Communism* (Stanford, CA: Stanford University Press, 1967), 181; for further indication of Zinoviev's influence, see Alastair Davidson, *Antonio Gramsci: Towards an Intellectual Biography* (London: Merlin, 1977), 199–202, 204, 205, 236, Antonio Gramsci, *Selections from the Prison Notebooks* (New York: International Publishers, 1977), 169–70, and Peter D. Thomas, *The Gramscian Moment: Philosophy, Hegemony and Marxism* (Chicago: Haymarket, 2010), 165–67.

10.   Severe criticisms by four who knew Zinoviev can be found in: Alfred Rosmer, *Moscow Under Lenin* (New York: Monthly Review Press, 1973), 54, 83, 182, 207–09, and a passage from the Conclusion of the French edition, quoted in Emil Fabrol, "The Prelude to Stalinism," in Alfred Rosmer, Boris Souvarine, Amile Fabrole, Antoine Clavez, *Trotsky and the Origins of Trotskyism* (London: Francis Boutle Publishers, 2002), 20–21; Victor Serge, *From Lenin to Stalin* (New York: Pathfinder Press, 1973), 53–56, and *Memoirs of a Revolutionary* (New York: New York Review of Books, 2012), 84, 132, 158, 207, 225; Franz Borkenau in *World Communism* (Ann Arbor: University of Michigan Press, 1962), 163, 203, 227; Angelica Balabanoff, *My Life as a Rebel* (Bloomington, IN: Indiana University Press, 1973), 220–24, 283. Balabanoff is the most unrelentingly negative—Rosmer, Serge, and

Borkenau who knew him better and longer, convey positive qualities
that provide a more rounded portrait. For more on Zinoviev, see
Georges Haupt and Jean-Jacques Marie, *Makers of the Russian Revolution: Biographies of Bolshevik Leaders* (Ithaca, NY: Cornell University
Press, 1974), 95–106. For James P. Cannon's critique of "Cominternism," see, "Internationalism and the SWP" in Cannon, *Speeches
to the Party* (New York: Pathfinder Press, 1973), 67–91, and at https://
www.marxists.org/archive/cannon/works/1953/international.htm.

11. Lars T. Lih, "The Ironic Triumph of Old Bolshevism: The Debates of
    April 1917 in Context," *Russian History*, 38 (2011): 200.
12. N. S. Krupskaya, *Reminiscences of Lenin* (New York: International Pub-
    lishers, 1970), 335.
13. Ibid., 348–49.
14. Ibid., 349–51; N. N. Sukhanov, *The Russian Revolution 1917: A Per-
    sonal Record* (Princeton, NJ: Princeton University Press, 1984), 280–
    89; Raphael R. Abramovitch, *The Soviet Revolution 1917–1939* (New
    York: International Universities Press, 1962), 30–32; W. S. Woytinsky,
    *Stormy Passage: A Personal History Through Two Russian Revolutions to
    Democracy and Freedom: 1905–1960* (New York: Vanguard Press, 1961),
    265–67; Alexandra Kollontai, *The Autobiography of a Sexually Emanci-
    pated Communist Woman* (New York: Schocken Books, 1975), 31.
15. Lars Lih, "Democratic Centralism: Fortunes of a Formula," *Weekly
    Worker*, April 11, 2013, http://links.org.au/node/3300.
16. Lenin, "A Militant Agreement for the Uprising," in *Revolution, Democ-
    racy, Socialism*, 174, 177.
17. Ibid., 174, 179, 180.
18. Lenin quoted in Paul Le Blanc, *Lenin and the Revolutionary Party*
    (Amherst, NY: Humanity Books, 1993), 117.
19. Lenin, *What Is to Be Done?* in *Revolution, Democracy, Socialism*, 143.
20. Lenin, "The Revolutionary Proletariat and the Right of Nations to
    Self-Determination," in *Revolution, Democracy, Socialism*, 233–34.
21. Levitskaya quoted in Leon Trotsky, *Stalin: An Appraisal of the Man and
    His Influence* (New York: Stein and Day, 1967), 53–54; James P. Can-
    non, "Happy Birthday, Arne Swabeck" (delivered in 1953), Cannon In-
    ternet Archive, http://www.marxists.org/archive/cannon/works/1953
    /hbaswab.htm; Maxim Gorky, *Mother* (New York: Collier Books,
    1962), 344; for Lenin quote from *What Is to Be Done?*, see Le Blanc,
    Lenin and the Revolutionary Party, 53; Lenin quoting Trotsky in "Once
    Again on the Trade Unions" (1921) in Lenin Internet Archive,
    http://www.marxists.org/archive/lenin/works/1921/jan/25.htm.
22. Georg Lukács, *Lenin: A Study on the Unity of His Thought* (London:
    Verso, 2009), 11–13.

23. Le Blanc, *Lenin and the Revolutionary Party*, 182.
24. For the United States, an initial (perhaps preliminary) effort in this direction is offered by Francis Goldin, Debby Smith, and Michael Steven Smith, eds., *Imagine!: Living in a Socialist USA* (New York: HarperCollins, 2013).
25. This point is emphasized in Cooper and Hardy, *Beyond Capitalism? The Future of Radical Politics*, 144, 154–55, 156. This is an issue wrestled with in Leon Trotsky et al., *The Transitional Program for Socialist Revolution* (New York: Pathfinder Press, 1977). On thinking this through regarding the United States, see Paul Le Blanc and Michael Yates, *A Freedom Budget for All Americans: Recapturing the Promise of the Civil Rights Movement in the Struggle for Economic Justice Today* (New York: Monthly Review Press, 2013).

Index

About the Author

Ashtyn Marino

Paul Le Blanc is a professor of history at La Roche College, has written on and participated in the US labor, radical, and civil rights movements, and is author of such books as *Marx, Lenin and the Revolutionary Experience*, and *Lenin and the Revolutionary Party*. He has also edited a volume of Lenin's writings, entitled *Revolution, Democracy, Socialism*. Other books include *A Short History of the U.S. Working Class* and *Work and Struggle: Voices from U.S. Labor Radicalism*. In addition, he has coauthored, with economist Michael Yates, the highly acclaimed *A Freedom Budget for All Americans: Recapturing the Promise of the Civil Rights Movement in the Struggle for Economic Justice Today*.